Aegean Summer

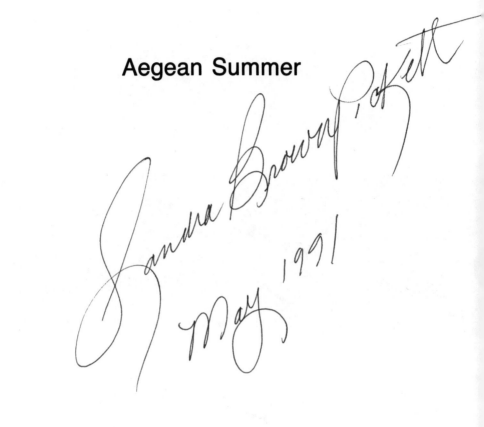

Sandra Brown Pofett

May 1991

THIS TRIP ON THE EVA
WAS MADE MID 1960's I MENTALLY
pieced together, Then found the date
Stated, finally, pg 174.

Aegean Summer

A FAMILY ODYSSEY

BY

MIMI LAFOLLETTE SUMMERSKILL

WITH AN INTRODUCTION BY NICHOLAS GAGE

PAUL S. ERIKSSON, Publisher
Middlebury, Vermont 05753

Manufactured in the United States of America

10   9   8   7   6   5   4   3   2   1

Library of Congress Cataloging-in-Publication Data

Summerskill, Mimi LaFollette.
     Aegean summer: a family odyssey / by
     Mimi LaFollette Summerskill.
          p.   cm.
     ISBN 0-8397-0105-5: $22.50
     1. Aegean Islands (Greece and Turkey)—Description and
travel—1981-   2. Wright family   I. Title.
DF895.S86   1990
949.9—dc20   90-36781
                                                         CIP

For my sons and daughters,
Richard, Bill, Robert, Helen and Wendy
all of whom I nurtured "over fool's mountain,"
and who in turn pushed and prodded and teased and loved me
into being a better human being.

Preface

Why did I keep a log that summer-of-the-yacht? Endless hours of writing in a cloth-covered notebook purchased in Greece, with my back braced against the wheelhouse as we skimmed the waves, or curled up on the bunk in my rose-wallpapered stateroom as the schooner bobbed gently in some remote bay or busy harbor—I wrote.

Always I have written, my poor children sinking under descriptions of and feelings about far-flung lands. Keeping the original, I would launch a copy to each offspring, and sometimes those copies were hard to come by—as in Oman. I wonder what I thought might become of all those witty pages!

And then I met Sam Vaughan. Sam came into my life via Kenya. One of his daughters participated in a student program I directed and she spent such a successful semester in Kenya that Sam came on my board of directors. And changed my life. I now know that this man is one of the great editors of the "books of our time" since World War II. When I asked one of his fellow publishers to comment on Sam he said, "There are damn few in our business like Sam." He is known for his soaring abilities and his modesty.

Sam urged me on in my writing and somehow, with many talented writers demanding his attention, he found time to tutor me in this difficult craft. He is also responsible for suggesting Alison Bond as my literary agent and it is my good fortune that this skillful woman took me on.

Finally, Sam suggested the manuscript go to Paul Eriksson, the veteran, distinguished publisher. It did. And here is the result!

But there are others to whom I am grateful, especially Sara Rau, an experienced editor whose husband is in the Foreign Service. As I was writing this manuscript in Greece, and the Raus were stationed there, Sara became my editor and forced me to rethink and rewrite. Day after day I sat at my table-desk in our house on a hill at Athens College. From there I could see Penteli, a mountain with massive scars on its flank resulting from removal of the marble used in the building of the Parthenon in the fifth century B.C. A sobering thought, yet one which urged me on in my efforts to describe life in the Aegean in the twentieth century A.D.

Through the birth of this book there was always John. John Summerskill, my beloved. Paying tuitions, welcoming offspring, active in his own profession and doing his own writing, John ever found time to encourage me in my new career. What devotion!

CONTENTS

x CONTENTS

Introduction

By Nicholas Gage

"I guess I was hunting for the simplicity the far side of complexity."

That's the reason Mimi Summerskill gave when asked why she decided to spend a summer sailing in Greece with her five children at a time when she was recently divorced from a husband who was confined in a mental hospital, in love with a married man, wooed by another, and struggling to support her children. She knew no Greek, but when she received a small inheritance of $30,000, she impulsively decided to spend the whole windfall on one vagabond summer. Inspired in part by her love of Homer's *Odyssey*, she elected to sail with her offspring and another recently divorced woman on a three-month tour of all the Greek islands she had ever wanted to see, renting an 81-foot racing schooner, the *Eva Maria*, with a Greek-speaking crew who were not accustomed to taking orders from females. Undaunted, she set out like Candide in search of simplicity, far from television, telephones, plumbing and the many distractions of life in California.

Luckily for us, Mimi LaFollette Summerskill kept a detailed journal of that summer and this book is the result. With her family, we share the discoveries and the beauties of the voyage that changed all their lives.

My native land of Greece has beckoned travelers with a siren song since the beginning of history. Julius Caesar, Cicero, Saint Paul, Lord Byron, Julia Ward Howe, Oscar Wilde, Edward Lear, Lord Elgin, Heinrich Schliemann, Chateaubriand, Mark Twain, Herman Melville, Gustave Flaubert—the list is endless.

These travelers came for many reasons—conquest, curiosity, admiration of Greek art and culture, longing for adventure, desire to help the Greeks or to steal their treasures.

It's fortunate for such travelers that the Greek word *xeni* means both "stranger" and "guest." *Philoxenia*—usually translated as "hospitality"—literally means "love of strangers," and it is the cornerstone of Greek culture. Any stranger who knocks on a Greek door will be offered the best the house can provide, even if it's only a glass of water, a piece of fruit or a shot of ouzo, before he is asked his business. But once the rules of hospitality have been met, the questions will come, for Greeks are endlessly curious about strangers. And the language barrier is easily surmounted by Greeks, who are so eager to communicate that gestures and facial expressions will serve if words fail. A visitor's few mangled phrases of Greek are applauded as a great achievement.

Whatever strangers are seeking when they set foot on Greek soil, their voyage usually provides an unexpected dividend—a greater understanding of one's self. It's hard to say why, but perhaps the reason is that cited by President George Bush in a speech: "Any American who goes to Greece has a sense of home even if he has no Greek blood himself, for every American has a kinship which is even more important—and that is a Greek heritage."

The best travel writers give their readers three things: a description of a physical journey filled with evocative detail that makes the terrain seem real to the reader; an internal journey that chronicles the emotional reactions, insights and discoveries of the writer; and finally, thanks to the author's discerning eye and pen, a vicarious odyssey into the reader's own mind, heart and emotions. That is why such books can be read and re-read with pleasure, offering something new each time.

There are a number of twentieth-century authors who have given me this three-part delight in their writing about Greece—Henry Miller, whose *Colossus of Maroussi* is a well-thumbed travel companion, both Gerald and Lawrence Durrell who have invested certain parts of Greece with such indelible descriptions of their adventures that I always see those places through their eyes, and Patrick Leigh Fermor, who, in works like *Mani* and *Roumeli*, often seems to understand us Greeks better than we do ourselves.

Aegean Summer by Mimi LaFollette Summerskill is a welcome addition to the bookshelf of vivid Grecian odysseys, because it is unusual in many ways. You might say that she follows in the footsteps of the intrepid English and American women of the nineteenth century who kept travel journals and sketchbooks of their Grand Tours as they visited the harems of Ali Pasha, the huts of wondering peasants and the encampments of sinister bandit-warriors.

"Impulsive" and "brave" are two adjectives that describe Mimi Summerskill. Her children, aged ten through twenty-two, were no less intrepid, learning to speak Greek, discovering the joys of reading and argument, sampling strange, exotic foods, and exploring the most isolated sites, even when there was no public transportation, their shoes had worn out and no new ones could be found in their size. Mimi herself discovered an ancient Minoan village on Crete where she thinks she might have lived in a previous existence, and when the family happened upon an exquisite beach in Ios, empty except for sheep, goats and a lonely *taverna* she immediately decided to buy a piece of land so that her family could build a home there, even though she had forgotten to bring along a checkbook.

Mrs. Summerskill has an eye for the telling detail; the gestures, phrases, and customs of the Greeks, the colorful mosaic of a farmer's market, the graceful play of a school of dolphins, the slow rhythm of daily life and the bustle of a small harbor as the fishing boats set out to sea. Her family read more than a hundred books as they sailed from island to island, and historical, literary and mythological nuggets from their reading are studded throughout this account.

That Aegean summer became a watershed for the family. The enforced intimacy of living together in cramped quarters and sharing their adventures created bonds of affection and understanding that would never have been forged in Menlo Park, CA. Afterwards, all the members of the family became world travelers, learning Greek and other languages, working, marrying and settling all over the globe. Mimi Summerskill did not expect that summer to be a rite of passage for her family and a great divide in her life, but she has managed to capture the magic of their odyssey in these pages with poetry, insight and great frankness. We, her readers, are the richer for it. During her family's Aegean summer Mimi Summerskill discovered the truth of Constantine Cavafy's famous poem *Ithaka* about Ulysses's voyage:

> Setting out on the voyage to Ithaka
> You must pray that the way be long,
> Full of adventures and experiences . . .
> But do not hurry the journey at all.
> Better that it should last many years;
> Be quite old when you anchor at the island,
> Rich with all you have gained on the way,
> Not expecting Ithaka to give you riches.
> Ithaka has given you the journey.

North Grafton, MA.

Prologue

"I hear you have a house on a Greek island." The professor was seated on my right at the small dinner party. "Is the house a reality or someone's fantasy? It's a long way from Princeton, New Jersey, to Greece."

"Oh, it's a reality all right. In fact, we built it."

"How in heaven's name did you choose Greece?"

"I didn't choose to build a house in Greece at all. It all began because I chartered a marvelous old wooden racing schooner and took my children sailing in the Aegean for a whole summer."

"Slow down," cautioned the professor, "I can't take it in so fast. Start at the beginning. How did you happen to charter the schooner?"

"Well, I was living alone with my five children in Menlo Park, California, next to Stanford University, and supporting them, when I inherited $30,000 from my grandfather LaFollette. So I took that money and chartered the yacht with its crew of five for the whole summer. About a month after we set sail I bought land on the sea on a small island which did not have electricity but did have the most phenomenal beach I had ever seen. And in the end we built a house. In any event I spent all my inheritance in one summer! I know it sounds crazy. In any practical sense it was an insane thing to do. Richard, my oldest son, had just finished Princeton with very little financial help from me and I had the others to help educate. . . ."

"So she spent all her inheritance in one summer and then married me." It was my husband, John, who joined the conversation. "The Greeks thought I was an idiot to marry a woman with five children. Worse, she had spent all her dowry!"

"So you didn't sail with Mimi?" The professor's wife turned to John.

"No, Mimi and a mutual friend, Ann Pine, were alone with the children. But I have been at the Ios house every summer since."

Across the table Homer Thompson, an archaeologist famous for his excavations of the Agora in Athens, joined the conversation. "You should see Ios where the Summerskills live. The island is mountainous and starkly beautiful. I did an excavation of a noble's tomb on the island next door."

"Ah, yes, Sikino." I smiled at Professor Thompson who was the only person present who knew the pull of the Aegean.

"I like it," the professor's wife spoke again, "I really like the idea that you — a woman alone — took five children and sailed away."

"I know it sounds irresponsible, but that summer changed all the children's lives and mine as well. It changed attitudes, professions, college curricula. . . ."

"Do you get to be there very much?" our hostess asked.

"Quite a bit. At least some of us are there every year. John and I went at least twice a year when we worked in Ethiopia, and these last few years while John was president of Athens College, we could go even more." I laughed, "But the ferry from Athens to Ios takes more hours than the plane trip from New York to Athens."

"Do you speak Greek?" the professor asked.

"Yes, fluent terrible Greek. Most of our sons and daughters have better Greek than we do. My oldest son, Richard, sounds exactly like an Ios peasant and speaks so rapidly that I have yet to understand a word he says."

"Daughter Helen's Greek is the best," added John, "she teaches it, too. Robert, Mimi's youngest, is totally fluent, but he doesn't read or write Greek. My youngest son, John Paul, has been on the island every summer since he was an infant and after working one summer on a Greek cement ship even he gets by in Greek. That's enough of the linguistic ability of our large family."

"That's right, you have eight children, is it, between you?" Even our hostess was confused.

"Exactly. And if you asked any one of them, you'd find Ios is a kind of core place for each. It is a deep love affair."

"But back to the beginning." It was the professor again, "I still want to know why you chose Greece for sailing? Why not the Carribean or the Bahamas or even the South Pacific?"

"I don't know. I really don't."

How could I tell dinner partners of the anguish over my first husband's illness, the loss of my lover? Or of years of decision-making and money-making and the lonesomeness of being a single parent, the complications in my love for John?

"I guess I was hunting for the simplicity the far side of complexity." In the mad twentieth century some people make it to simplicity. When they do it is a very personal thing. There is no map.

"I suppose I wanted to run away but I couldn't leave my beloved offspring so we all ran away together. Not all of us ran joyously. Twelve-year-old Wendy went kicking and screaming."

"Tell me more about the schooner," said the professor. "Did she have a motor? cotton sails? how long was she?"

"Eighty-one feet of sleek elegance and, yes, the sails were cotton and heavy! The *Eva Maria* is an old-fashioned schooner built of wood in the 1930's in Scandinavia."

"She's still around then?"

"Oh, yes. Actually there is a recent and fantastic story about the *Eva Maria* and her treasure."

Now the whole table listening.

"Well, not long ago we were in Athens, and the governor of the National Bank of Greece came for dinner. He commented on a picture on our livingroom wall — the *Eva Maria* in full sail."

"I know that schooner," he said, "the new owners are friends and I often race with them. How do you happen to have a picture of the *Eva*?"

"I chartered her for a summer just after the original owner died. Actually I chartered the *Eva* with an option to buy her — some kind of insanity on my part. It is just that she is so beautiful."

"You should have bought her," my banking friend said. "The new owners recently replaced the teakwood deck. Between the deck and the hold they found three bars of gold — enameled black — and two priceless sets of sterling flatware. The owner — I guess you know he was Egyptian Greek — decided to hide some of his wealth when Nasser came to power in Egypt."

Yes, I knew the tragedies created for many families when Nasser decided that all foreigners must leave Egypt. In many cases those Greek families had been two centuries in Egypt. But selfishly I found my thoughts racing to reconstruct those months we sailed innocent of the wealth under our feet.

Yet I knew the real wealth of the summer could never be measured in ounces of gold. It had much more to do with sunsets on the blood red sea; changing our backyard at will; taking parts as we read some of the great Greek tragedies aloud sprawling about the deck; a ten-year-old son — desperate for American food — learning to peel, cut and French-fry potatoes. It had to do with letters shared, screaming family fights, abortion, and daily marketing. Those months on the sea were the same, yet totally different for each of us. But magical for all.

I did not know that those three months sailing would be my "rite of passage" which led me into the ancient Mediterranean world and a new life. That summer among the mountaintop islands of Greece and Turkey became the Great Divide in life. On one side were my childhood, young womanhood, college, marriage, babies, struggle — and on the other side of my private and mythical wall was a new marriage, to John, and a rambling stone house on a remote island which became the center of our worlds.

PART ONE

BEGINNINGS

❧ *1* ❧

Pioneers

I come from a line of strong-minded people. Both my father and grandfather were highly successful men, in the accepted sense. They were opinionated yet loving, and were putty in the hands of the strong, serene women they married. As a child, I never felt that my father imposed his will on my mother — or his children — except in matters where one's parents always prevail when one is young.

My family name was famous in those days because Robert LaFollette had founded the Progressive Party and he was highly visible in the political world as Governor of Wisconsin and then as Senator from that state. Everyone knew my name. Sometimes I got upset as people always either adored or hated Bob LaFollette and often it carried over to me. I was me — not him. But I understood. It was my heritage.

We lived in Colfax, a town of 3,000 in eastern Washington State. My father was a lawyer. Many evenings Daddy would lean over the banister and call, "Helen, aren't you ever coming to bed?" Perhaps Mother was sewing and we would be grouped around the fireplace, telling stories, giggling, and putting off our studies or practicing music. Daddy would call again, "Helen! Please come!" And she would go and we knew, that as totally as we were loved, they came first for each other.

How I treasure the small stories Mother told me about their lives together. She showed me her tiny notebook on "love making" during their first year of marriage. I was about to be married and she told me that when she married she knew nothing about sex (her mother had died when she was eighteen) and how gentle Daddy had been. Many times she told us the story of how she always took the ribbons from her dimity nightgown, after the lights were out, and rolled them up. In the morning she would get up and brush her waist-length curly hair, put the ribbons back in the gown, and get back into bed. So the tiny notebook appeared — from a nineteenth century box of Grandmother's (the picture of an old-fashioned douche on its cover) where it was kept tucked among the corkscrew curls cut from Mother's head when she was a little girl. Each page of the notebook bore check marks. Each mark, dated, was a love-making time. It was easy to determine they made love each and every day — except during her menstrual periods. My life began with one of those marks!

Just before I married, Mother told me her sexual "fantasy." "There will be many times, Miriam, when you won't feel like making love. When there are small children and you've worked all day . . . well, I always pretended I was in the Palace Hotel in San Francisco in a gorgeous suite, dressed in silken robes, sitting on a chaise longue nibbling bonbons and waiting for Daddy to arrive." Dear God, how many times in my lifetime have I thought of that fantasy! Once, in her seventies and driving along El Camino Real, Mother said to me, "My only regret in life with your father was that I never took off my nightgown when we made love." Who could resist a mother like that?

Such a woman! Welsh by heritage, she had brown curly hair long enough to sit on (until she cut it in the 1920s, thereby engendering such fury in my father that he did not speak to her for three days). Mother had the clear light skin of the English and china-blue eyes. Her father was a Congregational minister in eastern Washington State and Mother was born in Colfax and grew up gently. She lost her only sister and her mother while she was still in her teens. Attending the University of California in Berkeley, Mother became a notable thespian, playing leads at the Greek Theatre in Berkeley, in San Francisco and Carmel. To this day I wear the Italian cameo given to her by a fellow member of the "Mask and Dagger" society — playwright Sherwood Anderson. But though she was offered a Hollywood contract with RKO to play the lead in a Rex Beach movie to be filmed in Alaska, Mother returned to Colfax, taught school for a year and married the handsome son of a local farmer — and U.S. Congressman — William LeRoy LaFollette. Ten months later there was me.

"It must be very exciting to have such a romantic background," said Mrs. Helfit, "have you liked being part Indian?"

I was startled and for a moment no one spoke at the elegant New York City dinner party.

"Helen, your daughter, told us the exotic story of your great-grandmother's capture by an Indian Chief," Mrs. Helfit plunged on, "and how your grandmother was born from their union."

Helen! Beautiful adorable daughter Helen who had inherited the ability of her Scottish grandmother, Helen Urquhart, to make a good story better.

It is true that my great-grandmother, Mary Melcena Taylor, had captured the heart of the son of a Navaho Indian chief as the Taylor family plodded the Oregon Trail in the mid-nineteenth century. All the Chief's negotiations to win the young girl for his son failed and the family proceeded to Eastern Oregon. For days, the Chief, his son, and a group of braves followed the pioneers westward. Eventually the Indians took leave of their new-found friends, although the wagon train harbored fear the rest of their journey.

Now Melcena, I was always told, was truly a great beauty, and soon another young man fell in love with her, a pioneer named Will Hamilton. Soon after the birth of their son, Will was murdered by another settler and thus achieved the dubious distinction of being the first man murdered in newly-founded Oregon State. Melcena soon married another pioneer, John Tabor, and one of their two daughters was my grandmother LaFollette. John Tabor left Huntsville, Alabama, in the 1840s to go west and fight in the Mexican War. He made the west his home and at the time of the gold rush to California John Tabor made enough money — shooting game for the miners' food — to take his stake and move to the agricultural riches of the northwest.

As children we all cherished the stories of our grandparents and great-grandparents. Vividly I recall the original one-room log house in the corner of the vast yard of John Tabor's proper farm house. Grandmother LaFollette sang us the songs of the pioneers, taught us Indian words (my Campfire Girl name was Totsyeen—the name of grandmother's best Indian friend), and recited poems of the early days. Most often we asked for the story of "the Indian Chief who loved your mother."

A story of family fame concerned a night in Washington, at the White House, during the first quarter of this century when my grandfather LaFollette was a Congressman from eastern Washington. Four ravishingly beautiful girls brought all conversation to a halt as they swept into a ball in the Blue Room of the White House. Two were LaFollette girls (my father's sisters) and two were cousins named Taylor. All four beauties sprang from the famous Mary Melcena, who did *not* marry the Indian Chief!

Life was enchanted in the far west during those years following the first World War. At least it was for children. Palouse County wheat farms produced more bushels of wheat per acre than were produced anywhere in the world. Paddle-wheel steamers still ran from ports like Wawawi and Almota down the Snake River to the Columbia River and on to Portland, Oregon. Besides wheat they carried fruit from the first apple, peach, and pear orchards of Washington—and passengers.

Grandfather Tabor started those orchards and he and his beautiful Melcena lived with their three children in Wawawi. Wawawi was a collection of farms cradled by the Snake River as it swept around the peninsula of silt in a great arc. Daddy grew up there with his six siblings, swam the rushing Snake River, attended a one room school. (Later when he was District Attorney he gave a speech at the school and found his name carved in letters an inch high across one of the old school desks.) The LaFollette family divided their time between Grandfather Tabor's fruit orchards on the Snake and Grandfather LaFollette's wheat farms on the bluffs above the river.

I am definitely a country girl. Washington State, where both sides of my family settled a century ago, is still remote from much of the rest of the States. The LaFollettes, Huguenots, had arrived in America in the 1750s. My Welsh grandparents came more than a century later.

My life was greatly influenced by weekends and summers spent on Grandfather LaFollette's wheat and cattle ranch—some eight miles from Colfax. My favorite spot in all the world, Grandfather's home ranch, nestled in among the famous Palouse Hills at the head of a long draw up from the Snake River.

Our visits to the "home farm" nearly always began the same way. At the round barn we turned off the main Colfax-Pullman road onto a dirt road. My sister Maryly and I giggled when we passed the round red barn because Daddy had told us "a man went crazy in that barn looking for a corner to pee."

On lovely summer days—once we had turned onto the dirt road—Daddy let Maryly and me get out and ride on the running board, straddling the spare tires set in the front fenders. We were 9 and 10 years old, my sister and I. Curly-haired blond brother Bill, at only 5, had to ride inside. How I adored riding in the wind with billows of dust rushing from beneath the fenders.

We passed the spot where the old fort stood and where the settlers collected during Indian uprisings. Soon we were at the "crabapple tree field" and then over the hill and past the red cow barn, across the willow draped creek, past the horse and hay barn, and the bunk house. The handsome square farm house sat on sloping lawns with cottonwood trees across the front and a grandfather willow weeping over the kitchen entrance. From a lower branch of the willow tree hung the heavy iron bell which one of the children would ring with vigorous delight before each meal.

Our cousins came shrieking out to meet us. Lauretta was thirteen and John, *my* hero, eleven, while Lavelle was Maryly's age. Their father was Daddy's oldest brother, a law graduate of the University of Wisconsin. He ran his father's ranches as Grandfather was in Congress much of the time. Since it was Sunday a big family dinner was being prepared and we children headed for the orchard behind the house and the gentle slope there. The red June apples were ready and black luscious Bing cherries as well. Whatever happened to red June apples? Bright, red-skinned, snow-white inside, and sweet. I suppose they were not commercially viable.

Three apples and fistfuls of cherries later we still found room for fresh peas. To the left of the farm house behind a row of poplar trees were the rows of vegetables. Plunking ourselves down in the dirt between two rows, we popped dozens of crisp pods, devouring the tiny sweet peas.

"Let's play Annie Annie Over." We followed John to the house and, with an old hard sponge-rubber ball, we divided into two teams. One took the front of the house and other the back. We were now eight children as neighbors had arrived for Sunday dinner. In "Annie Annie Over" one tries to throw the ball over the house. Grandfather's house was three stories high so mostly the boys had to throw. If the ball went over *and* one of the other team caught it *before* it hit the ground he raced around the house trying to touch members of the throwing team before they could get around to the catcher's side.

John threw the ball and called "Annie Annie Over." It came back on our side. He threw again and called. All was quiet. Had they caught it? Suddenly a shout erupted from one member of our team as they saw the enemy rounding the corner. Amid the scrambling and shouting we lost one member of our team to the opposite side so now they were five and we were three.

"Could someone go to the spring for butter?" Aunt Edith called, "and I would like Lauretta to help getting the food on." I happily volunteered for the spring run. Ambling down the lawn and across the dirt road and a few yards into the field I lifted the wooden hatch, descended the three steps and sat on the lowest one enjoying the cool and delicious scents of buttermilk, the mint growing nearby, and the freshly churned butter. Filling my bowl with butter from the wooden bucket, I also filled a glass with buttermilk for my father. It was his favorite drink—next to hard cider.

Aunt Edith was supervising the laying out of food on big tables in front of the house. Aunt Edith did not like the ranch. She was a city girl and soon her oldest daughter would be the mainstay at the ranch house. Aunt Edith liked her friends and her bridge. She was always sweet and patient with us children and we were always fascinated by her marcelled hair and the tiny round spots of rouge on each cheek. Our own mother had mops of natural brown curls and no make-up.

After the bountiful lunch even the children dozed and later I would go with John to the triangle field and bring in the milking cows. I sat close by on a three-legged stool which matched John's while he milked. Once in a while he would shout, "Here it comes," and he tried to hit my mouth with a stream of warm sweet milk. Later we girls gathered eggs. In the dusk we played "Bear," a kind of hide-and-go-seek game carried on close to the house. How disgusted we were that Lauretta had opted to sit and listen to the "boring conversation" of the adults. Later the rhythmic put-put of the generator would lull me to sleep, but sometimes I awakened to the ranch dogs barking. What a lonesome but safe sound. Like a train whistle in the night.

Harvest had not started yet, so after milking in the morning we younger children would all creep up the steep farmhouse steps to the second floor and climb in bed with cousin Lauretta, who would tell us stories.

The dawn was still a hope when I followed cousin John to the cow barn the next morning. Calmly chewing their cuds the patient animals waited to be milked. (Years later, waking up a baby to nurse and so relieve my swollen breasts, I thought of those cows.) Fresh hay smell mixed with the warm smell of cow greeted us as John climbed to the hayloft and pitched down their breakfast. Soon John was pulling and squeezing the long streams of milk into the metal bucket, his head resting against the flank of each cow in turn. He filled both buckets and we turned the cows loose. They headed up the road, shepherded by me, to the triangular field with its lazy little brook. John staggered with the filled buckets, making for the back porch of the farm house and the separator. We were all in awe of that separator that took the place of the large shallow pans into which the milk had traditionally been poured so that later the cream, which rose to the top, could be skimmed off. The family still slept, though the dawn was brilliant now. The noise of the separator soon wakened the household.

After breakfast Uncle Tabor drove into Pullman, the nearest town, to look for a "jigger" for the combine. Harvest would soon start and the regular hired man, Floyd, was taking a few days off before the long grueling days of harvest began. We children worried about Floyd as he lived all alone during most of the year in the many-bedded bunkhouse. His shower was an oil drum, bottom punctured like swiss cheese, strung up in the rafters of the machinery barn across the dirt road from the bunkhouse. But soon the beds would be filled with harvest hands — the men who moved south to north following the seasons and the ripening grain. When I was young it took a lot of men to run the combine. One man drove the horses, one punched hedder (raising or lowering the cutting bar), one jigged the sacks, packing the wheat firmly, and another man sewed the sacks. Then, of course, men drove trucks filled with the sacked wheat.

One fresh summer day we children decided to surprise Floyd. He had gone into Pullman for some farm machinery parts. The crabapple field was not planted to wheat that year. It was the largest of the fields on that 1500–acre ranch and since, in those days, one could only grow wheat every other year on the land, Uncle Tabor had planted it to hay. The hay had been cut but not shocked. Handling the hefty bundles of hay, standing them in teepee form, was hard and hot work. Itchy, too. John and I worked one direction around the field and Lauretta and the little girls the other. When our fresh day turned boiling hot, we ached to stop. The laden crabapple tree gave some puckery relief and we kept going. A lifetime later we met and gazed back over our labors. Hundreds of tent-like shocks stood proudly behind us. They were safe now from dew and would be easy to pitch into trucks.

The annual Pioneer Picnic was one of life's great delights. The Fourth of July picnic, Thanksgiving, and dances at the Grange followed close behind. But the Pioneer Picnic had a class of its own. After all, it drew people from all over the Palouse country whereas all the events at the Grange were of local farmers. That large pioneer gathering was usually held in Smuck Park in Colfax, and before the harvest season. Practically every farm family in the county arrived by ten in the morning. Various contests of strength, prowess in horse-breaking, skill in milking cows, in catching a greased pig, plus many games on horseback along with delights such as sack races and egg races, kept the young occupied.

Best of all in my small girl heart was the hog-calling contest. Hogs were held in a corral at one end of the park. Men would line up and, one by one, have their turn at crying the long wail-like WHOOOOOOOEEEEEEEE, WHOOOOOOOEEEEE, followed by a gutteral "PIG, PIG, PIG."

I could not take my eyes off of each contestant as he would plant his feet, take a big breath, and begin his wail. The contest was won by the one whose voice carried farthest — the pigs determined that.

I began to practice hog-calling. To this day it is one of my talents and over the years my children have been summoned to dinner, or alerted to my presence in an unexpected place, like JFK airport, by WHOOOOOEEEEEE, WHOOOOOEEEE. I forego the "Pig, Pig Pig!" My call often momentarily startles people standing near me, but before they can identify the source I have assumed my best dignified lady look.

Until I became a pig-calling fanatic we children used a "call" our mother taught us from her childhood. She and her sister, Miriam, made up the call along with their best friends in Colfax's grade school. When you wanted a friend to come out and play, or walk to school, you would call, "Hick (pause) taminica honica saw debunk dela toohoo" in a piercing monotone. Honest! that call, along with an early-developed and often-used "pig latin" (I really was into pigs!) are now performed for my grandchildren.

How can any culinary event in the world hope to equal the marvel of joint farm picnics? Each and every woman from each and every farm arrived at the Pioneer Picnics with potato salads, some form of meat, often meat loaf, jello salads (always melting), jars of pickles, relishes, and cakes and pies and cakes and pies and cakes and pies. It was as if the proof of one's cooking ability lay in cakes and pies. And of course, homemade bread. It so inspired me that for my whole adult life, no matter how busy, I have baked most of the bread our family has eaten. It was years before I discovered that my children, with thick, home-made, wholewheat bread sandwiches in their school lunches, often traded with other children for the commercial, squishy Wonderbread.

Now about the men in my life. I can only say I adore them. I have fought my men, sometimes won, sometimes lost, but I have loved and cherished my father, my grandfather, the father of my children, my husband, my sons and my grandsons. And when I read from an interview with Germaine Greer, "I still hope to have a meaningful relationship with a man," I wonder what the hell *that* means.

Naturally Daddy Roy, my father, was my first male love. How straight he sat a horse. He was always most at home breaking ponies or fixing things. His hair, dark and wavy, was worn in a pompador—like his cousin's, Bob LaFollette.

When I was five I crossed Washington State by train with my father—oh joy, the upper berth! Daddy was to try a case before the Supreme Court in Olympia. How many trial lawyers would take a five-year-old to court? Daddy bought me a coloring book and for hours I sat under the lawyers' table in the Supreme Court. I can still picture all those legs! Years later I heard my father prosecute a rape case during a "Jury Session." A jury was convened to hear all the criminal cases which had accumulated during six months. After the rape case I went to my father and asked: "What did the other lawyer mean when he asked, 'Have you ever tried to thread a moving needle?' "

Daddy had lurid stories of cases during those prohibition years. Some I recall. Others I cannot because he sent his daughters from the room to protect their virtue while he regaled the adults with the tales.

Often, unless we went to grandfather's ranch, our weekends were spent on the vast sheeplands of the McGregors who, my father claimed, had the best library in the State. The McGregors also had innumerable Basque sheep herders and a foreman named Jock McCrea who drank a quart of whiskey a day and . . . well, they kept talking about his women. Jock lived well into his ninety-second year.

As a teenager I rode in the rumble-seat with my first love, Jim; had my first kiss sitting on the running board of the sheriff's car; fished in the wilds of Idaho (caught two trout on one cast). My father taught me to drive at 12 years of age so I could get out of the wilderness if he were injured. Sometimes our whole family took the five day train trip to Washington, D.C., to spend Christmas with aunts and uncles in Grandfather's great stone house on Wyoming Avenue in Washington, D.C.

Schooltime meant practicing my violin two hours a day, modern dance lessons, and trips to Spokane (our city) for whistling lessons (yes, really). Mother's philosophy was "a busy child is a happy child." I adored picnics—not Sunday school—and longed to grow up.

My values are still rooted in smalltown life and the Depression years. I simply cannot break the habit of looking at the right hand side of the menu *before* I contemplate food choices. Disgusting. The money for my first year at Stanford University was a divorce case fee paid Daddy and it totalled $600. My children still ask, "Tell us about your allowance at college." Five dollars a month, it was, and with it I purchased silk stockings, went to movies, and sipped chocolate milk shakes.

After two years at the University I went on a trip with my Mother and a young sister to Hawaii. Falling in love, of course, I dreamed of returning to the quiet shores of Waikiki—and did! I lived and worked in Honolulu for two years before the War—World War II, that is (I'm feeling sensitive since a grandson just asked me if I was the first person ever born). I was a radio announcer on KGU, an affiliate of NBC in Honolulu. I Interviewed celebrities —even Errol Flynn—at Waikiki, football players during half times, and conducted several serious morning programs. I was the only female announcer.

Magical years, when the world was innocent and Waikiki boasted three hotels only: the Royal Hawaiian, the Moana, and the Halekalani. My love affair ended, and I went back to the mainland to Stanford University, fell in love once more, got a degree and a husband! Ah, how romantic I was, and yet—like my Mother before me—I was a virgin when I married at twenty-three.

My wedding dress was white velvet and I later made Christmas stockings for the children from its train. My Welsh grandfather had built the Congregational Church in Colfax and was its minister for many years. I was married there. In that red brick church I had gone to summer Bible School, acted in plays, surreptiously read tiny O. Henry books during the sermons. And there I was, walking solemnly down the aisle on my father's arm (he dressed in tails from *his* marriage) as he bowed and smiled to every second person.

Everyone in the County knew Daddy. He was born in Whitman County, his father a Congressman, and I, his daughter, had been Queen of the Rodeo one year, so they mostly knew me too. We were a "pioneer family," and when Daddy campaigned for office he sang Harry Lauder songs and we children did the Highland Fling while mother presided at the piano. Much of the county population attended my marriage and those who could not get into the church stood on the pews in the Sunday school wing.

After all the wedding festivities we, bride and groom, drove the sixty icy miles to Spokane and the great old Davenport Hotel. We had been there about an hour when Daddy telephoned. Two things. He had been worried about the December roads, and he had not given me any "pocket money" for my honeymoon. He arranged for the hotel manager to give me $50. Daddy always felt women should have money of their own. He wanted to start me out right.

So I was launched. A virgin alone in a room with a man. But a man she loved. I recall only how nice it was to make love. Wondrous. Sort of wicked. Exciting. Happy.

My handsome new husband was bred by centuries of Scottish ancestors. One of his uncles had already presented me with a book called "The Urquharts," which begins with the mating of Adam and Eve and proceeds through its many pages and centuries to chronical begettings right down to the current Urquharts in the twentieth century. Tragically my new husband, Richard Urquhart Wright, was a manic depressive. Only those who have lived for years with someone so afflicted can understand the confusion, the loneliness, and the adaptability demanded of the partner. Sometimes I've wondered—did my sheltered and idealistic childhood help give me the stability to cope with the next two decades, or were those years harder for me because I had expected another kind of life?

❧ 2 ❧

Country Girl

With what innocence I married Dick, that winter of 1940–41, just as Hitler's armies were invading Poland, overrunning the Low Countries and subjugating France. The whole western world was falling apart but my worries were confined to furnishing my tiny cottage in the woods above Lake Washington in Seattle.

Dick had graduated from Stanford University the spring before and gone to work for The Carnation Milk Company — at the enormous sum of $150 a month. The war was a tiny cloud on the horizon of each day as I learned to know the western part of my state. Our marriage united two old Washington families. Well, old for the west. Dick's great grandparents had come from Scotland in the 1840s, sailing six months around Cape Horn of South America to begin a new life in the Northwest Territories, just south of what, a decade later, would become a village named Seattle.

"The United States is bound to enter this war." My father was being realistic. "Perhaps Dick should apply for officer training."

The recruiting officer for the Naval Supply Corps officer training at Harvard Business School ignored the medical mention of Dick's few month's of depression during his college years, and eight months after our wedding we found ourselves bidding a weepy goodbye to our honeymoon cottage as we headed eastward. Dick would have six months training to become an Ensign in the Navy of the United States of America.

In those days a naval ensign was not allowed to marry, so the three already-married young officers had to find quarters for their wives. I found a flat with a Radcliffe senior girl and returned to college life atmosphere, except that my new husband shared my narrow bed on Saturday nights when he was permitted a "night off." My job at the Old Corner Bookstore in Boston brought in just enough money for me to buy Dick a watch for Christmas. I gave book reviews too, traveling all around the Boston area by train. Lonesome, cold and lonesome.

On December 7th I was returning to my apartment with kidneys and mushrooms for dinner when a shopkeeper told me of Pearl Harbor. No! No! Impossible! That peaceful tropical naval station where I had spent so many days sailing and so many evenings dancing. As I raced back to my apartment to tune in the news, I remembered, irreverently, a New Year's Eve dance I attended at Pearl Harbor a few years before. As I left the festivities, I thanked my hostess for a splendid evening and volunteered that "Your hard cider was the best I've ever had." She looked startled. "You mean the champagne?" Country girl!

But even with the destruction of that magnificent harbor in Hawaii and all it implied for my country, my own problems came first. Dick was irrationally depressed. By the time he finished the course at Harvard he was in bad shape — yet he passed the course easily and off we went to the naval base at Corpus Christi, Texas. Living in ticky-tacky pastel colored houses — row after row of naval officers on a stretch of desert — where all men left each morning for one of the three air bases surrounding Corpus and where most women were pregnant. The only air conditioned building in town was the Nueces Hotel and many of us gathered in its lobby evenings to read books or just talk. But before the year was out Dick went into a very deep depression. I was eight months "with child" and night after night I would get up when I felt Dick leave our bed. Some instinct told me to be on guard for often I would find him staring into the bathroom mirror. I would stay awake as long as my husband did. It was only a week until Dick was catatonic and had to be hospitalized with round-the-clock attendants.

"Do you want your husband to stay in the Navy and be treated or would you prefer him to have a medical discharge now? We don't want men like him in the service." I sat in front of the base commander's desk in my homemade maternity dress, appalled at the Commander's lack of sensitivity, far from home and family, but at least I had the sense to say, "He should stay in the Navy for treatment." Within a few days Dick was sent to Washington, D.C., to St. Elizabeth's — the naval mental hospital. It was early 1943, the battle of Tunisia raged, and the massive bombing of Berlin began. Alone in Corpus Christi, I was a long way from those events *and* from my home and family in Colfax, Washington. Soon my mother flew down to be with me at the birth of my first child.

Even with all the anesthetics mothers were given in those days, I heard the doctor's voice as I lay on the delivery table in that inhuman position prescribed for delivering mothers. He was saying that my baby looked "like a halfback coming through the line" as my first son popped into the world at the SPAWN Hospital in Corpus Christi.

My mother found me in tears when she came to visit her new ten-pound grandson, Richard LaFollette Wright. "Oh, Mother, I so wanted to nurse my baby and I don't have any milk." Mother was exasperated, "Didn't the doctors or anyone tell you that the baby must nurse to bring in the milk?"

In the early forties mothers were not encouraged to nurse, the hospital staff were impatient with the fumbling of new mamas, and doctors warned — if one insisted on nursing — "Never feed the baby more often than once every four hours."

How would Richard and I have survived without my common sense mother who encouraged me to nurse "whenever the baby is hungry." An experienced woman, she knew that large babies had to eat often (she'd borne five) and, most of all, *she* was so confident that *I* didn't feel guilty going against the rules of the day.

Four weeks later I flew on a once-a-week commercial plane which came through Corpus from Mexico City enroute to Washington, D.C. My seatmate was a middle-aged Mexican man who, when I tried to feed Richard without baring my breast, pulled out a picture of a large family and, beaming, said, "Mine!"

For three months I lived in a tiny apartment in Washington and visited my husband daily. The grounds of St. Elizabeth's were lovely and we walked and talked. With electric shock Dick gradually got better. (Years later I was to question the electric shock treatment for a number of reasons — most particularly they did not seem to change the length of Dick's depressed periods). But oh the despair I felt attending the Saturday night dances the hospital gave for its inmates! Richard, my son, was my normality in those horribly abnormal days.

Dick received his medical discharge in June and we drove west to take up residence in the tiny town of Carnation, Washington — just east of Seattle. There, in our little farm house ($15 a month), surrounded by black and white cows and white fences, Dick worked and regained his health entirely.

Maybe it was all over — those times of depression. Perhaps the doctors were wrong in Washington, D.C. when they diagnosed Dick as a manic-depressive. When the chance came for Dick to go to Stanford law school the next fall, we packed our newly canned peas and applesauce, baby furniture, and clothes into a just purchased-trailer ($12) and, with one baby in arms and another on the way, we set out for Palo Alto, California. My father helped us buy a home in neighboring Menlo Park and Dick began selling real estate with a classmate from Stanford (law school was six months away). Perhaps it was best that Dick never entered the law. He was successful at real estate. People trusted him and he had many friends in the area dating from his years at Stanford. So our second son was born, William Urquhart, and two years later baby Helen joined her brothers. Much of the time all was normal — mad confusion!

We were a young successful couple. Wasn't I often featured in the San Francisco *Chronicle* modeling some I. Magnin gown? Didn't we belong to the Menlo Country Club? Didn't Dick play in the Bing Crosby tournament at Pebble Beach?

We both adored our rambling redwood house on San Francisquito Creek with Stanford's 8,000 acres our backyard. We worked hard caring for our family, gardening, and earning a living, but there were months and months of shattering loneliness for me and really no one to share it with. The doctors had not been wrong in their diagnosis of Dick's illness. In a couple of years he had become depressed again. The cycle would begin in November and would end in early spring. Usually Dick was treated as an outpatient and then I would drive him home and, when he felt better, accompany him to the office.

Fortunately Dick was seldom manic, as those were the terrible times. One drink affected him like five and he could spend thousands of dollars — which were not in our bank account — in a day. I worried about his driving and once he undressed in the San Francisco airport and the police brought him to jail. The hassle getting Dick removed from the jail and taken to the hospital was horrendous. No one understands mental illness very well — not even the doctors — and certainly not policemen!

What is most difficult to understand is that once a spell of either depression or mania is over — it is over. I would try to pick up friendships and outside activities as if nothing had happened. I wondered how much the children even noticed when their beloved father who played with them, worked with them, taught them golf and imbued them with his fineness, suddenly withdrew from all activity. At least when they were small I believe they did not notice at all, in that self-centered way of children.

So, in time two wars were fought and won and I had borne three sons and two daughters. A friend once commented, "Mimi? no, she is not a Catholic. She is the Protestant's answer to Catholicism." Well, I wasn't that either. After five large healthy children — the last weighing more than twelve pounds at birth — I had my tubes tied.

Gradually I became less resilient and less supportive of Dick. The birth of the last two children added work and responsibility. There was no escape. Yet we tried, or rather *I* tried twice during winter depressions, to run away as a family. When there were only three children we spent a winter on a friend's cattle ranch in eastern Oregon. Later when Robert, the baby, was a year old we went to another friend's home in Hawaii for a few months. Those months away didn't help Dick, as his spells ended anyway after a few months no matter where we were or doing what, but they did help me. It seems incredible that we could survive financially during those years, but we managed, as the nature of the real estate business is feast or famine.

In 1959 at Christmas, Dick became very ill and had again to be taken to the Veterans' Hospital in Palo Alto. After only a few months I knew he could not come home again. And I could no longer live on all those levels, support the children, "stand still" for them, and take care of Dick. One of the tragedies of mental illness is how love flies out the window. I guess loving has much to do with the loved one's own feeling of self. Care, concern, and duty remain, but in the end my own survival came first.

Gradually I learned to live with myself—the self that was going to be divorced. One weekend after Dick had been in the hospital more than three years, Richard and I went to Carmel. Gentle, lovely Carmel-by-the-sea, was only a couple of hours drive from our home. I was determined to tell my oldest son of my decision to divorce Dick. A weekend at the ocean seemed like a good opportunity. We hiked and swam and drove down to those great old sulfur baths in the Big Sur and eventually I got up my courage. Struggling with each word I told Richard of my intentions. "Mother, we children have known for months!" Rick looked at me kindly. "It's OK, Mom, just hang loose."

The terrible-for-me day approached. Divorce was for those others—not for me! And deliberately to seek a divorce from someone who was ill—appalling! The case was to be held the day after Helen's birthday. On the night of the family birthday dinner this drama took place in our dining room where the table was festively set for the celebration:

—Our Siamese cat leapt onto the dining table

—Robert, age 8, entered the dining room tossing a baseball.

—I leapt at the cat and felt terrible pain in my left ankle, assuming Robert had thrown the baseball and hit me.

—I hit Robert as I fell to the floor in considerable pain.

—Robert fell down too, yelling and crying.

I had pulled my Achilles tendon leaping for the damn cat and after Robert and I sobbed in each other's arms, and my garbled apologies, we struggled through the birthday dinner and my always-lopsided homemade birthday cake. I fell into bed with the doctor's words ringing in my head, "You'll be in a wheel chair for a week or more."

The following morning I arrived at the County Courthouse in San Mateo County. I was pushed by Richard—pushed in my newly-rented-from-the-hospital wheel chair. Disaster—there was no elevator in the courthouse and the courtroom was on the second floor. So I arrived in court carried by Rick who deposited me in the front row—both of us amused and embarrassed. The judge listened patiently while I explained I was not permanently crippled. The divorce was granted, but the court ordered that I should be financially responsible for my ex-husband. That was fine and I went home and cried and cried for the beautiful young man I'd married — and for me.

⚮ 3 ⚮

Mistress

To be quite literal I guess I was a mistress twice. It's hard for me to categorize myself. Somehow a woman with five children isn't most people's — or my — idea of a mistress. First there was Charles. And without Charles and the wisdom and patience I learned from our loving, I could not later have stood still for John.

In any event, Charles became my lover some eighteen years and five children after my marriage to Dick. It was very much like "How to Make Two Lovers of Friends." We'd been friends, our two families with nine children between us, for a number of years. Both Charles and I had mates with emotional problems. And one day we came together as if preordained. Perhaps it was in response to the old adage "You have to get to give."

What a magical mysterious business it is, being in love. Each day had a golden border — a border knit from lovingness. There was another adult in the impersonal world who cared for *me,* shared with *me,* listened to *me.* The sound of his voice alone gave meaning and impetus to a day. Somehow the loving support we gave each other tided us over a few years and gave a warm glow to very trying times. Charles used to call me as he arrived at the train station in San Francisco each morning. That few minutes of talk would give me strength to fulfill my day's duties. I felt like a woman — a desirable woman. Later, when I took a temporary job at KQED (the educational TV station) in San Francisco, Charles and I would take the same train and hold hands under the *Wall Street Journal.* I would walk him part way to his office on the waterfront (where he ran a conglomorate of companies), have coffee in a stevedor's bar, and wander happily back to my temporary job, idly marveling at the persistence of weeds which had forced their way up between cracks of sidewalk cement. Recently I saw Meryl Streep in "Falling in Love." Many people discounted its message. Not me! That's how it was — except complicated by nine children!

But the world always seems to claim its pound of flesh and, since neither Charles nor I could leave our dependent spouses, we left each other. The months that followed that separation were agonizing. Hearts do break and it hurts, physically hurts. Much of the time I watched my hands work as if they were separate from my real self. I felt disembodied, floating with no base, no hope. How could I live knowing Charles also lived and ate and slept and longed. Our separation seemed against life.

Finally I filled my evenings, after bedding the children, by writing a book to Charles about our love. I sent it to him — that manuscript — and later he telephoned, "I took your treasured book with me to New York. I read it there and again when I returned to San Francisco. Yesterday I walked to the middle of the Golden Gate Bridge, tore the pages in pieces and threw them to the winds. It took me a long time."

I kept a copy, but I have never re-read my efforts. Not even yet. And what amazes me about people is that four years after loving Charles I met John. How could I have ever gotten involved again? To love a married man. Had I not learned?

Every hour of those four years before my divorce was jam packed! Filled with football and basketball games, teacher conferences, markets and meals, and stories read aloud, and an endless stream of English *au pair* girls — some competent, others all but hopeless. I especially remember Elizabeth. From Hampshire. "Mrs. Mimi, I can't wash the kitchen floor. I never have. My mum has a char woman for that." Little did I care. It was just one more job for me and Elizabeth added another pair of hands.

Living alone with the children — and the Elizabeths — and with Charles gone, I faced reality. Even if I worked full time at KQED I would not make enough money to support my family.

So a business was born. My mother thought of the idea. It was a travel service for companies. The electronic boom was just beginning in the area now known as Silicon Valley—between San Francisco and San Jose. Many of the executives of those companies were Stanford University graduates and my friends. So I called on them—Dave Packard and Bill Hewlett, the Varian Brothers, George Long, the President of Ampex, and others. I offered to start a service based on the campus at Stanford, to replace their own expensive-to-operate travel departments. How I hated those appointments. Hated asking them to accept on faith that I could do something and do it well!

The birth of "Travel Desk" was agonizing as I was painfully launched into the business world. At first I had two partners. Each man was a specialist in his travel field; one partner had been 20 years with United Airlines and the other—a Dutchman—had spent his career advising international travelers. It is one thing to have friends willing to help a new business but the service offered must be tops. My job would be the business end. My partners only lasted one year. Neither could accept the responsibility, the risks and decisions of their own business. But they brought, during our year together, a lot of knowledge to "Travel Desk," and some excellent staff.

"You want to borrow as much as $300,000 at a time. With what for security?" asked the loan manager at Wells Fargo Bank in San Francisco.

"You see my company must pay the airlines every two weeks but often the companies for whom we do business only pay us once a month. Here is a list of our clients."

"Hmmm, reliable companies. I see you have seventeen in all. I know many of their presidents. Well, I guess we could give you a $300,000 line of credit on non-notification receivables."

"On what? I don't understand non-notification receivables."

"It means that we loan you the money to pay your customers' bills to the airlines but we don't notify—let's say Sylvania Corporation—that we are doing so."

"OH!" and so I was launched in the world of high finance.

At the end of each business day I would say good night to the thirty-two members of my staff, ride my bicycle up the lane of eucalyptus trees on the Stanford campus, across the bridge and on down San Francisquito Creek to HOME. I learned what it is to come home dead tired from an office after a day of decisions which meant economic success or failure, a day of phones and people wanting everything. I learned how sweet a clean and orderly home can be, even if you have to hold your evening scotch and soda above your head, surrounded by eager offspring.

Gradually the tasks of living—starting the business—running the home—playing with children, lessened my anguish but not my loneliness.

One day John Summerskill, on a visit from Cornell University where he was Vice President, appeared in my office. He was an old friend of my beloved friend, Ann Pine.

I can never counsel my children sensibly on "love at first sight." It happened to John and me. We fell deeply and permanently in love in one day. We fell in love from such a different base than the first time around. Somehow a few important things were all that mattered. We had grown up. But it was scary too. John had a family in Ithaca, New York, but his marriage had long been unraveling. Both he and I had been raised to respect marriage. Indeed we still do! After John flew east, and even as we wrote long loving letters to each other, we faced the improbability of our marriage. So what to do? Was I willing to be a long-term mistress—more or less cutting off the possibility of marriage with some other man? Yes. Mature lovingness, undemanding, supportive with a large dash of laughter, is hard to come by. And all my children liked John and never questioned their mother's relationship.

So there I was, a mistress again. For a long time, too, as it was to be five years before John and I would marry even though we spent the last of those years living as a family while John was president of a major California university.

✴ *4* ✴

The Dream

"Mom, hey, mom," yelled nine-year old Robert from the big bedroom he shared with Zachary. "Make him leave me alone. I can't finish my homework."

Zachary, son of my friend Ann, had just turned four. During the past year, he and his mother had been part of our household. They had come for a visit when Ann separated from her husband and they were still with us more than a year later. That year on Mother's Day my youngest son, Robert, drew a colored picture of a butterfly under which he printed:

There are mothers
There are mothers
All through the air.
Wherever I look
One is always there.

Multiple mothering, the family — not couples — was the core of our lives.

As I turned from my half-packed suitcase to settle Robert and Zack's fracas, I heard Bill, my second son, call to Ann who was keeping me company in the bedroom. Bill, then a student at Stanford University, said, "Ann, could you come into the living room and talk to me about Christ?" Ann, who was Jewish, muttered to me, "Damn, I wish I'd never suggested that Bill take the New Testament course. It was bad enough last semester with the prophets. Now it's Christ, always Christ."

"Your reward for having studied the Bible," I observed. At least the girls were quiet. Daughter Wendy was closeted in her bedroom with a group of other giggling eleven-year-olds and her sister, Helen, eighteen, was out with her friend Jim. The fair Helen was in love, a condition the rest of us hoped would pass quickly, at least with this particular dull, conservative male.

How, I wondered, in the midst of my big, demanding family, would I ever be on the plane for India the next morning? "Never mind," I told myself, "it's business and survival — you'll do it somehow." Air India had invited me, as the owner of the second-largest travel business in California, to be their guest for three weeks of touring India.

While finishing the packing and making last-minute arrangements that evening, Ann and I had found ourselves composing an essay entitled: "Why I Want to Go to Law School." This for the benefit of my oldest son, Richard. Richard had graduated from Princeton in June, taken the national law school examinations, which he passed handily, and had been admitted to Boalt Hall at Berkeley. Now the university had imposed this ridiculous essay requirement and we had no idea how to reach Richard, wandering in Europe. Well, soon the younger children would go to bed and Ann and I would pour ourselves some Scotch and invent our most profound reasons for going to law school. Our efforts would be sent to Boalt Hall in Richard's name.

I loved being a mother, tiring and frustrating as it often was. Mothering was the thing I did best, and it seemed a profession of enormous value to me. And I liked it. As my life changed I found myself sometimes resenting my new role in the business world. It was a hard and harsh world out there earning money. Home and family are the cushion, the support that renew the wage earner.

That night I had my dream again.

It was not long after meeting John that I inherited the money from my grandfather. Though my life was full to brimming with daily chores at home and work, and I was keeping afloat financially, I felt a deep need for space. I was confused in my relationship with John. I felt trapped by daily events — I could not see a future for myself. For the children, yes, but not for me. And I, who seldom dreamt — at least to remember — kept having the same simple dream. Night after night I dreamt I was walking down Market Street in San Francisco and would fall down on the sidewalk. Immediately passers-by would rush to care for me. Then I would wake up. No need for professional advice on that one!

Slowly the reality of my inheritance worked its way into my subconscious, milled around a bit picking up support, and gradually I knew that, one way or another, those dollars were going to be my magic carpet to freedom. Since it was unlikely that the kindly souls of Market Street could really "take care" of me, I would take care of myself. Even as did Candide, I would find my simplicity.

But where would I find simplicity? In the past few years I had traveled, as guest of each country, to Portugal, England, Israel, and now was enroute to India for a month. I had spent a month 'down under' as a guest of Qantas Airline. On my arrival home from that trip and at the San Francisco airport, I was met by all of my children plus a guitar-playing friend. Totally ignoring me, they stood in a line near where we exhausted passengers awaited our luggage, and they belted out "Waltzing Matilda."

Those voyages were mini-escapes, but they did not offer peace, or time for contemplation, much less time to read.

A serendipitous evening provided my escape route. Slides presented after dinner at a friend's home showed the Cycladic Islands of Greece in all their whitewashed glory, with the vivid blues of the Aegean ever in the foreground.

All the bits and pieces seemed to come together as I replaced the Market Street dream with that of a sailboat billowing on a turquoise sea. And in one night I knew we — the children and I — would flee to Greece where it is warm and gentle and we would have no cares and no telephone. Simple. On my way home from India, I would stop in Athens and work out the details.

PART TWO

THE ODYSSEY

✱ 5 ✱

Love at First Sight

Devising a summer adventure for seven people in the Greek islands was not quite as hare-brained an idea as it seems, considering that I supported my family and paid my bills by doing just that sort of thing for other people. For five years I had run my own travel agency which catered only to the needs of business executives. In fact, my trip to India that fall was at the behest of the Indian government which had invited the owners of ten other travel agencies, plus a few newspaper reporters, to see their country.

It was my first trip to India and I was enchanted. We saw the Taj Mahal by moonlight, stayed in palaces and on houseboats in Kashmir and all the time were treated as VIPs. Toward the end of the three weeks we were taken to Madras, famous for its cloth and the center of the movie industry of India.

In later afternoon we all boarded a turbo-jet and took off for Bangalore. Our pilot took off without enough power and when we were fifty feet or so off the ground we crash-landed. The struts of the Fokker Friendship collapsed and we scooted along the runway as the metal underbelly of the plane burned. Immediately the cabin filled with black acrid smoke. As we crashed, I thought "thank God for seat belts." Almost immediately my only concern was to get *out* of the belt, and fumbling for my purse, I stood and tried to kick out a window. I heard an American voice over and over, "Don't panic, don't panic," and one by one we climbed out an escape window as a crew member yelled "run." Gaining the edge of the runway I watched the fire truck arrive and spray foam, and a bus came and took the twenty-six passengers (half Indians, the rest foreigners) back to the terminal. When we got inside I realized that I was still sucking the candy given us before take-off.

Madras is a "dry" state in India but we foreigners had between us eight bottles of scotch. We drank it all in the next four hours as we waited for another plane to fly us north.

A few days later on our final day in Kashmir, at the end of our Indian adventure, one of my luncheon companions held up a small basketball. "Look at this. I picked it up on the runway in Madras after our crash. I wish I knew whose it is."

"It's mine!" I shouted at the startled woman. Son Richard had given it to me his senior year at Princeton when his basketball team—led by Bill Bradley—had won the NCAA Championships, and I wore it on a golden wrist-chain.

After the crash I did not want to fly again. But I did—often. With palms wet from fear and my heart pounding I clutch the person—often an unknown person—seated next to me at take-off. On that first flight after the crash—the long, long flight from Bombay to Athens—the marvels and anguish of those weeks on the sub-continent faded as my whole being concentrated on being with son Richard, FAMILY!, after my scare. Then, there was the excitement of actually planning our big next summer's adventure.

As soon as I landed in Greece I felt at home. How much of that feeling was the hospitality of the Greek people, how much the excitement of seeing Richard, how much the upsurge of emotion all people in the western world seem to feel when they return to the source of so much of their art, architecture, and thought? I couldn't sort out my emotions at that moment, nor did I wish to. All I knew was that my middle-of-the-night instincts back in San Francisco had been on the mark. Greece, I felt sure, was right for us. It was time to go shopping for our yacht.

"Mother, you keep spelling it 'yatch'," complained Richard, peering over my shoulder as I scribbled postcards to Ann and the children. "If you can afford to rent it, you can at least spell it correctly."

In addition to being a good speller, a loving (if sometimes critical) son, tall and handsome Richard also had the ability to get things organized. He found a retired sea captain who was a

broker for persons wishing to buy, sell, rent, or hire boats of all
varieties. Through this broker and friends living in Athens, we
saw a veritable fleet of seaworthy vessels. We inspected fat
"caique" yachts, sleek motor-powered yachts, and small jib-
headed sloops. We saw Anthony Quinn's wonderful square
yacht, built like a house, and were tempted.

One captain, hoping to entice Richard to rent, described the
antics of a French group he had recently transported through the
Aegean.

"They had an extra girl, *pedhi mu* (my boy), and every night the
men rolled dice for her favors."

"Interesting," said Richard, a bit wistfully, "but *we* are a
family."

Then we found our yacht. The elegant, slender *Eva Maria,* as
impractical as she was lyrical, seduced us from the minute we
saw her. She was an eighty-one-foot racing schooner built in
Scandinavia in the thirties for a wealthy Greek from Egypt. No
nylon sails had she! The *Eva* had heavy cotton sails and only
recently had acquired her first motor—a Volvo. Because she
drew eleven feet of water she would not be able to moor in all
harbors—but never mind. Her tasteful decor reflected the fact
that she had always been a private yacht. The owner had died
recently and his heirs—two daughters—were unsure whether
they should keep their father's old love or opt for the convenience
of a power boat. We were the beneficiaries of their indecision.

That night the captain-broker introduced us to "No. 17," a
well-known bar near Syntagma (Constitution) Square in Athens.
Drinking icy martinis in front of the open fire we took the leap.
We would charter the *Eva Maria* for three full months, long
enough for us to gain a discount. Moreover, we would charter
her with an option to buy—a decision we would make after the
first month of sailing. Instead of $200 a day ($18,000 for the
three months) our contract was for $15,000 for the summer and
that included a crew of four. I had decided again. The $15,000
would be applied against the $45,000 purchase price. Obviously
I had gone clear overboard!

Immediately the papers were signed the sheer impracticality of
my behavior crashed on me. Was I crazy to be throwing away

my small inheritance for a three-month vacation? Richard had received little financial help during his four years at Princeton, and could anticipate leaner times in law school. In Munich, he had lived on a hundred dollars a month, so close to the poverty line that when he visited his girlfriend in Bonn, he was forced to borrow clothes for dinner. Helen was a sophomore at the University of Colorado and Bill was still at Stanford. Wendy and Robert had years of education in front of them, and . . . and . . . There were countless *reasons* why I should salt away the money. But I was fed up with reasons.

After five years of being practical, I was bone tired. For five years I had supported the family, not by choice but by necessity. I had started a business, earned the money, and been father and mother to the children. Only when I was forced to abandon the conventional feminine role had I begun consciously to realize the joys and special strengths of being a woman. Before, I had simply been one.

Now, with one stroke of the pen, I had given myself a reprieve. All through the long summer months, the children and I would be together, idling the days away in a world without meetings, planes, timetables, alarm clocks, telephones, television, unpaid bills . . . all the accoutrements and double-edged blessings of this modern world.

Thoreau had his Walden; Huck and Jim had their raft on the Mississippi; Candide and Cunegand cultivated their little garden near Constantinople. The Greek islands and the *Eva Maria* would be our way.

Months earlier, on a trip to Scotland, I had read Homer's *Odyssey* for the first time. My reaction to that experience must have been yet another unconscious nudge toward Greece. As Robert Payne writes in *The Gold of Troy,*

> In every age, men have read Homer but never has he been read so widely or attentively as in the present age, and with good reason. He holds the mirror up to nature. The world he describes is the world of today, for little has changed in the thirty centuries since the burning of Troy. The fires burn; the besieged make their sorties; everywhere the cries of the doomed can be heard. We are all Trojans; and Homer, the blind wanderer among ancient islands, describes our present plight with

excessive brightness. It is not that he was a prophet; it is simply that no one else has ever described the human condition with such starkness and majesty.

With a signed contract in my suitcase, I said good-bye to Richard, and flew back to San Francisco, my head spinning with happiness, some lingering uneasiness, relief, and anticipation. We, "the besieged," would make our sortie in less than nine months. Then we would sail the seas of Homer and wander through the islands Odysseus knew. Perhaps in the end, we, like Odysseus, would find our Ithaca.

⋆ 6 ⋎

Hoist the Sails

Sailing yachts look incomplete when their sails are furled, but even with her rigging exposed, the *Eva Maria* had a purity of line and natural grace. I felt sheer pride of possession when we boarded her in the early afternoon of June 9, 1965, in Pireaus, Greece.

Only an hour earlier, we had arrived at Athens airport, the tiresome plane trip from San Francisco behind us. Our mound of luggage was delivered quickly. Richard awaited us with Tom Singer, a friend who would sail with us for a few weeks to instruct us in the Greek language. Richard, so very tall (6'4") and slender . . . Richard, who had become father as well as son in our family. I was glad he had been able to spend a year in Munich following his graduation from Princeton. He needed time for himself. Now he would have a chance to be part of our summer idyll, after so many years of discipline and purposeful endeavor.

I had seen him last in February before I returned home from Winston Churchill's funeral in London. Munich is not exactly on the direct route between London and San Francisco. One of the few advantages of the travel business is the chance to have two almost-free passes each year on every airline! When a foreign correspondent friend called and asked if I could fly to Churchill's funeral, I barely hesitated. "Give me an hour to be sure Ann can be with the children and to get an airline pass. I'll call you right back."

In those days in London seeds were sown for lifelong memories. Churchill had written the plot and planned the staging for one of the great productions of all time. It was the end of an era. Though my correspondent friend could have gotten us directly into Westminster

Hall to view Churchill lying in state, we chose to join the people's line which was sometimes two miles long. We entered the queue at three in the morning. The end of the line was along the Thames and directly across the river from the Parliament buildings. We found ourselves in the middle of a diversified group. There were women in evening dress on the arms of tuxedo clad males, families clustered with children dressed for school. Old people, young people and it was cold! Human snails all, we edged forward, talked, cursed the weather, discussed history. Across the bridge, through Victoria Park where—with Sylvia Pankhurst's statue gazing on approvingly—we were handed tea in paper cups by Ladies of the Volunteer Flying Corps. "Sugar, dearie? Here, let me stir it for you."

At the end of the long funeral day—London on foot; cannons going off in parks; golden carriages and finally the procession on the Thames, I bid Churchill and London farewell as I flew off to see Richard in Munich. Rick took me to his apartment, little more than a garret actually, and I noticed to my maternal distress that he was unable to stand up straight except in the very center of the room. "Ah well," I reasoned, "it will be good training for the yacht."

Now we were actually seeing the yacht alongside the dock in Piraeus, the harbor of Athens. "Isn't she something!" The *Eva Maria!* Her four crew members dressed all in white with the ship's name blazoned across their shirts waved as they bustled to and fro with the provisions we had ordered from a shop in Athens. We added our nine pieces of luggage to the heap of other supplies and went on board to meet the crew.

Captain Antonio was a solid, middle-sized, middle-aged man from the small island of Kithira, off the tip of the Peloponnese. The sea had been his life, as it is for so many island Greeks. Shaking his strong, wind-chapped hand, and knowing that he would be responsible for our safety throughout the summer, I thought how sad it must be for him to be separated from his wife and sons for three months. I had yet to learn that on islands such as Kalymnos the sponge fisherman regularly bid farewell to their families after Easter and return—if they are lucky—late the next fall.

The two sailors, both named Nikos, greeted us shyly.

"*Kali mera* (good morning)," said Nikos I.

"*Kalos erthite* (welcome)," said Nikos II.

All we could do was smile at them eagerly, burdened as we were by a total lack of a common language.

In tandem the two Nikoses presented a slightly comic sight. Nikos I was balding and skinny. Nikos II was quite short, but his unimposing stature was more than offset by the fierceness of his mustache. Such a bellicose appearance was not mere bravura we soon learned; he had fought with the Greek resistance when the Germans occupied his native Crete during World War II.

Yorgo, our steward, was a handsome, open-faced young man who had sailed with the *Eva* for the past three years. One of his duties on this cruise would be to help us out in the galley since we had decided not to hire a cook. With only eight mouths to feed and four women on board, we had reasoned that a cook would be excessive baggage . . . a grave mistake we soon found out.

At that moment, though, nothing mattered except being on our yacht in Pireaeus. Ann and I looked at each other, shook our heads in mock bewilderment, and began to laugh with sheer delight.

"We're really here . . . actually in Greece," I said.

"Really here," Ann echoed, "what a yacht!"

Even twelve-year-old Wendy (whose friends had gathered to weep copiously with the help of a few cut onions at her departure from San Francisco) whooped excitedly as she raced around the yacht with young Robert, exploring every nook and cranny.

"Oh, look," she shrieked, "my room has its own ladder." Our nubile bud disappeared into the stateroom which she would share with her older sister, Helen, while Ann and I checked out the master stateroom. It was a spacious room, papered in rose and white fabric, with its own "head" adjoining. A dressing table separated our wooden-sided beds whose linen sheets had hand-embroidered borders representing waves. Down the main hall from our quarters there was another single stateroom, another bath, and a cozy wood-panelled salon which would serve double-duty as a bedroom for four and a dining room when the weather forced us below deck.

The Captain's quarters near the wheel also served as a chart room. Farther along in the bow section were the crew's quarters. The galley, we noted, was small and narrow.

"No cook?" I mused briefly, then put the thought out of my mind. At the moment I was enchanted with our yacht and its elegant teakwood deck.

Part of the *Eva's* grace was the effect of her narrow prow and even narrower stern. Even at the center she was only sixteen feet wide, which left a minimum of space for topside activities. Still, we could manage outdoor meals with a small table and four of us seated on one side of the boom and four on the other. A deep blue awning covered the dining area, while deck chairs placed toward the stern allowed space for sunning and relaxing. Midship hung two small boats, a handsome well-shaped wooden dinghy and a speed boat, *The Albatross.*

In less than an hour we had stowed all our food and gear and sailed out through the narrow neck of Pasalemani Harbor, the harbor guard tooting us into the broader waters of the Saronic Gulf. Even though Paselemani Harbor fascinated us with its freighters, ocean liners, tugs, fishing boats, and yachts, we were glad to be at sea. A brisk breeze blew away all traces of the heat and odors of the teeming port.

"Would you like to hoist the sails now?" Captain Antonio asked, looking directly at Richard.

"Yes, let's hoist the sails," I answered.

Ignoring me completely, the Captain continued to stare at Richard. Richard looked at me, and without exchanging a word we grasped the delicate cultural complexity of our situation. Could I, a woman, tell a Greek sea captain what to do? Never! So I nodded almost imperceptibly at Rick who then replied to our captain in his most decisive voice, "Yes, Captain Antonio, hoist the sails."

Immediately the two Nikoses and Yorgo were at their posts, and with all able-bodied males on board pulling their hardest, the heavy white sails unfurled and we were underway southeast along the coast of Attica.

We continued to play our chain-of-command charade throughout the summer. I would make a decision, sometimes singly and sometimes in family conference, whether to anchor in a bay or at dockside; whether to stay in port or move on immediately; whether to sail to the next island or to change course. I would discuss my decision with Richard, who would then discuss it with Captain Antonio (with Tom Singer acting as translator in the beginning). Only then would the plan become operational.

Several hours after setting sail, we turned into the harbor of a small, uninhabited island near Sounion and dropped anchor for lunch. Robert, our youngest, instantly clambered over the side and dived into the sea. Just as instantly, he popped up again.

"It's salty!" he shouted in amazement, bobbing up and down like a cork in the clear green water. A veteran of California swimming pools since he learned to swim at fifteen months, Robert was a newcomer to sea water.

The four of us followed Robert into the sea and swam noisily ashore, the first of many such expeditions. Striking out across the expanse of sand, each of us went his own way, stooping occasionally to examine a bright pebble or shell and letting the noonday sun bake the wetness out of our skin and swimsuits.

I felt as buoyant as I had in the water, sensing in an almost physical way the evaportion of the cares I had accumulated in past years. I knew then with complete certainty that my decision to come to Greece had been right. "It feels right," I told myself, pondering the miracle that had brought me, my offspring, and friends to this tiny Greek island. More miraculous yet, I realized that when we tired of this particular spot, we could sail somewhere else in our elegant *Eva Maria*. As Rick said earlier, we had the luxury of "changing our backyard at will." A whole world studded with islands beckoned, and we had three months in which to explore it. This summer would become our "island in time."

My fantasy came jolting to earth as an enormous sow appeared on the horizon of our "uninhabited" island. She gazed at us with disinterest, waded into the sea where she wallowed briefly, and then sauntered on. There's nothing like a pig to put paradise in perspective.

The magic spell broken, Wendy drew our attention to tar on her foot, the sticky black residue discharged by a passing tanker. Yorgo, who had just arrived in *The Albatross* with our picnic lunch, showed her how to remove it by scrapping it with one of the many cockleshells which abound on Greek beaches. Robert, who watched this operation with fascination, rushed to help Yorgo spread the cloth and lay the dishes. Never before had I known him to set a table without severe parental pressure. He had obviously entered into a new stage of hero worship with exposure to this resourceful young Greek. Yorgo, for his part, patted Robert on the back and smiled broadly at the rest of us.

"*Ee skia mu,*" he said with amusement.

"He says Robert is his shadow," Tom explained. And so he would remain for the rest of the summer.

On to Sounion we sailed in the golden twilight. The majesty of Poseidon's temple high on the southernmost tip of the Attican peninsula was a reassuring sight now that we were sailors under his protection. Poring over our guidebooks and histories, we wondered out loud how many sailors for how many centuries had looked shoreward to that magnificent marble edifice. The discussion on deck continued:

When Thesseus passed this way after slaying the Cretan minotaur, did he pay homage to the god of the sea from the prow of his ship whose forgotten black sails billowed so fatally? The guidebook said one legend names Poseidon as the real father of this great hero.

Did the Persians, who destroyed an earlier temple on this site, have their own god of the sea or, with their roots deep within the Asian landmass, did they reject the importance of such a deity? The Greeks, whose lives and livelihood always depended on the sea, set about rebuilding the temple immediately, and it was standing there when they defeated the Persians at the Battle of Marathon in 490 B.C.

Did the Crusaders turn their backs on this pagan temple as they rounded the Cape on their way to Byzantium? Or did those Christian warriors fail to realize that this was the sacred precinct of the ruler of the seas and brother to Zeus?

Would Poseidon guard the modern sailors on the *Eva*—or persecute us as he had persecuted Ulysses on his journey from Troy back to Ithaca?

This game of questions and answers became academic, however, as we sailed into the center of the lovely horseshoe bay of Sounion and dropped anchor just below the temple.

The following morning was windless so we put to sea using our Volvo motor, and we arrived shortly at Kythnos, one of the northernmost islands of the Cyclades group. Again, the knowledgeable Captain Antonio steered us into a hidden bay whose water was so pure, so clear, and so inviting that we raced for our suits and plunged in. We were dying to swim naked, but sensed that our crew would be shocked.

Yorgo and Robert took *The Albatross* to a nearby village for gas and supplies. They returned with the makings of a feast: village bread and two huge lobsters. After boiling the lobsters and garnishing them with tomatoes, potatoes, and eggs, Yorgo presented the platter on deck as proudly as any maitre d'hotel in a three-star restaurant. And no meal was ever better. We ate it all, including the garnish and the hard crusty loaves of bread.

After lunch we talked about our cooking problem. Yorgo, the mainstay of our galley, had thus far served as steward, chief purchaser of supplies, sailor, and pilot. Of all the crew, he was obviously the best sailor. We agreed that as soon as we reached Mykonos we would lighten his workday by taking over the shopping and cooking.

Too happy to nap, I sat on deck all afternoon, my feet braced against the ship's rail. A high wind came up, and we seemed to fly toward our destination, Syros. Small islands, close and distant, appeared and disappeared as fleetingly as shadows cast on the water . . .

Was it really me—flitting between Greek islands without a care in the world? What a few years since the perimeters of my world were the continental United States and Hawaii. When my sister, Maryly, and I were twenty and twenty-one Daddy offered us a summer in Europe . . . to broaden our horizons. The Depression was ending and Daddy was finally being paid in cash instead of potatoes and old cars! That was 1938. But our European summer fell to Hitler's invasion of Czechoslovakia. Instead Maryly and I took a three month's driving trip around the United States. The highlight of our great adventure was a month in New York City with Daddy's sister, Suzanne LaFollette. We nieces and nephews adored our beautiful and bright Aunt from the East. Suzanne had never married, although the family gossip was that she was the mistress of a famous writer for many, many years. "No man," she would admonish us girls, "is worth losing more than one night's sleep over."

Ten years before our journey East, Suzanne had published a book which created quite a stir, *Concerning Women* (recently republished). But her main career was in the field of editing. William Buckley recently wrote a tribute to Suzanne, "She was a very beautiful woman, with a hilarious sense of humor . . . and a trunkful of anecdotes about her glittering editorial apprenticeship and career: an editor of *The Freeman,* under Albert Jay Nock; secretary and editor of publications for the commission of inquiry into charges made against Leon Trotsky in Moscow trials (The Dewey Commission); managing editor of the *American Mercury;* managing editor of *National Review.* When teased about her political move from the left to the right, she commented, "I haven't moved. The world has moved to the left of me."

Suzanne, with many other writers and artists, made the Chelsea Hotel in Manhattan their home. Maryly and I were put on the floor above Auntie Suzanne's apartment in the studio of her brother—our uncle—and there we slept amid unfinished sculptures and exotic paintings. John Sloan and his tiny wife, Dolly, lived right next to Suzanne, and Maryly and I both came under the great painter's spell and loved the long evenings when he or Ben Stolberg would regale us with stories. Ben's favorite was how he sat on Franz Joseph's knee. He couldn't remember why.

Constantly in awe, what with the Empire State Building, Jones Beach, and the Second Avenue "El," Maryly and I distressed our beloved Aunt whenever any intellectual subject arose. One morning she told us that we were going to have dinner that evening with Alexander Kerensky. In unison we asked, "Who?"

"God dammit!" Suzanne pounded the table, "You children from the west are so ignorant!"

Of course she was right. Colfax High School was certainly not the center of learning and somehow even at university we managed to feel very far, indeed, from Europe and its problems (to say nothing of the rest of the world).

Strangely, Alexander Kerensky was to become a dear friend of mine in the 1960's. He moved to Stanford and wrote books about his period of history. He used the Hoover War Library and he and I had lunch every Friday—for a number of years—always starting with a martini. I loved his tales of childhood. Alexander and Lenin were from the same town and Lenin's father was principal of the high school and Alexander's father principal of the lower school. So the two boys had gone to each other's father's school. "But," Alexander would hasten to remind me, "Lenin was twelve years older than I." Then he would tell how his mother worried that he would be a hairdresser as he loved fixing his two older sisters' hair. Over the years I wondered, after learning the history of Alexander's love life (the story of three women), if the world would have been different (at least the history of Russia) if Alexander had not been in love with his wife's cousin during the brief time he was President of Russia. It takes a lot of time and energy to be in love! One time when Alexander came to our house for dinner he was playing ring-around-the-rosy with the younger children and I worried he'd fall in the fire pit because he had terrible myopia. "Rick," I instructed, "go rescue Alexander from the children." "O.K. Mom, but isn't it fascinating to watch him. It's like seeing history on the hoof."

Richard had spent the summer of his 16th year in Russia as a member of the first group the Choate School sent to live and study there. Later Alexander insisted I study Russian so Richard and I could talk, and he got me a tutor named Mr. Passion! My lessons were in Alexander's office in the Hoover Library. In 1966, on my birthday, Alexander came for dinner. He was to leave the next day for New York and spend time with his publisher. He looked so frail and smaller than usual and I worried that I might not see him again. As he left I said, "Alexander, I love you." Bowing over my hand he replied, "Ah, my dear, it is too late."

Gazing at a fast approaching Aegean island I wondered where Alexander was — as I blithely wandered among islands. Maybe in Liverpool with his second son while his first wife read aloud to him? I wished he could have joined us on the *Eva* for a few days. He would have loved every minute.

It was late afternoon when we dropped anchor in a small cove off the southern coast of Syros, which placed us in a convenient position for our ongoing voyage to Mykonos the following day. A quick consultation with the *Guide Bleu* informed us that this island had dominated sea transport in modern Greece until the

1870s, but had gradually given way to Piraeus after that time. Its large port, Ermoupoulis, is the capital of the Cycladic islands, and those who spend time ashore can see a replica of the Milan opera house, many magnificent old homes, and a few delightful remnants of Venetian architecture. Instead of visiting those wonders, however, we peered through binoculars to see if we could identify the hills which an American named Pearson had recently tried to reforest with pine trees. I had read his book about his dream of a green Syros — and his struggles with the Greek bureaucracy. His project was also and repeatedly thwarted by the goats who ate the succulent new pine needles.

That evening at sundown, sipping ouzo over ice, I read Mary Renault's *The Last of the Wine*. It was the perfect book for the early days of our Greek summer. In all her historical novels, Mary Renault makes ancient Greek life easy to enter. I felt I must read quickly, however, if I were to make my way through even a fraction of the impressive library we had brought with us. In addition to the books we carried from San Francisco, Tom and Richard had ladened our shelves with their own weighty volumes, including the *Life of Cellini* and all Churchill's war books! We had at least twenty books on Greece and three on yachting. We had Aldous Huxley, Herbert Muller, Robert Graves, and assorted Durrells (Gerald and Lawrence). We had history books, both Turkish and Egyptian. We had *Moby Dick*, *The Life of Gandhi*, and *Winnie-the-Pooh!*

At the sound of happy giggles, I looked up and saw Wendy, seated on the chartroom steps, reading aloud to Robert from *Seventeen*. "No television," I said to myself. "Thank God."

Wendy wore a dress made of two bath towels, her fifth costume of the day. At twelve, she was a wondrous mixture of budding teenager and little girl. Physically she was well-developed and incredibly beautiful, with olive skin, deep brown eyes, and very curly blond hair which she had tried to iron straight several times in the past year. Emotionally, she was totally self-absorbed and refreshingly open about her topsy-turvy emotions which were in transition from childhood to sexual maturity. Shortly before we left Menlo Park for Greece, I had gone into her room to kiss her goodnight and tuck her in bed. As

I bent over her cheek, she had turned her head, kissed me squarely on the mouth, and wiggled her tongue.

"Wendy!" I said, drawing back in shock.

"Just practicing, Mother," she answered cheerfully.

"Yes," I mused, "a summer with a big sister, two mothers, and three brothers — younger and older — is a sound prescription. And at such an impressionable age when all the pressure of our culture seems to bear down on such small shoulders, how important to have a little time — time just 'to be.' "

I turned my gaze to the other members of our extended family who lay on a row of air foam pads: Ann reading *Bitter Lemons;* Richard, a book about Joseph Kennedy; and Tom Singer, *Zorba the Greek* (in Greek).

Tom, a classmate of Rick's from Princeton, would sail with us for two or three weeks. His professorial mien was enhanced by a lush chocolate brown beard, carefully nurtured during the past winter as an instructor at Athens College. It contrasted becomingly with his blue, blue eyes. We were lucky to have him to bridge the gap between ourselves and the crew. We spoke English. They spoke only Greek. The fact that among us we also spoke French, Italian, German, and a bit of Russian, did not help one iota.

Tom rose to admonish us: "Remember you must all know the Greek alphabet by morning."

We had protested the assignment earlier, but to no avail. We abandoned our various books for the small, gray, Greek grammars and soon we were making tentative forays into the complexities of Greek written and spoken letters. It was reassuring to learn that the first and last letters of the twenty-four character alphabet are *A (alpha)* and *O (omega)* and that explained the origins of our common phrase for the beginning and end of things. But how to remember that *Z (zeeta)* follows *E (ephseelon)* or that π is pronounced "pee" and not "pie" as we had always assumed? With repeated corrections from Tom, we began to make slow headway. We realized that "Pi Phi" sorority sisters would be "pee fees" in Greece and that the cohorts of Phi Beta Kappa would be more correct to speak of their fraternity as "Fee Veeta Kappa."

This was only the beginning. Real lessons would commence the next morning during our sail to Mykonos to pick up Bill and Helen who were joining us after finishing their university exams in the States.

7

All Together

Sometimes blind faith becomes a self-fulfilling prophecy, as happened on the mid-June morning we sailed into Mykonos. We were absolutely sure that Bill and Helen would meet us there, although we knew that the two of them had begun their flights on opposite coasts of America and after meeting in Athens, as we hoped they had, they were supposed to have discovered the ferry boat schedule and were supposed to have boarded it—all this without speaking or reading Greek.

We docked the *Eva* against the cement quay which jutted into the bay and waited for the ferry which materialized on the horizon. Within thirty minutes it landed and disgorged a mob of unruly passengers, including Helen and Bill who had traveled third class "with the vegetables, chickens and goats," as Helen described it.

Our wild and demonstrative reunion caused the passengers on three cruise ships to stare at us in amazement. After dispatching their heavy luggage ("My God, more books?" I wondered) to the yacht, we repaired to a seaside *kafeneion* for drinks and talk.

"It's a good thing you met us," Helen said, sipping a thirst-quenching, delightfully cold Greek beer called Fix, "we were down to our last drachma."

"Ah, youth!" I murmured and marveled that my daughter's faith in events outmeasured even my own.

"And your exams?" I asked. "How did they go?"

"Oh fine, I think," she said. "But it's good to be out of Colorado and here in Greece. I'm going to sleep for a week."

Helen did look tired, yet blooming, as only a nineteen-year-old can. With long black hair shining down her back, black eyes and olive skin, she seemed a Mediterranean. But she isn't, at least not to our knowledge — though one would suspect that some Greek or Roman, in centuries past, climbed the family tree in Wales or Scotland.

Bill, two years older than Helen, and a year younger than Richard, was as tall as his older brother. But instead of dark hair and eyes, he had brown curls, blue-gray eyes, and a guileless, light-the-world smile. Looking at him across the small marble table, I remembered how I complained to the naval doctor in the fall of 1943 about a lingering nausea. I suspected stomach flu, a diagnosis which caused arched eyebrows and a skeptical smile.

"Perhaps you are pregnant," the doctor gently suggested.

"Oh, no," I answered, glancing down at Richard in my arms, "I already have a baby."

"Is your husband with you?" he asked, for those were wartime years.

"Yes," I admitted . . . and so, before long, was Bill.

Arriving in Mykonos Bill had already missed his east coast love, Katy, whom he had met and wooed the past spring in New York. He had studied one semester at New York University on leave from Stanford where he was a history major. Even thoughts of Katy, however, could not dampen his enthusiasm for the long, lazy days in Greece which lay ahead. During the last six years he had worked every summer without a break before or after the academic grind.

As we finished our Fix beers (the butt of many jokes that summer), we watched the tourists from the cruise boats. Looking confused and ill at ease, they wandered in and out of the gaudy shops, examined the merchandise which hung on racks in the street, and now and then glanced up at the famous windmills. Some actually walked the length of the half-moon waterfront before settling down for a drink. They had "done" Mykonos.

We, with a whole summer at our disposal, were just beginning to explore a Greek island. First, we observed the Greek men in the coffee house to see if they showed signs of hereditary baldness. Bill had read one of the works of the geographer Strabo and learned that this peripatetic scholar of the first century B.C. had been struck by the prevalence of baldness on Mykonos — so much so, that for centuries afterwards his fellow Greeks had referred to a bald man as a *Mykonian*. Not so in the twentieth century, we concluded. A luxuriant growth of black hair covered the pate of every Greek we saw.

Next we looked at the village itself. It was our first exposure to the architecture of the Cyclades and we were dazzled by its whiteness. Whitewash, the staple of every Greek village house-holder, is twice as white as paint. Even the sorriest, rain-stained building becomes virginal with a few swipes of the long-handled whitewash brush.

Whiteness was everywhere: white cubistic houses, white cu-polas atop square white churches, white sails turning against circular white windmills, white birds perched on white dove-cotes, white steps interrupting narrow white lanes. Our aching eyes welcomed the brilliant patches of red geraniums and ma-genta bougainvillea and lingered on the coolness of gray shadows cast across various surfaces. But even the shadows from white-washed walls are different; by moonlight, they seem phosphor-escent.

"Let's leave this tourist scene," Bill said abruptly. "After all that time on a plane and ferry I feel like walking."

Eight people walking together is complicated anywhere, but the narrow lanes of Mykonos forced our family to march along in single file like a giant sixteen-legged caterpillar. The provocative streets led us heedlessly this way and that until we lost all sense of direction. Even the general location of the harbor became a mystery. Suddenly Richard, who led the procession, stopped and turned to face the rest of us.

"They did it on purpose," he said.

"Did what?" we chorused.

"Built the streets this way," he explained. "In the old days, pirates were always a threat to the islands, so they designed this maze to confuse them."

"Well, they certainly got it right," shouted Ann who was bringing up the rear of the caterpillar. "Except, now we're the confused ones."

"No wonder the cruise boat people stick to the waterfront," Helen observed.

Being lost in Mykonos was exciting—half fun house, half picture postcard. Tiny balconies sagged under the weight of potted plants and flowers. A large olive oil tin full of basil caught our attention and drew us into yet another byway. Thick-necked grapevines sprang from small squares of earth, each vine producing enough greenery to shade a whole balcony or small courtyard. Hanging everywhere were bunches of grapes ripening slowly in the summer sun. Now and then we encountered an adventurous cruise boat passenger who had also penetrated the maze, and we would all turn sideways to let him pass.

After ten or fifteen minutes we found ourselves in front of a shop belonging to Joseph the Tailor. After the requisite preliminaries—introductions, pleasantries, and small cups of coffee—Richard ordered much-needed summer trousers to be made of navy blue-and-white striped denim.

"The trousers will be ready on the morrow," said Joseph with a flourish.

Had he learned his English out of Shakespeare, I wondered, but before I dared ask, a row of handmade sandals caught my eye. Each of us bought a pair and put them on. Our exploratory expedition would be a good occasion to break them in.

We decided to leave the village and to investigate the countryside, with thanks to Joseph who walked us to the edge of the maze and pointed to a donkey path leading up the hill. Up and up we walked, struggling over the loose rocks scattered between stone walls until we eventually arrived on a plateau high above the village. Resting on one of the inevitable stone walls, we looked down and marveled at the distance we had climbed.

In the field behind us a woman drove four mules round and round a stone threshing pit filled with wheat, while her husband sat on the largest of the stones watching. Through the still, hot air Greek music blared . . . but from where? Sharp-eyed Wendy quickly solved the mystery.

"See, there it is. On the haystack," she said. "In the baggie." Sure enough, a small transistor radio enclosed in a plastic bag brought a bit of the modern world into this bucolic scene.

In the field on the other side of the path red poppies bordered a plot of potato plants. Figs were ripening on a gnarled tree with smooth gray bark. Farther down the hill there was a patch of tomatoes, as red as the poppies. A large pig dozed in a stone enclosure, and goats rested in the shade of a stone wall. In the distance several old stone windmills with thatched roofs had been converted into homes.

Below us lay the village, quiet and withdrawn now that most of its three thousand inhabitants took their siesta behind cloth-draped doors. The somnolence of the afternoon, accentuated by the hypnotic buzzing of cicadas, was catching, at least so far as the feminine contingent of our party was concerned. Ann, Helen and I sat down and rested our backs against the broad stone walls. Wendy curled up and put her head in my lap.

To the southwest we could identify the two islands of Greater and Lesser Delos, which we would visit the next day. How was it possible, I wondered, that these small rocky outcroppings could once have been the political and religious capital of the Cyclades, which in turn constituted a flourishing civilization more than four thousand years ago?

As Robert Liddell, an authority on the eastern Mediterranean, has written,

> The Aegean is the heart of the Greek world which, since the dawn of history, had looked for guidance to the sanctuary of Apollo, on the island of Delos. Round this small island circle the Cyclades, and to this fact they owe their name. These link up with other islands, forming stepping-stones to East and West. In ancient times (and even today in this mountainous country) it is the land that separates, and the sea that unites.

Ann and I pulled books out of our bags and began to compare facts.

"Did you know," I said, scanning my Blue Guide, "that in ancient times there were only about a dozen Cycladic islands with Delos as their capital? And that today there are thirty with Syros the capital?"

"How come?" Wendy asked sleepily.

"Because this whole area is really a submerged plateau and the islands are the peaks of hills. As the level sank over the centuries, more peaks became exposed."

"And did you know," I continued relentlessly, "that these islands were once heavily wooded, but now are rocky and barren, containing mainly olives, figs, and grapevines?"

"How come?" Wendy asked again, this time more faintly.

"They cut down the trees, I suppose," I replied. "They must have needed wood for ships and didn't think to plant new trees. Or if they did, the goats may have devoured the seedlings. Remember the problem that Henry Chauncey's Harvard classmate had when he decided to plant a pine grove on Syros?"

"Here, let me read some," Ann said, taking the book. "Did you know that many of the islanders are Roman Catholic rather than Greek Orthodox?"

"No. Why?"

"The Venetian connection," she said. "And here it claims that the inhabitants of these harsh and glorious islands are of a purer Greek strain!"

"Whatever that means," I said, glancing down at Wendy who had finally fallen asleep. Helen, too, was nodding.

Ann and I fell silent, each of us left with her own thoughts. To me, the history of ancient Greece seemed curiously unrelated to the simple scene before us at that moment. But at least I could understand why Apollo, the god of the sun, had been the chief deity here. The sun was the key to a farmer's existence, bringing warmth and energy and growth to all things. Now, as it rested low in the late afternoon sky, its rays bathed all of Mykonos and the two islands of Delos in golden light.

I basked in the warmth and felt something akin to perfect contentment. Here I was, sitting on a stone wall on Mykonos, surrounded by those I loved best, watching a farmer and his wife at their timeless labor behind a simple stone house which they themselves had built. Life was reduced to its basic simplicity — love and the eternal struggle for survival, but survival with grace and dignity. Here, surely, I had found the simplicity that was my reward for cutting through all the layers of modern life to achieve this voyage. Here, at last, I thought, was the simplicity that lies at the far side of complexity.

Yet, how arrogant of me! Was my idea of simplicity only a reality for myself? For the farmers I was watching it was simply their life. Their *only* reality. The barren earth providing existence, the church a beacon to an afterlife which is supposedly less harsh. These simple strong peasants built their stone houses, worked to eat, to buy a donkey to lessen the work load, to provide clothes and books for their children and "prika" (dowry) for their daughters.

Of what did the peasants of Mykonos dream? Of Athens? An apartment? A car? More years of education for their children? A machine to plow the land? Would they finally get those wishes and then long for the simpler days? I thought of my Grandfather LaFollette who rode his horse west from Wisconsin at the age of sixteen, who homesteaded two years later and made a substantial fortune on wheat. Self taught, he went to Congress to represent the eastern part of Washington State. He also became a trustee of the University of Washington. His seven children all had university educations and became lawyers, teachers, writers. Would the same thing happen to the peasants of Greece if they had money — or at least a way to make it?

In my family the land continued to be the core of life. We all returned to "the ranch" to work and to feed the soul. None of the seven children of my grandparents had escaped the pull of the land, and that pull had been passed on to me. "Here I am," I thought, "infecting my own children with the same disease — a passion for the land."

I was roused from my reveries by the antics of a baby donkey in the field next to the threshers. It raced around the enclosure and stopped suddenly in front of Tom and Robert who were leaning on a stone wall. Then it gazed at them mournfully, uttered that painful drawn-out wheeze which donkeys make, and cavorted away. On the next lap, Tom held out a handful of grain which the donkey approached, gingerly, its ears standing straight up. Then in a flash, Tom jumped back and shouted wildly, "He bit me!"

Back we went to the *Eva Maria,* stumbling over the loose rock in our new sandals. While Wendy and Robert showed off the yacht to

Bill and Helen, the rest of us consulted with Yorgo about one of the "heads" which was not functioning. As we talked, Tom entered the one working facility and locked himself in. Moments later we were startled by the sound of muffled swearing coming from that direction. Yorgo went to investigate and after ten minutes managed to extricate a hot and angry Tom. He explained that he had pumped the flushing mechanism so hard that he hit the door handle which fell off and disappeared in the toilet bowl.

"First the donkey bites me and now this," he moaned. "Attacked by both cultures."

That night Ann and I stood on deck watching the activity along the quay. Wendy and Helen had gone to their room, Helen to unpack and Wendy to chatter. The boys had gone ashore to find a taverna where they could sit, sip Turkish coffee, and observe the venerable Greek custom of the *volta,* or promenade.

The townspeople, dressed in their Sunday best, strolled along the wide dockfront. Children of all ages ran and bicycled or sat quietly on their grandparents' laps watching the passing parade. Mothers pushed babies in buggies and strollers, and old men played with worry beads, which they held behind their backs as they walked. Sometimes whole families strolled together, but more often several woman and girls kept company, as did the men and boys.

Seized with the spirit of the occasion, Ann and I decided to walk the plank ashore and join the women.

"Fantastic," I said as I hooked my arm in Ann's. "We are actually all together. Here. On Mykonos. We did it."

As we walked along the seashore, we talked about our friendship which had led us to this unforgettable day on Mykonos.

"Who would have thought that a popped button would have brought us here," I said, and we laughed, remembering the night we met seven years earlier at KQED, the Educational TV station in San Francisco. I had been excited and a bit scared about doing my first stint of volunteer work. My job was to play Girl Friday to the staff and guests of a weekly political show hosted by Casper (then Cap, later the Knife) Weinburger. Minutes before the principals were to appear, I looked down and realized that a crucial button was missing. It would never do to be popping out of my blouse in such surroundings.

Before complete panic set in, a young woman in tight jeans and a red cotton shirt appeared with thread and needle and efficiently repaired my blouse.

"I remember exactly how you looked," I reminisced as we paused to admire Petros, the famous Mykonos pelican. "I thought you had the most enchanting dimples I'd ever seen."

"I used to admire them myself," Ann replied, "until the time a date who was studying dentistry told me that dimples are simply muscular deformities."

We recalled that after the TV show we crossed the street to Al's Bar to relax and get acquainted. Ann told me that she, too, worked at KQED as a volunteer, but that she had been there long enough to know the ropes . . . literally the ropes, since one of her jobs was to drag around the cables for the cameramen during the shows. We also discovered we lived less than five miles apart on the peninsula — Ann and her husband on the south side of the campus of Stanford University, I on the north side. So we talked and talked, and our friendship was born.

Never were friends more different! Ann was born in Astoria, New York, of Russian Jewish parents. She could whistle down a taxi with two fingers in her mouth and she knew how to cope with the hazards of the New York subway system. She was a graduate of New York's famous public school, the High School of Music and Art.

I was lucky to have well-educated parents, a fine home library, and a chance to visit my grandparents in Washington, D.C., once a year. We were also blessed by living in the west before the Second World War when the pioneer spirit was still a reality rather than a legend. Nevertheless, the Palouse country was an isolated and provincial part of America, far from the urban mainstream.

Given such radically different heritages, it was a miracle that Ann and I had felt such immediate rapport. But there it was, and we didn't question it. Not that we always agreed on everything. We often fought, sometimes violently, about everything from the nature of God to what wine went best with chicken. Our children must have gained a liberal education listening to those quarrels through many a long evening. Ultimately, though, we learned to understand each other's world and to live in relative harmony.

Strolling back toward the *Eva,* Ann and I waved to the boys who were lingering in a waterfront taverna playing tavoli, or backgammon. Then we walked the plank back onto the deck of the *Eva Maria,* and descended the ladder into the girls' stateroom for goodnight kisses, and I slept on the knowledge that we were all together again.

✲ 8 ✲

Among the Ruins

The next day the wind picked up, and I could imagine that the two Nikoses had released Odysseus' Bag of Winds left carelessly on deck by Captain Antonio. But instead of driving us away from Ithaca, this wind—a moderate gale—sped us from My-konos to Delos in only thirty minutes.

Even the clouds, forming and reforming in swollen masses, seemed to be racing with us. As we swept along in our yacht with its sails billowing, it was easy to picture a vessel out of the past making the same voyage to drop off a diplomatic delegation from Athens or a supplicant in search of oracular advice. The day was sparkling clear and for a while we could see the island of Tinos brooding on the horizon to starboard and big Syros poking its mountainous head up behind Delos. How lucky we were to be on a sailing yacht. That reality made it easier to envision the sailing vessels of other centuries which had plied the same waters.

We entered the strait which separates Lesser Delos, the sanc-tuary island, from Greater Delos, or Rheneia, and pulled up to a small boat dock. We were relieved to see no cruise boats spilling out their sightseers. We would have Delos to ourselves. We waved at the fishermen who were repairing their nets on the dock and headed toward Mt. Kynthos, the highest point on the island.

Along the way, we stopped and draped ourselves over various chunks of marble while Ann read aloud from the Blue Guide. We already knew the myth surrounding the origins of Delos as a religious center. After the philandering Zeus had seduced the goddess Leto, she became pregnant, which caused Zeus' wife Hera to fall into a jealous rage. She made sure that the poor pregnant goddess would be turned away from every island on which she sought refuge. Only small, insignificant Delos welcomed Leto, and it was here that she gave birth to the Divine Twins: golden-haired Apollo, the god of light, harmony and beauty, and Artemis, the goddess of woods and hunters.

I could sympathize with Leto, having been a mistress. It is not an easy role. Yet those periods of my life sharpened my understanding of what it is to be a woman.

Ann's voice brought me back to Delos as she read about the cult of Leto which the Ionians from Asia Minor had brought to the Cyclades nine or ten centuries before Christ. Their goddess was of Asiatic origin, which perhaps explains why she was so beautiful and why she managed to seduce the most powerful god of the Greek pantheon. Eventually the entire island became a sacred precinct in which great religious festivals and games were held every four years in honor of the mother and her offspring.

We read a little, then climbed a little, up the four hundred feet of winding stone path, past pastel-colored mosaic floors of once-grand houses, to a temple on the summit of Mt. Kynthos. Most of it lay in ruins, but a part of one column still stood.

The children took turns sitting on the column, and when they wandered off, I climbed on it and stood there like a caryatid — the Delian Leto. The wind buffeting my body was strong enough to make my balancing act precarious, but a sense of exhilaration chased away all fear. I was the queen of the world, the hub of a wheel, with Delos spread out at my feet. I pictured a flotilla of boats bringing mainland Greeks to worship. There they were, landing at the seaport, walking slowly in formal procession to the Temple of Apollo, stopping for ceremonies at the lake and then continuing past the row of archaic lions (which looked more like panthers to me). Now and then one of the pilgrims left his delegation to visit the home of a prominent Delian. In one of those ruined houses below me a rectangular marble table and marble stools remained, waiting forever for the next dinner guests to arrive.

"Look Mom, over there! We aren't alone after all."

The sound of Robert's voice brought me back to modern Delos. He had gone off looking for the sanctuary of the Delian oracle — second only to the Delphic oracle — and he had found farmers instead. From my perch, I could see clear to the end of the three-mile long island. Many fields had been cleared — centuries of picking up rocks — and planted. Each field contained a threshing circle and a small stone hut.

None of us wanted to leave our mountaintop, so we sat talking about the thousands of men and women who had come to worship on Delos over the centuries. This mecca of Classical Greece reached its pinnacle in the fifth century before Christ. Then, as its spiritual attractions declined, its commercial stock rose. Strabo said that "by the second century the great religious festivals were in essence trade fairs on a heroic scale" and that Delos "became the slave market of Greece with as many as 10,000 slaves changing hands in a day."

It was harder for us to imagine that time when the harsh calls of the Roman merchants and the cries of the captured echoed through teeming narrow streets. Religious ceremonies seemed more in keeping with the sun-bleached rocks and ruins all around us.

Robert had given up his search for the oracle. He prodded Ann to "read more about pirates." As she described this later era in the island's history, we devised an imaginary scenario: a black-sailed ship moving silently into the narrow strait at night to disgorge the plunderers; a quick foray into the temple or nobles' homes; then a furtive scramble back to the ship, and away.

On our visit nothing remained to tempt a pirate, unless he happened to have connections in the international art market. These weathered stones housed little more than numerous large lizards which looked like small crocodiles scurrying here and there. Had the gods deemed that lizards, above all other living things, should prevail after Leto and her twins left for good?

On our descent from the summit we paused to observe more Delian wildlife — a two-inch wide column of ants which stretched across our path. The rank and file of Delos' ant community were transferring grains of wheat from one of the fields to their anthill. A single ant would carry a wheat kernel as large as himself for a while, then turn it over to a colleague who relieved him temporarily of his load.

"Like Huckleberry Finn, Mother," said Robert, "an ant gets his friend to help."

"Bravo, Robert," I thought, congratulating myself on bringing some Mark Twain reading on the trip.

Down on his knees, Robert continued to examine the ants.

"Some of them push the wheat and some of them pull," he observed.

"Hmmmm," I replied, "just like human beings. Aren't some of us pushers and other pullers? At the moment I am a pusher. Look how far ahead Rick is."

Farther down the hill, Wendy made her own discovery.

"Come quick," she shouted. "Look what I've found."

We ran down to the spot where she was examining a magnificent spider web almost a yard in circumference. The spider had attached each end of his web to a column in the corner of a roofless mansion and was curled up in the center. We stopped to marvel.

"Doesn't that make you think of *Charlotte's Web*, Wendy?" I asked.

She nodded in delight. I had reminded her of one of her favorite books. It was one of my favorites, too. I had read it aloud at least five time, once to each of my progeny.

As we continued down the hill, we caught sight of Richard who had left us earlier to investigate a cistern under the mosaic courtyard of a noble's house. As we came closer, we noticed that he was lounging with his back propped against a perfectly preserved white marble fertility column. Its square base contained a relief of a fertility bird on one side and, on the other, a bride being led home. On top of the column was a gigantic stone phallus, "balls and all" Bill observed. Once, when we were in Rome, Richard had thrown a coin into the Trevi Fountain, uttering the wish that he remain virile until he was ninety. His pose now against the fertility column reminded us of that wish. We began to laugh and tease him.

"That is some god you picked to worship on Delos," said Helen.

"I hope it's symbolic," retorted Richard, laughing himself. "Now back to the teaks" (a reference to the teakwood decks on our yacht). This phrase, coined by Richard in the shadow of his phallic symbol, became our instant rallying cry. For the rest of the summer, "Back to the teaks!" triggered a mass return to our floating home, the *Eva*.

✶ 9 ✶

Lessor's Blues

Back on the teaks we took stock. One week down, twelve to go. We liked the Captain, he liked us. More important, he liked to sail.

The *Eva Maria* seemed mostly fine — nearly new sails, nearly new motor, deck in good shape. But there were small, nagging problems. Refrigeration was handicapped by a flying fridge door which stayed shut only when roped around. One toilet leaked copiously, terrible with bare feet. A water ski was cracked and the canvas deck chairs split, in serial order, as we tried them one by one. It seemed foolish to head out for three months in less than tip-top shape. We decided to return to Piraeus for repairs.

Sounion was again the perfect stopover and no sooner had we dropped anchor than we were all over the side swimming toward the shore directly under the temple. Ann and I dove first and we kept looking back over our shoulders at the children strung out behind. Richard dove last, just the rest of us spotted a speed boat. I screamed and all of us madly waved arms and shouted as the driver of that big ugly boat headed for the open spot where Rick was still underwater. When Rick surfaced terror was on his face.

"That Goddamned kid! His motor brushed my face."

I could barely swim I was so furious, my stomach churning and my legs like jello.

"This is no place to panic," I thought, "turn over on your back and float." My motherly instincts reasserted themselves just then and I called to the children that Rick was really all right and they should keep swimming. Rick floated near me and we swam slowly in to join the others.

After that experience it was good to have the steep climb up the cliff amidst wild flowers. Soon we emerged at the Temple of Poseidon. We were all in our swim suits, hair dripping, standing in a line, and looking terribly serious. A photographer had one of those ancient tripods with a black hood and a plastic birdie he kept squeaking as he took our picture. I looked at the camera, but my eyes were really looking inward trying to cope with my emotional reaction to the near tragedy. Pump, pump went my heart as I tried to breathe deeply and seem calm.

As we were swimming back to the *Eva* the same speed boat approached. The young Greek driver, his Scandinavian girl-friend beside him, had been sent out by the Harbor Master to apologize. Richard blasted the young Greek verbally, his voice deep with anger. I knew I was disturbed in my soul, but I even surprised myself when I was able to reach up and slap the young man driving the boat. It was the first time I had ever experienced such a feeling of total, mindless fury. Fury at the utter stupidity and carelessness of his act.

Back in Piraeus at last, and anchored once more in Paselemani Harbor, I went ashore to call the yacht broker, Captain Louis, and to report our problems. We talked for some time and he assured us: "All will be fixed immediately. Just go ashore and have a good time. You will sail again by tomorrow afternoon."

Much relieved and heartened I returned to the *Eva* to find the children working on a song called "High Noon at Paselemani," to the tune of *High Noon* from the film of the same name. In those days much sewage ran directly into the harbor and it was an odoriferous anchorage as the words of the childrens' song dramatically described. I rallied my troops: "Why don't we all go ashore and explore Piraeus? Port towns are interesting and we need to purchase some essentials."

A Greek chorus shouted "yes" and we merrily embarked on a group adventure. We bought a garlic press, plastic storage boxes for the fridge, yogurt, stamps, and maps. Though the Captain has a complete set of nautical maps, we wanted a good large map of all Greece and hoped to find one which would include the Sea of Marmara and Istanbul as we had designs on that eastern stronghold of the Roman Empire. I wanted to post the map in the salon and enter along its edge the ports or bays where we slept each night and the approximate mileages traveled.

Arranging to meet at a seaside taverna, Ann and I split from the family to buy bikinis. We had discovered that we were the only females in the whole of Greece wearing one-piece bathing suits. Because Helen had lived in Switzerland when she was sixteen she was "liberated" and owned two bikinis. She had brought one for sister Wendy as well.

It was fun shopping in Piraeus. It felt like a small town with families strolling and shopping that June evening. Along the waterfront were stores carrying merchandise related to the sea. We passed shops filled with brass fittings for ships; shops for making sails; other filled with wine barrels and sacks of dried beans and peas. One shop had only spices, nuts, and raisins, all in vast quantities. Between rows of shops: a taverna or coffee-house, a few more shops, and so on.

Finally, back two streets from the harbor, Ann and I found a whole street of small stores selling ladies' garments. What a chore—trying on bikinis. Ann found a pretty black suit almost immediately, but most were too small for me and I struggled in and out of a dozen, finally choosing a printed brown and white number, not too bikini-ish and covering most of my stomach wrinkles. Five babies over ten pounds *does* stretch one!

Piraeus was best at night with ships and yachts lit up and citizens strolling the quay. We had a feeling that all Piraeus was outside enjoying the summer night. We ate ashore and returned happily to the *Eva* knowing all our problems would be solved and we would soon sail again.

Since there were to be workmen on the yacht that last day, we decided to spend the time in Athens. The younger children had never seen the Parthenon, Tom would guide, and I had a date in late afternoon with the broker and the owner of the *Eva*. I had to make my final payment for the summer rental.

"Come on," Tom suggested, "let's take the subway into Athens." Right across from the ferry harbor in Piraeus is a domed building which houses a few shops and the train-subway for Athens. It runs from Piraeus to central Athens and on out to the suburbs. The "subway" is mostly above ground, it is inexpensive, and much the fastest way into the center of the city.

It was five o'clock when Ann and I arrived at the broker's office near Constitution Square in Athens. We climbed the now familiar steps to the second floor to find one of the young female owners and her husband waiting for us as well. As we sat waiting for Captain Louis to finish a phone call I managed to sneak appraisal of the husband sitting opposite me. He was casually but expensively dressed — pale yellow slacks with a perfect crease, handsome white sport shirt open at the throat, shiny new white espadrilles. He greeted us disdainfully and in perfect English, and returned to reading his magazine. "How," I wondered to myself, "can he look at once so slick and pompous? Is it the oiled back hair?" Suddenly I noticed that he was reading his magazine upside down!

Captain Louis turned to us. We asked, "Things are now in order on the yacht?" "Yes, yes, all is in order." Thus reassured we decided to resume our voyage.

When we stood shaking hands all around, the owner extended a flabby hand: "I am sorry you don't like my yacht," he smirked. I was irritated by this insipid remark and by the fact that we had had to return to have things fixed which should have been in perfect order when we originally sailed. I drew myself up:

"You completely misunderstand me. We adore your boat. It is *you* we do not like."

We made a hasty exit, leaving him gaping, raced down the stairs (stifling giggles) and went into *The Delphi* bar for an ouzo.

Upon boarding the *Eva* later we found that NOT ONE THING HAD BEEN FIXED. I was totally flabbergasted. For the first time I was face-to-face with the Byzantine character. I had totally assumed those men were as good as their words.

"But he *said* everything was in order!"

"Well, two men did come and try to fix the toilet," said Bill philosophically.

I went to look at the toilet. Water still oozed out from under, the fridge had not been touched. The same spit canvas deck chairs lay in disarray about the deck.

"What do you suppose it is? Are they taking advantage of me because I am a pleasant, trusting American? Do they think I am totally naive? Is it because I am a woman? Damn it! What now? I don't like being duped."

Richard had been in the wheel house talking to Captain Antonio.

"Mother, the Captain is very upset. He wants to help but he does not know how. He is Captain, but he is 'just an employee.' But we *aren't* employees. Would you like me to go into Athens tomorrow? Also, you could stop payment on your check."

"Yes to both questions." I was still seething. "I'll cook hamburgers for dinner. Robert," I barked, "you start making that ersatz catsup of yours." Maybe cooking would calm me.

Richard and Yorgo took the speed boat ashore and Rick called Captain Louis to say payment was being stopped on the check. Richard said he was going to Athens early next morning "to talk." The Captain, enormously encouraged, said he would arrange things in Piraeus.

Wow! ACTION. Five "technicians" had been on the yacht the day before to see the toilet leak and report that it could not be fixed unless the yacht was put in dry dock. As Captain Louis arrived early the next morning with a plumber, suddenly it *could* be fixed. In ten minutes the toilet was repaired. A new fridge arrived with Captain Louis *and* a new set of water skis *and* a bolt of blue canvas. Almost immediately a tiny boat bearing a sailmaker drew alongside and for several hours he sat on deck making new strong covers for the chairs. In record time all was in order.

As we hung around watching, Richard suggested that he should go back to Athens with Captain Louis, settle with the owner and get us back on the high seas. It was several hours before the two men returned. Over a drink of ouzo Captain Louis told us their adventures.

"Your son told the owner of the *Eva* that you wanted three extra days of sailing since you'd wasted time on repairs. But Mr. X kept vacillating and I could see Richard was getting angry. Finally Rick stood—he is very tall—and said to Mr. X, 'When I talk to you, you must look at me' and then Richard kept talking very strongly and at the end of the tirade, Mr. X said O.K., O.K."

Rick broke in laughing, "He even asked what else he could do to help us." Captain Louis was still shaking his head over the afternoon's events. "Mrs. Mimi. Your son is wise. He will be a millionaire before he is thirty years old."

Later when I teased Richard about his "wisdom," he said, "It wasn't wisdom, it was fury and I remembered reading about DeGaulle whose philosophy in such instances was to *use* your temper — not lose it."

We sang Captain Louis the newly polished version of "High Noon at Pasilemani" before he headed back to Athens and we chugged out to sea and the nearby island of Aegina. Everyone was beaming — what with our new fridge, sittable chairs, solid doorknobs, Captain Antonio may have been the happiest of all. His weatherbeaten face was one large wrinkly smile as he yelled orders to his crew.

I sat in one of the new comfy chairs and speculated about the past three days. At least they proved that Americans believed in direct action. We had not allowed ourselves to be run over by an irresponsible motorboat driver or by an opportunistic businessman. But those had been very emotional days, and now I wanted only to sit and gaze at the sea.

"Mother, would you like me to make some French fried potatoes for dinner?" Robert was constantly hungry. "Yes, darling. I'd love it!"

For the next hour Robert sat cross-legged on the deck, laboriously peeling and cutting, a shock of straight brown hair neatly covering his eyes. My world was right.

✶ 10 ✶

Saronic Gulf

Free at last from the noise and bustle of Piraeus, we headed our refurbished *Eva* into the Saronic Gulf. Everything was ship-shape. We decided to head southwest into the Saronic Gulf and take a look at the islands closest to Athens.

Richard and I, arms hooked around the main mast, braced ourselves against the wind.

"I *guess* we chose the best island for tonight," Rick mused. "I know you want to get going, Mother, away from civilization, but it does seem too bad not to visit Salamis. Perhaps we could just sail into the bay."

We were headed to Aegina to see its great temple and then to other islands in the Saronic Gulf.

"Come on Mom," Rick persisted. "Salamis is historic. Imagine Xerxes arriving from Persia with four thousand ships. It seems impossible that they could all have fitted into the Saronic Gulf, much less the Bay of Salamis. Did you see it on the map? It's small."

Indeed, we could see the real Salamis Bay to starboard, but I was not to be deterred by either Xerxes or Richard. Even Themistocles, that Greek leader who trapped Xerxes's fleet in Salamis Bay, could not have lured me there. Still, I was curious.

"How many ships did Themistocles have?"

"Only three hundred," Rick answered as Robert arrived to snuggle against me. "What an achievement to defeat four thousand ships with only three hundred!"

The whole Saronic Gulf seemed filled with mountains, some of them islands and some of them the peaks of the Peloponnesian Peninsula. Like most foreigners, we originally had lumped all the Greek islands together. But now, as we began to formulate our vague plans for the summer's sailing, we were learning that there are several main groupings and that each has its own flavor. Our plan was to spend a few days in the Saronic Gulf, whose islands had been involved in historic Greek battles because of their proximity to Athens. Then we would explore the Cyclades before crossing the open sea to Crete. This schedule would bring us out of the southern Aegean ahead of the full blast of the *meltemi*. The famous *meltemi* wind is peculiar to the southern Aegean beginning around July 1 and continuing for about six weeks. The wind cools the islands but is frequently so strong that sailing is impossible.

On our first leg we were sailing directly toward Mt. Oros, the conical mountain of Aegina. A "mother" caïque, painted fire-engine red, passed close to us, her five "babies" in tow. The fishermen waved, their palms facing inward — the sort of motion I might use to say "come here." One doesn't wave, in rural Greece, with the palm out. This motion, called a *moondza*, is considered a curse on the person *and* his whole family.

Richard and Robert disappeared together and I stood alone at the mast, thinking about the wonderful walks we would take during the summer. Such expeditions had already become part of our on-shore routine, with Bill usually setting the pace for the rest of us. Once our destination had been agreed upon, Bill's single-mindedness plus his very long legs would carry him to the front of the pack. It reminded me of Bill with one of his old girlfriends. Barely as high as his chest, she never walked beside him, but always slightly behind — at a trot. Like Bill's girl, we followed along at various distances and speeds.

Another oddity of these family hikes was the reaction of the Greek farmers. No sooner would they see us than they would ask, "Are you Germans?" What experience or training, we wondered, had convinced them that only Germans are capable of walking beyond the tourist attractions of a village or town. Although we were never able to discover the origin of this cultural stereotype, we took glee in destroying it: "No, we are Americans."

On Aegina we anchored for the night in the village of the same name and took a short walk in the twilight to examine ruins of the ancient temple of Aphrodite which stands at the edge of town on a small peninsula. We sat awhile thinking about Aegina's history. Her sea power had been greater than that of Athens in the ninth century B.C. The minting of coins was developed in Aegina. It was incredible that this small fishing village where we sat had been such a power in its time.

Our main excursion on Aegina was to the Temple of Aphaia on the western side of the island. Sailing along the fertile coast we could see one orchard after another of pistachio and almond trees, their green leaves contrasting with the silvery, ever-present olives. As we neared Agia Marina, the village below the temple, the vegetation changed with pines covering every hill.

We scorned the cries of *ela tho, ela tho* (come here, come here), from the donkey drivers who urged us to mount. Instead we began our trek through the pines on foot. The air, under the lacy fragrant pines, was deliciously cool and that was fortunate because it was hot and the climb steep.

The Temple of Aphaia captured my heart. I found its proportions perfect and its location atop a hill inspired, with views in every direction. The bay below was full of tiny ships, their white wakes cutting the blue water into a jigsaw puzzle whose fluid pieces shifted continuously. In the distance I could see Athens. I could even see the white scars on Pendeli, the mountain where the ancient Greeks mined the marble for the Parthenon.

"How beautiful the town of Athens must have been in the old days," I said, eyes squinting. "Imagine the Acropolis surrounded by empty plains and crowned with the Temple of Athena. What a setting, with those three massive mountains forming a protective circle and the sea in front!"

Richard sat down quietly beside me and handed me the binoculars.

"Look, Mom," he said. "Not only can you see the Parthenon from here, but there is Poseidon's Temple at Sounion. I wonder if the three temples were built deliberately as points to a triangle."

Each of us had found his own column for leaning and thinking. It takes time and quiet to contemplate the centuries. I thought of the thousands of inhabitants of Aegina who had so threatened Athens with their sea power that, at the beginning of the Peloponnesian War, the Athenians evacuated the enemy en masse to Thebes . . . away from their beloved sea.

Helen and I walked back to the harbor ahead of the others, to see that lunch was served before the afternoon's sail to Poros. We were "on duty." In the pine woods we discovered how farmers secure the resin for *retsina,* the white table wine of Greece. We found several pine trees whose trunks had been scored, the bark cut away in long strips. At the bottom of each scar was a rough-cut piece of tin bent into bowl shape. Into the tin dripped the blood of the tree, just like the liquid from sugar maples.

Sailing on to the island of Poros we went directly toward the Peloponnesian Peninsula whose rugged mountains rose steeply from the sea. I took the binoculars and with the help of Captain Antonio found the small village of Troezen, the legendary birthplace of Theseus, nestled into the mountainside just before the island of Poros.

Soon we were in the narrow passage between Poros town and the village of Galatas on the mainland. We had to navigate carefully as there were many boats of every size shuttling between the two villages in haphazard fashion. There was no berth for us in Poros so we anchored and Yorgo rowed us to shore. Although my leg muscles were still sore from the Aegina climb, the children urged me on and up through the maze of whitewashed streets of Poros. Steps ran to the right, turned sharply left, sometimes cut into the rock of the mountain. Finally clear of houses we climbed over boulders to reach the clock tower atop the town. It stood, white and proud, on the highest promontory of the village, affording a panoramic view of Poros with her red-roofed houses. To our right along the Bay we could see the old summer palace of King Otto, now a naval academy. Vast olive groves and lemon orchards lay on the far shore, clothing the lower reaches of the Peloponnesian mountains.

The family spread out, each to his own rock perch. We watched the sky turn shades of mauve and pink and then fade into the brilliant reds and oranges that come only after the sun had disappeared behind the mountains. Dusk found us fumbling our way down and happily staggering into a taverna. Sitting by the sea in Poros was like being on a lake shore, surrounded by land and placid water. We ordered fried squid and Robert was horrified when an ink-like substance oozed out. This summer he was living on bread and eggs and, daringly, he began to eat tomato salads "because I like to soak up the dressing with my bread."

The next day we sailed on to Hydra through the Strait of Poros which is protected at its eastern end by a tiny island called Bourdzi, with its ruined Turkish fortress. We had heard almost as much about Hydra as we had about Mykonos, both islands being notable in modern times as artists' colonies.

After only two hours we approached the dry, inhospitable bulk of Hydra island. I couldn't even imagine a town on such steep, rocky terrain. Then suddenly we rounded a corner and were face to face with a village of such staggering beauty that I thought it a flight of fancy. A tiny, perfectly round harbor crowded with white yachts and fishing caïques in all their colorful dress acted as the stage for a natural amphitheater filled with spectacularly lovely homes. How some of those stone houses clung to the sheer mountainside I could not fathom.

Now we had found the perfect walking island, as cars were forbidden. After quickly packing a picnic lunch, we wandered the village streets for a little while and then struck out to the west. The rough path rose high above the sea and then descended to a small village, Kamini, where we paused at a seaside taverna for drinks and instructions for continuing our hike.

"Yes," the taverna owner encouraged us, "it is a good walk. The path keeps going west and after you pass the old arched stone bridge, you can circle behind the mountain and return to Kamini."

It was a long walk doing it "our way," which meant stopping to swim off stony beaches a number of times. The boys loved stony beaches as they provided endless raw material for rock skipping contests.

Was it all a creation of my brain? The remote path, an island where even motorcycles were forbidden? The sea was lacquer blue and gently undulating, and the rocky shore was edged with shaving-cream foam.

Back in Kamini Ann and I abandoned the children and climbed high in the village where we discovered a back road into Hydra town. For two hours we walked and climbed, marveling at the homes. Many were of natural stone, others were plastered and painted in pale yellow. All the roofs were of tile and in many places we could peek into lush courtyards.

Hydra was completely different from Aegina and Poros whose modest homes were inhabited by fishermen or farmers. On Hydra one could see signs of wealth both past and present. I wondered how islands so close together could be so totally different.

As we strolled, we played our own game of Monopoly, buying and selling at will.

"There. That's the house I want!" I would say to Ann. Then it was her turn.

"Look over there. That's mine. Do you want to trade?"

When we tired of Monopoly, we pictured the great sailing vessels harboring in Hydra during the Greek War of Independence. Or we looked for landmarks, such as the home where George Washington's nephew had been a guest near the end of the eighteenth century. Yes, George Washington's nephew "slept there!"

"Enough is enough, my leg muscles demand a rest."

"What about feet?" Ann countered, "By the end of summer we'll be in shape to climb Mt. Olympus."

But how I relished using my muscles instead of my brains. "Can you imagine not being here? What if we hadn't left everything and taken the risk?"

⋆ 11 ⋆

Our Floating Home

My feet dangled over the side of the prow. The deep quiet was broken only by the sound of waves slapping the hull and an occasional voice giving an order. My "log" was in my lap, but my mind refused to concentrate. Looking sternward, I chuckled. Here we were on the most elegant yacht in Greek waters, famous for her racing ability, but for us it was just a happy home.

We were not sailors like the Bill Buckleys, the Sterling Haydens, and the Johnsons (of National Geographic fame). We were not sailing to sail, but to be together, to have ease of movement — for the sheer romance of it all. If (according to Henry Beard and Roy McKie) sailing is: "the fine art of getting wet and becoming ill while slowly going nowhere at great expense," then we weren't sailing. We were seldom wet, no one had been ill, and we were very definitely going somewhere — lots of somewheres. And it was expensive.

Our "home" was 81 feet long and that is very long. Just imagine your living room, dining room and kitchen all hooked up in a line, most likely not as long as the *Eva*. She wasn't very wide, even in the center.

Getting to my feet I walked back to where Rick and Robert lay in the rowboat slung above the deck on the port side. They had a blanket drawn up under their chins and Rick was giving Robert oral arithmetic problems. "Ten plus three, plus eight, minus five, plus six, plus six, divide by seven, plus twelve. . . ." Planting a quick kiss on each son's cheek I continued my inspection of our home. How handsome the teakwood deck with its weathered grey narrow boards. Look at the patina on the wheel! How, I wondered, could a fiberglass or aluminum hull ever compare to wood? All our brass fittings shone and I could imagine the enormous trees in northern Sweden cut for our masts.

Off our stern we flew a Greek flag to show that the *Eva* was of Greek registry. The forward mast flew two flags: an American flag indicating *our* nationality and another flag showing our location — mostly a Greek flag in Greek waters.

Every night Yorgo made up the four bunks in the salon in case the young men, Bill, Tom and Rick, wanted to sleep below. Often they split their nights starting on deck with their air mattresses and sleeping bags (nights were cool in June) and, as dawn arrived, they went below to escape the light. Robert seldom slept below and he placed his sleeping bag as close as possible to Yorgo's on deck.

The night we sailed from Poros we all decided to sleep on deck. It was too magnificent a night to go below with a full moon shining on the massive mountains of the Peloponneses.

Earlier we all spent time in the salon where, while sharing some plump black cherries, Helen regaled us with the story of her adventures in Rome the summer she was seventeen. Helen is a marvelous story teller with the ability to make a good one better with embroidery and poetic license. That summer, two years earlier, a group of university students chased Helen down the Spanish steps in Rome. They had just finished their exams and were exuberant and lusty. Helen fell and rolled to the bottom of the steps, bruising her legs. A young plainclothes policeman saw the whole scene, helped her collect her belongings, and invited her for a cappucino. Then the policeman began to make his approach (in that totally direct way of the Italian male) and Helen fled again, running this time all the way to her pension. From the frying pan into the fire!

"Dammit," Bill yelled, and we turned immediately to him.

Bill's problem came from another source than brotherly concern:

"I can't get my cherry stem tied in a knot with my teeth. I've been trying ever since Helen started talking."

We roared with laughter: "Don't give up, Bill. You know it can be done." At one time or another we had all accomplished the feat of tying a cherry stem in a knot using only teeth and tongue.

We had been taught by an older Italian friend, a woman of great beauty and elegance. Careful to choose a long-stemmed cherry, Elizabeth could tie the knot in less than one minute. On the yacht we discovered this was an ideal way to keep the children occupied when long periods of quiet were needed.

Even though we had lived very close as a family, on the *Eva* we were beginning to know what closeness really meant. There was no place to tell a secret. It was all air ducts and open hatches. We spent a lot of time together, indeed all of our time together, sometimes dividing into pairs or smaller groups. We were discovering the pleasures of the Greek *parea*—one's company of friends. We were sharing literally everything as we read each other's letters (the recipient reading aloud); discussed each book we read, often declaiming cherished bits; planned excursions and meals; and talked and talked and talked.

We had a little Telefunken battery radio with us, but it wasn't much in demand. It was more fun to go ashore and join a *kafenion* crowd and sometimes luck out as a musician arrived and Greek dancing began. Going ashore also gave the possibility for private talks and confidences.

I adored sitting on the stern of the *Eva* as we floated at quayside. Local people would walk past, stopping to stare at one yacht and then another. We looked at them, they looked at us, and it all seemed to work. It was equally pleasant to walk down the gangplank and become a participant in the sport of yacht watching.

But reading was certainly the favorite pastime as we methodically plowed through all those books. Sometimes the main problem was to choose among the rave notices given by previous readers. "Mom, *please* read *The Loom of History* next. It's the best history book I ever read." Or, *"The Gold of Troy* is really good, Mother. . . ."

There were wonderful places to read, beginning with my own bunk. I was charmed by the pink and white stateroom and loved lying there reading or taking a siesta, in spite of the occasional head poked through the hatch above with one inquiry or another. I loved reading on deck, too, lying on a mat or in a canvas chair. When we anchored I would seek out a *kafenion* and sip a cool drink while reading, or wander further afield and walk out to the end of a dock, dangle my feet in the sea and read . . . or just stare at the undulating water.

One day I asked Robert, "Do you miss television?" He thought a moment. "Yes, I sort of miss it, especially on the weekends. But I can't remember when the weekends are."

He spoke for all of us. What a lovely world when all the days were weekends.

I had not ventured to sleep on deck until the night of the full moon. We had decided that we would all sleep "up" as the night was truly magical with the high mountains of the Peloponneses- like giant silver shadows against the bright sky. Before going above in my printed-in-shades-of-pink-knee-length-nylon nightie, I paused in the salon to look at our map. I wanted to know where the night's sail — from Poros to Serifos — would take us. We would re-enter the Cyclades that night, this time from the west.

I put my sleeping bag down next to Ann and drifted off. I was vaguely aware of our 5:00 a.m. departure from Poros as Ann murmured: "I can't sleep for watching the dock, the moon, the clouds, and the Captain stepping over bodies."

"Were those raindrops?" I felt my face and listened to the sound of the wind in the sails. I dozed again to be awakened by the rush of the sails being lowered. It was *really* raining and Captain Antonio shouted that we should shove everything down the hatch and get ourselves below as well. In the middle of the confusion he observed in all seriousness:

"*Then vreki steen Junio. Pote.*" (It *never* rains in June.) We fell into our beds and stayed snuggled until 11:00 in the morning and our arrival in Serifos. My first try at sleeping on deck had aborted.

Our days took on a vague sort of pattern.

"Greek lessons," Tom would call.

"No, not this morning."

"Yes, every morning. Of the dozen verbs we chose to learn you only know 'I am' and 'I want.' You don't even know how to say 'I *don't* want'."

So we gathered around on our mats, with our little grey books, to struggle with verb endings, feminine endings, masculine end- ings, neuter endings. When Tom suggested we try to learn ten new nouns a day Helen laughed:

"Mother, do you remember when you used to make us take a list of ten new English words to school each day, and we were supposed to know them all by dinner that night?"

I remembered. It was during those years when the three older children were pre-teen. Every morning during the school year I would arise at six-thirty and go for a bicycle ride, my only time alone during the day. . . . That enabled me to cope with the next hour when I would make lunches, cook breakfast, braid hair, and nurse a baby. I made the new word lists for the children the night before and stuck them in their lunch sacks.

"Boy, it was a lot easier to learn those English words," Helen complained, "I wish I had taken that beginning course in ancient Greek this year instead of waiting for next."

"I have a system," said Richard who claimed the most recent expertise in languages since he had studied two at once — German and Russian — the past winter. "I always find an association for a new word."

"What do you mean — association?" Bill asked skeptically.

"Well, take the hardest word we had yesterday, *efiemarietha* (newspaper). Just remember that it is two girls' names put together and then the ending will come easily after you've said the word out loud a few times."

"Hmmm," Bill pondered, "but how do I remember to associate the girls' names Effie and Marie with the word for newspaper?"

By that time we were all involved and Tom told us two horror stories about word association. One was the man who learned to say "thank you" in Greek, *evharisto,* by remembering "Harry's toe." The trouble was it came out "Harry's toe" forever — not recognizable in Greek.

Tom continued: "The worst language story I know is about one of the American teaching fellows at Athens College. He just refused to study the Greek language and contented himself with learning only one word. That word was *episis* meaning "the same to you." No matter what anyone would say, my friend would respond with *episis.* Come now, back to work."

It is very important that you all learn to say *katalaveno* and *then katalaveno.* "I understand" or "I don't understand." These words come in handy every day."

I gazed fondly at Robert who was struggling to pronounce *katalaveno.* How marvelous, I thought, for him to have the two

FRONT: HELEN, MIMI, RICHARD. *REAR:* ROBERT, WENDY, BILL

AN AEGEAN ODYSSEY

THE *EVA MARIA*

JORGO AND CAPTAIN ADONIS

ROBERT

RICHARD HAVING WON HIS BATTLE WITH THE OWNERS

HELEN'S 19TH BIRTHDAY IN *EVA* SALON. COSTA'S ON VIOLIN AND YANNIS PLAYS THE BOUZOUKI.

MIMI AND ANN

BILL AND APOLLO'S HEAD. MUSEUM ON ISLE OF RHODES

WENDY IN HER BOY-WATCHERS

MIMI. CORINTH CANAL

ROBERT IN LIFEBOAT (HIS "NEST")

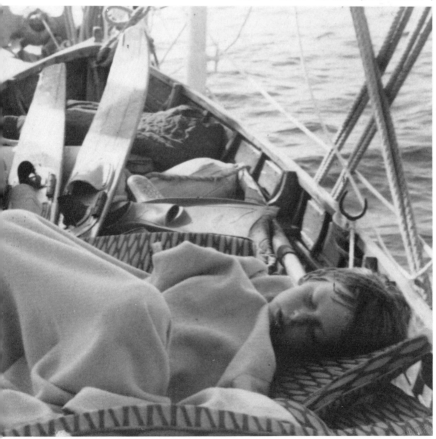

BILL, TOM, RICK BALANCING ROBERT. FIRST WINDMILL EXCURSION ON IOS

STEPS TO HIPPOCRATES' TEMPLE, KOS

young men, Tom and Rick, forcing him to concentrate on sounding out the letters the syllables, and finally the whole word. Actually Robert was getting ahead of us all. He spent so much time with Yorgo, the sailor, that he was already communicating easily in simple Greek. Both Robert and Wendy had already completed the beginner's course in Greek profanity . . . or so I was told.

We were also discovering that it took a fair amount of time to keep ourselves and our clothes clean. Besides the inevitable bathing suits, in assorted colors and sizes, flying like signal flags from various ropes on the *Eva's* deck, there were always undies, socks and shirts, drying in the breezes, destroying the sophisticated image of the yacht.

One eve, as Ann and I sat in the golden light, we could hear great cleanliness commotion below. The girls were washing their hair. Soon they emerged, hair done up in towels, bodies wrapped in blankets.

"Boy, it feels good to be saltless," said Helen, brushing her black locks, "what a production to take a shower!"

Indeed it was. The procedure:

"Yorgo, thelo ena douch." (Yorgo, I want a shower.)

"Amessos." (Immediately) And he would come on the run, beaming happily as he flipped on switches and prepared to man the hand pump.

"Etimo," (ready) Yorgo called to the bather who proceeded into the small tub-shower, sat on a small stool, and in turn yelled:

"Etimo." Yorgo would begin his pumping. Almost immediately the pumper and his helpers would start yelling, "Aren't you through? Hurry up! Are you washing your hair again?"

Finally the bather would emerge, triumphant and clean. Well, at least superficially clean. One day I noted that Robert's whole neck was grey and over his violent protests I took soap and a wash cloth to prove it really *was* dirt. Although exposed many times each day to water, Robert had not been personally involved with soap since we sailed.

It was difficult enough for all of us to wash our hair in the small shower, but for Rick and Bill it was impossible. We had discovered that you could wash hair in the sea, using *Prell* (not a good recommendation I fear). But have you ever tried to wash hair while treading water? In hair-washing one normally raises both arms above the head and both hands scrub away. This causes a swimmer to tip over like a top-weighted toy. One hand has to stay "finning" in the sea while the other scrubs hair. Or you *can* call a friend to scrub while you concentrate on staying upright and afloat.

Another method is to get a plastic bowl of water on deck, douse the hair with suds, and then dive into the sea for rinsing. But this method never lets one have even an hour of salt-free hair.

Conversation about such mundane matters as hair washing consumed a great deal of time as we sat together on deck talking endlessly. We were really learning from the Greeks. Like Robert who one morning asked,

"When are we leaving?"

"Robert, we'll make a Greek of you yet," Tom commented hopefully, "then you will just sit happily for hours."

"And not even talk? Or read?" Although Robert was dubious about the joys of sitting still I noticed that he would climb into the dinghy slung on deck and lie for long periods watching the sails and the sky . . . dreaming ten-year-old dreams . . . probably about food.

We also *talked* a lot about food and shopping. It took much of our time to shop and prepare the food for eight people three times a day. We loved much of the shopping, but we all felt negative about the constant cooking. The alternative was to eat ashore, but we were better cooks than most taverna-keepers, and it was certainly less expensive to eat on board.

"We should have hired a cook." I fretted. "Maybe even now. We'll see."

We were sharing the cooking, with Ann, Yorgo, and me as chefs, and menus depended very much on what was available in the markets of the very small villages where we anchored.

On Serifos we shopped in the only store in port, a combination taverna-grocery. Its small front veranda was covered by a grape-vine and invited some preshopping sitting.

"Let's have a drink before we shop." How fantastic it was not to hurry, to have no deadlines, no meetings, no telephones. As we divided two large *Fix* beers and Robert and Wendy drank their orangeaids, the proprietress brought three saucers of food: chunks of cucumber, cheese, olives, hot peppers and tomatoes.

By then we knew she was just being kind in serving us some mezes because only when you order ouzo is it required that the establishment serve some kind of food. We had eaten, with our ouzos at various times, morsels of bread, squares of turnip, and slices of squid pickled in oil.

"Run along, my loves—go have another swim. Ann and I will shop. There is no way all of us can get inside this store."

"I'm afraid there is little to buy in any event," Ann observed. "I'm glad we bought those three chickens on Poros yesterday."

"Thank goodness we can always find onions, lemons, and garlic," Ann's theory was that any food could be made palatable with these ingredients especially if you added mustard, the good strong Greek mustard. But we were to have little variety during the summer as the village Greeks ate only the foods of the season. The lowly chicken became our best friend as we roasted him, fried him, and boiled him. Robert's main worry was the catsup supply and when I had cooked hamburgers one night he could barely manage to eat without his precious red sauce.

Inside the dark interior of the shop on Serifos, dusty shelves sagged against the walls, and great gunnysacks hunched on the floor filled with everything from flour to beans. Along one wall were *denakes*. These tins, five gallon and square, and topless, held olive oil, olives in various sizes and colors, dried fish, and other mysterious things. We bought a kilo of rice which our lady shovelled out with a conch shell. Then she shyly offered us as a *doro* (gift): some newly picked spices.

Even though we did not see any fresh vegetables, we found that if we asked they were sometimes produced from a back room. "Look," Ann giggled, "there is imported Carnation milk again! What an Aegean excursion *that* salesman had!"

Back on the yacht we surveyed our purchases, some tomatoes, one cucumber, an old whisky bottle filled with local family wine. Ann and I poured some Scotch from our stores and sniffed an inviting aroma wafting up through the hatch. The three plump Poros chickens, plucked by Yorgo and stuffed by me (over Yorgo's protests) were roasting for dinner. We had prepared them "island" style, rubbing olive oil and lemon juice into the chicken and over the chunks of potatoes surrounding them in the pan. After a liberal application of oregano, salt and pepper, they were baked a little more than an hour. In most villages such a dish would be prepared by the housewife in mid-morning and taken to the baker where it would be shoved into the cavernous mouth of the village oven along with many other similar pots prepared by other housewives and taverna owners.

Once we discovered this village cooking system, we understood why the food in tavernas was so often cold. Sometimes the taverna food was quite good but it was always cool to cold, unless it was fresh grilled or fried fish. So when we ate ashore we usually ate fish along with peasant salad (tomatoes, cucumbers, onions, feta cheese, and olives) and island bread, with fruit for dessert.

On entering any taverna in all of Greece our procedure was invariable: stake out the table ("In the sun, the shade? inside? what do you feel like today?") and proceed immediately to the kitchen, en masse. What should we have? Always there was *Tzadziki* (grated cucumbers mixed with yoghurt and garlic), *taramo salata* (fish roe mixed with bread and olive oil), usually a baked dish, either *mousaka* or *pastichio* (macaroni and cheese and hamburger meat), perhaps baked, or overbaked, chicken, or beef. Often we would be shown a tray of fresh fish which would mysteriously appear from a fridge.

Our orders were always massively confusing to the waiter, even to us! Everything would arrive and be plunked in the middle of the table, with a basket containing bread, paper napkins, and exactly enough knives and forks to go around. Wine would come from a barrel — or one of several — and was usually served in a gold-tinted aluminum pitcher, by the litre. Emulating the Greeks we ate from all plates, sampling this or that, never leaving a single morsel. I adored going to tavernas as inevitably the owner would take a personal interest in my enormous family and we would end up sitting at our table while he meticulously added up the *logariosmos* (bill) and shared our wine.

On the other hand eating on board was a delight, too, especially our traditional breakfast following a long sail. When a sail of several hours was indicated, the Captain would leave at dawn. If the sea was rough we stayed in our bunks, or sat on the teakwood deck, feet braced against a rail, facing into the wind, licking the salt spray from our lips. Each of us would be wrapped in his own world. But as the hours progressed all thoughts would eventually turn to food.

Immediately upon anchoring we set out to realize our food dreams. Each person in the galley had an assignment as we prepared a big omelette made with potatoes, onions, canned bacon from Holland, and cheese. With the omelette we would serve a platter of deep red tomatoes, quartered and sprinkled with oregano, with a couple of loaves of fresh bread which one child would have been dispatched to buy. If we anchored in a villageless and breadless bay, I made biscuits on board. Then there would be fruit and fresh coffee from our brought-from-America drip-coffee-pot. It was always silent as the family fell to.

✻ 12 ✻

Serendipity

Once upon a time our family owned half a vacation house on a plot of land in the coastal mountains of northern California. A family contest to name the house wasn't getting anywhere until the day I encountered an unknown word — *serendipity* — in a biography. The word had such a pleasing ring that I ran for the dictionary. But I couldn't find *serendipity*. Finally I tracked it down in the San Francisco Public Library, which contains what surely must be the world's largest Webster's. There, in fine print after *serenata* was "serendipity, *n.* (coined by Horace Walpole) after his tale *The Three Princesses of Serendip* (i.e., Ceylon). The Princesses displayed an apparent aptitude for making fortunate discoveries accidentally." My persistence not only increased by word power but assured me victory in the contest. We named our house "Serendipity."

Now as we sailed toward Ios, eight thousand miles from the San Francisco Public Library, I was about to encounter serendipity once more. Once more it centered on a family place, a plot of land. Not that I had any intention of buying land in Greece! The long summer's sail was madness enough.

As we sailed through a long narrow neck to Ios harbor we saw immediately that Captain Antonio had been right. This island was indeed fair. A lighthouse to portside and a sparkling white church to starboard welcomed us. Past the church the bay hooked to the right and broadened. A small port town offered anchorage. Higher up, the village wrapped itself around a conical mountain which was nippled on the very top by the dome of a tiny chapel.

I wandered ashore to inspect the telephone office, the two tavernas, the office of the port police, and a sprawling white house on an acropolis rising directly behind the port. Walking along a quiet stretch of beach, I saw a wide valley of agricultural fields, outlined in bending and rustling bamboo, and a large farmhouse framed by cypress and eucalyptus trees. The silence was broken now and then by the bray of a donkey or the peal of a distant church bell. Looking back to the port, I could see the soft orange glow of kerosene lamps as dusk began to fall. My heart felt at home as I walked back toward the glowing portholes of the *Eva*.

Both family and crew had mysteriously disappeared so I went below and climbed onto my bed, bent on finishing *The Gold of Troy*. The *meltemi* wind was blowing so fiercly that even the mountain-protected harbor of Ios had whitecaps and the wind made ghostly noises as it attacked the vents and hatches of the *Eva*.

I tried to read, but my mind kept leaving Helen of Troy to center on another Helen—my own. It seemed to me that our great escape had become a sort of homecoming to Helen. Before leaving the States, she and her dull young Stanford man, who had haunted our lives for years, had "broken up." We were all relieved, Helen most of all, and now she bubbled with a rediscovered delight in life.

Tonight was the eve of Helen's nineteenth birthday, and I tried to recall how it felt to be in the last of one's teens. I could certainly recall how *I* had felt that day nineteen years ago when she was born. June 21, 1946, was the longest day of the year—by calendar time and by my own inner clock. All day I sat by the side of a friend's swimming pool, dangling my feet in a manner of speaking, and holding Helen "on my lap." She was born late that same night, weighing 11 pounds, 10 ounces—the second largest of my children. Afterwards, I am told I asked everyone who entered my room, "Are you sure it's a girl?" I was ecstatic to have produced a baby girl after two boys.

For days my heart kept sing-songing, "I've a daughter, a daughter, a daughter." For the first year Helen had almost no hair, but with determination I pasted big pastel bows to her head with scotch tape. No one, but no one, was going to mistake my daughter for a boy! Now, nineteen years later, there was absolutely no possibility of mistaken identity and I treasured the thought that my daughter and I were becoming sisters in the secret society of womanhood.

Gradually, the yacht came to life. Pots and pans clattered and Robert yelled for instructions about the correct side for knives as he set the table. Ann and Rick came in and curled up on my bed for a pre-dinner *ouzaki*.

As we sat down for dinner, Tom and Bill arrived from their trip ashore with two Greek musicians in tow.

"It's a treat for Helen's birthday tomorrow," Bill announced. Soon the salon burst into music as the two middle-aged Greeks played the violin and a sort of long-necked mandolin called a *bouzouki*. The *bousouki* player, Yannis, was of slender build with a heavily lined face. He told Tom he was the miller of Ios and invited us to visit the mill the following day.

"Come early," he encouraged, "the wind is stronger in the morning."

The other musician, plump and rosy-faced, Costa, beamed as he drew the blackened bow ferociously across the strings of his violin, held, not under his chin, but halfway down his chest. Exactly like the country fiddlers of my youth in Washington State. Myself a violinist for many years, I was fascinated by Costa's homemade instrument with its beautifully carved pegs. He let me play for a bit and the children all yelled for "Pop Goes the Weasel." I dutifully performed.

Handing the violin back to Costa, I curled up on the divan, remembering the western music of my childhood. My father had "played the fiddle" in his campaigns for political office. He would "fiddle" while mother accompanied him on the piano. After he warmed up his audience with his musical offerings he would give his campaign speech. As Costa's violin gave forth its plaintive shrill melody over the repetitive chords of Yannis' *bouzouki*, I realized that the effect was not very different from western *Grange* music. The monotony of both kinds of music soothes the spirit while it encourages the feet.

When the musicians paused for a rest we offered them beer — a real treat on the islands where wine and *ouzo* were cheap, but beer was dear. While they drank, Richard played "On Top of Old Smoky" on his guitar and we all sang.

After dinner, we moved up on deck where the crew joined us. Far, far into the morning hours the music continued, sometimes inspiring Jorgo and the Captain to dance. A few times they lured the boys to join them — no mean feat on our small deck. I retired before the end, lulled to sleep by their monotonous tunes.

Following Yannis' advice to visit his windmill when the wind was strongest, we got up at seven and climbed down the ladder to the girls' stateroom and sang "Happy Birthday, Helen." It was also a ruse for getting our daughters up, as the absolute quiet of their nest — as well as their ages — predisposed them to sleep late. The isolation of their stateroom had become an escape hatch for all the children — a place to nap, to read, or tell secrets. Even there a confidence had to be whispered if it was not to become general knowledge.

I went ashore to the miniature telephone office where an equally tiny operator, about four feet ten, sat on a raffia-bottomed chair, her feet dangling at least six inches above the stone floor. After yelling *"embros"* (go ahead) endlessly into the mouthpiece of her antiquated phone she finally aroused Athens for me. I took the phone to shout in turn to Captain Louis, our broker, telling him to please forward our mail packet to the harbor master in Crete as we expected to be there four or five days hence.

Then I joined Ann and together we paid a visit to one of the harbor tavernas to arrange Helen's birthday dinner.

The owner of the taverna was the soul of cooperation. "Will fish, potatoes, and salad do?" he asked.

"Fish, potatoes, and salad will be fine," I replied. "Now what about a cake?"

"A cake?" he repeated with a sudden frown. "No. No cake. We don't make *glyka* (sweets) here on Ios. They come from a bakery on Paros. You must order ahead."

Ann and I looked at each other, crestfallen. Whoever heard of a birthday without a cake. "Do you think we could concoct something in the yacht's galley?" I asked, without much enthusiasm.

"Are you kidding?"

"Well, what are we going to do?" As we stood pondering our problem, several ladies of the port joined us, curious to know what was happening. They were all fascinated to learn that the five young people, who by now had arrived to help plan the birthday dinner, were my *paithakia* (children).

"How old are they?"

"Which ones are yours? *All* of them?"

"Where are you from?"

"Do you own the yacht?"

The questions came one on top of another and I was hard put to answer them in my halting Greek. By the end of the question-and-answer session, however, the women had become involved enough in our family situation to agree to jointly concoct a cake worthy of Helen's natal day. Much relieved, we began our ascent toward the mill, on the ridge above the village, first by path and then by stone steps.

The steps were at least eight feet broad so that we took three strides forward and a step up, three strides forward and a step up, to follow our own yellow brick road to our own City of Oz.

There were definite signs that our road was also used by donkeys. As if the prove our deduction, a Greek woman approached us on her donkey. She was dressed in the inevitable black mourning garb (in the extended family system of the villages someone has always died recently). Sitting sideways on the wooden saddle, she looked at us curiously, smiled broadly and clattered on down the mountain, her left foot rhythmically kicking the donkey's side in encouragement.

Here and there the road was bordered by a carefully built dry stone wall wide enough and solid enough for sitting.

"Let's stop and rest," I said, "I'm hot in spite of the *meltemi*." So my family humored me, and we spread out on the next section of wall which was shaded by eucalyptus and feathery pepper trees. Below us the blue bay shimmered under the sun. A few caïques and a small yacht bobbed about like children's toys in a bathtub. The church of Saint Irene stood guard on her headland. The acropolis of the big white house in port was circled with terraces of trees. In the background rose the small Cycladic island of Sikinos. A confused rooster broke the midmorning silence.

"This island has style," Richard said suddenly, putting into words what all of us felt.

Ios did possess that elusive characteristic — style. The difference from Serifos, where we had hiked the day before, was obvious, yet hard to pinpoint. Was it the more substantial houses here, greater number of trees along the paths? Was it the higher mountains or even our own higher spirits? I didn't know, but somehow there was magic in the day.

On up we trudged. Well-dressed, courteous villagers passed us, trying hard to contain their curiosity. Many of the homes on Ios could be classified as villas, and the higher we got the more elaborate they became. Many had two stories, with wrought-iron balconies and white marble lintels around the doors. Even the less elegant ones had doors painted bright red, green or the blue of the Aegean. Their doorframes were often painted with a sparkling mixture of marble dust and water to resemble real marble.

Many doors sported dried wreaths of flowers left over from May Day. "So," I wondered, "our May Day custom of flowers comes from Greece?" The stones in front of homes were *damased* (the Greek word for checkers is *ntama* and it appears that this word, peculiar to the Cyclades, comes from *ntama*). The stones, called *plakes,* were to us flagstones and every seam had been whitewashed creating a checker board pattern. It was a delightful sight, these whitewashed patterns which we discovered existed inside homes as well as outside. They gave a fresh look to paths and floors, like newly laundered curtains in a room.

In the beguiling town square with its one shade tree, we gathered around two tiny tables under a brand-new awning and ordered "our usual" from Costa, the taverna owner. Costa's father, a handsome white-haired old gentleman in brown baggy pants, sat nearby on a bench leaning against the building with both hands clasped on the cane in front of him. Robert took a polaroid picture of this *papou* (grandfather). When the old gentleman saw his image emerge only seconds later, he hoisted himself to his feet:

"*Ela, Ela tho,*" he called out to his relatives in the taverna. They all emerged to exclaim over the wonderful instant photo, passing it from hand to hand while *papou* pounded Robert vigorously on the back, giving him full credit for the miracle. As we left, Costa's family was busy putting the photo on the wall of the taverna with sticky flypaper.

As we passed the open doors of tiny shops we saw a man sitting in a chair by an open fire soldering a lamp, a carpenter hammering together rungs of a chair, and a baker placing freshly baked loaves on a shelf to cool.

"Oh, can we buy some cookies, Mother?" Wendy and Robert asked, made hungry by the seductive bakery smells. But once more we discovered that sweet things were not an Ios specialty. Only bread was available. So we bought a kilo, still warm on the inside and crisp on the outside, and divided it among ourselves.

Up and up we continued, past a small square where a dozen older men sat talking in the sun, then past a smelly abatoir. Suddenly we were confronted by steps worthy of the Parthenon. "There has to be a temple at the top of such impressive marble steps," Tom speculated. "Do you suppose there is one and no one has told us?"

Side by side we mounted, breathless from the climb and anticipation. No temple greeted us, but Yannis's windmill stood at the back of a wide open space, its sails spinning rapidly. Strung out along the mounting ridge were twelve more mills. The two closest to Yannis's were working and the next two had furled sails. The remaining mills were in various states of ruin.

"There must have been a huge population on Ios if they needed that many windmills," Helen exclaimed. "And look at the terracing for fields of grain. What a location the miller chose all those centuries ago when they first built these mills!"

As far as we could see in every direction terraces created geometric patterns as they swirled around hills and mountains at various heights. And dotting the landscape at frequent intervals were tiny chapels (more than four hundred according to the townspeople). Ios was still seducing us with her topography and picture-postcard architecture.

I lingered behind as the rest of the group made a dash for the rickety stairs of Yannis's windmill to escape the wind which was blowing even more strongly than before. I remembered that Yannis has told us that his ancestors built this round stone building over five hundred years ago.

"Incredible," I said to myself. "This building stood here well before Columbus landed in the New World, and here it is today, still squeaking along as it grinds flour for the islanders' bread."

I climbed on all fours up the well-patched steps, whose lifts glowed with a soft patina worn by five centuries of footsteps. Two flights up, on the floor which held the millstone, I found my family wide-eyed with awe. Each person sat on a sack of wheat and each person was already covered with a thin coating of flour. Tom translated, as Yannis proudly explained where the parts came from and how the mill worked. "The millstone," he said, "came from Milos. It has always been in the mill. On the other hand, the axle is new."

"How new?" we asked.

"Quite new," he assured us. "It came from America in 1918."

We asked him about output. "On a good windy day," he answered, "I can grind about 100 kilos of flour."

Suddenly he interrupted his lecture and darted over to brake the sails against a sudden gust of wind. The sail brake was a thin round log of hardwood about two feet long, which Yannis operated with his foot as he sat in a taverna-style chair close to a square hole in the floor. Below this hole was a box which caught the flour as it came from the millstone. This box also had a hole in its floor to which a gunnysack was attached. Yannis pushed the flour from the box into the sack with a broad wooden paddle. "Can I do that?" Robert asked. Yannis handed him the paddle and rose to pour fresh wheat into the box above the millstone.

The wind howled around the mill, yet we felt safe inside its heavy stone walls. The creaking wooden wheels slowed down, then raced again. The roof of the mill was thatched — wooden beams rising to a peak, with bamboo reeds between. The wind was so fierce that small pieces of kalami (bamboo) and chaf from the wheat whirled around our head. Everything inside the mill was wood including the dowels and pegs.

"See how the wheat in the trough above the mill shakes down all by itself," Helen observed.

I stood to look at the angle of the trough and passed out a handful of wheat to each of the children and Ann.

"Chew it," I admonished, conjuring up a picture from my childhood in eastern Washington's wheat country. "Your grandfather Roy always carried wheat in the pocket of his business suit. Instead of smoking he chewed wheat, even when trying a case."

When we eventually decided to leave, Yannis braked the sails to a halt and came outside the mill to bid us goodbye. We looked back to see him winding in each of the small triangular sails. The *meltemi* was welcoming summer with a big blow.

So delighted were we with Ios that we dawdled as we retraced our steps. Robert spotted an octopus clothespinned to a line, looking all too much like a ragged mop. An elderly lady stopped us to exclaim over my Madras patchwork skirt, saying over and over,

"Poli orea, poli orea. Tha to kano."

"She really likes your skirt." Tom told me. "She says she could make *that* kind of skirt."

Half way down to the port, Robert cried: "Mother, mother, look! A hotel. You and Ann are always looking at hotels. Let's go see this one."

Robert was often not only our "reporter" but the member of the family who urged us to new places and situations.

Obediently, we all climbed the curving steps which led through a bower of flowers to a tiny hotel on a broad terrace. The hotel owner was nowhere to be seen but a guest sat in the open doorway of his room, writing on a small spindle-legged table. He looked up and saw us milling around. "May I help you," he inquired in perfect English. "My name is Otto."

And that is how we met Otto who, in turn, introduced us to our destiny. He quickly explained that he was a teacher at Reed College in Portland, Oregon, but that he came to Ios every summer to write. This summer, he said, he was translating *The Metamorphosis* for an off-Broadway production in the fall. We talked on and on about the charms of Ios. "Have you been to the beach at Milopotas?," Otto asked, obviously warming to his subject.

When we shook our heads, he continued, "Then you haven't seen the most exquisite spot on the whole island. It's an easy walk from here. Why don't you join me a little later today?"

"And why don't you join us for lunch on the yacht beforehand?" I asked.

We strolled back to enjoy gin and lemon juice (a drink we found palatable without ice), sour pickles, and olives. As we lolled on the deck, we discussed theater. Ann had majored in drama at Ithaca College and Cornell and was delighted to have a knowledgeable companion in Otto.

"Don't talk so much," Robert nagged at the adults, "we want Otto to take us to the beach he talked about."

"Soon, Robert. It has been a big morning and Helen's birthday party is tonight. Let the adults rest a bit. Why don't you and Wendy walk out to the church of Saint Irene on the point, and then we'll leave for Otto's beach."

I nearly missed my destiny that lovely lazy afternoon, as I had grown accustomed to the delightful Greek habit of siesta, especially when lunch was substantial. Fighting off my desire to read and sleep, I donned a swimsuit with a cotton dress on top and joined the others as we again mounted the stairs to the village — a good steep climb of twenty minutes. This time we did not go clear into the village but followed a rough donkey trail below the windmills and on past the island's graveyard and three small chapels. Then, after abruptly rounding a corner, we found ourselves confronting a view of such splendor that I could only gasp, "What if I hadn't come!"

The Bay of Milopotas, an almost perfect semicircle, was bordered by a wide white sandy beach longer than ten football fields. Behind the beach, fields were cultivated, neatly parceled off by stone walls and, every now and then, a clump of enormous old eucalyptus trees intruded on agriculture. The smell of freshly threshed wheat rose from the valley. Tavernas at either end of the beach seemed like sentinels protecting that glorious bay whose water was a kaleidoscope of blues.

We spread our towels near the sea and waded into the water. The soft, fine sand sifted through our toes until gradually the water became deeper and we could no longer touch ground.

What a perfect beach for small children! On a point of rocks back toward the village appeared to be a white castle. Otto told us that a French film-maker had only recently completed it. With its crenellated tower outlined brightly against the brown hills, its tiny beach, and a massive statue of Pegasus standing guard, it looked more like a movie set than a summer house on a Greek island.

Inspired by the Frenchman's castle, we set to building our own in sand, all nine of us digging, mounding, and molding the forms that materialized out of the deepest recesses of our nine respective imaginations. Now and then, we stepped back to admire our creations. "You can definitely tell that our castle was built over the centuries," Rick commented at one point. "Look how the styles vary."

Then we built a vegetable garden, all criss-crossed by tiny stone walls of pebbles, like those we had seen from above. Of course, we built a moat and then irrigation tunnels to water our garden. As we were putting the finishing touches on the magnificent edifice, Bill suddenly shattered our trance with a blood-curdling whoop.

"Man the walls!" he yelled. "The goats are coming! Fill the moat! Raise the drawbridge!"

We stood in a circle to protect our creation and forced the invading herd of goats to break ranks and detour around either side, bleating and tinkling their bells in protest. A sheep-dog added to the din by yapping at their heels. The bow-legged shepherd bringing up the rear was exceptionally short and stocky, with skin like weathered leather. Waving a staff as tall as he was, he introduced himself as Andreas and told Tom that he brought his herd down from the mountains twice a day for water. "See the river," he said, pointing directly behind us, "It has fresh water all year round."

The danger of the sheep and goats trampling our castle had passed so we decided to visit the small taverna on the rocks a few hundred meters ahead. Pausing to pick up pieces of pumice which had floated over from volcanic Santorini to the south, we climbed the rough cement steps to the Drakos Taverna. There we were welcomed with Greek peasant hospitality. Because the Drakos' oldest son had recently produced his first child, a boy, we were all treated to *ouzo*. When it was determined that Irene Drakos, like me, had three sons and two daughters, we all felt compelled to drink again. Irene prepared French-fried potatoes, the only food she had on hand. Wendy and Robert couldn't have been more excited had it been a four-course meal. They had not encountered that American staple in any Greek taverna so far.

Jorgo Drakos led us up another batch of stairs onto an inviting terrace above the sea. He had been working all winter on the four simple rooms which surrounded the terrace. He proudly showed us the two cots in each room and the separate "douche," or shower room. We also inspected a toilet room in which, once seated, one could not close the door. But the terrace was glorious with geraniums and ice plant, the sea was indigo blue, and the waves below looked like whipped eggwhites as they crashed on the rocks. Jorgo told us that the price of each bed would be fifteen drachmas a night (about fifty cents then). Not bad for a room with the wind and the sea as companions.

"Tom," I said idly, gazing back toward the valley, "ask Yorgo if there is any land for sale in this bay."

"Oh, yes, over there," Yorgo replied and pointed to a plot of land outlined by stone walls directly behind our sandcastle. "My friend owns it. I wish it were mine with all that good soil for growing beans. It's nearly nine *stremata* (over two acres), and there's a river next to it." Still gesticulating, Yorgo outlined the land for us and pointed to the river where Andreas was still watering his goats.

"I would like to buy it," I said suddenly.

Just like that I said it, "I would like to buy it."

The words slipped out before I had a chance to even form the thought in my head. Until I heard my own voice it had never occurred to me to buy land on any island, Greek or otherwise.

"How much does his friend want for it?" I asked Tom.

"He says about 180,000 drachmas ($6,000).

"Good. That's a feasible price." Swooping into the taverna, I collected the children and we went to see the land.

"Our own land?"

"Yes, our own!"

"Here on Ios?"

"You said the island had style, didn't you?"

"Really, Mother, do you think it's possible?"

"Everything's possible."

"We could build our own home . . . our own castle?"

"Yes, darling."

"Really, Mimi, it's crazy . . . but wonderful."

"Crazy *and* wonderful."

We all talked at once, and our excitement mounted as we gingerly picked our way, barefoot, around the perimeter of the field. The property fronted on the beautiful beach of white sand but it *was* filled with string beans.

Tom tried to moderate our enthusiasm with a touch of realism. He told us about other foreigners who had tried to buy land, and failed. "You'll never do it," he said pessimistically. "A piece of land this size has probably been divided so many times that eighteen people own it now. What do you think Yorgo?"

After conferring with us for a moment, Yorgo shook his head skeptically. "Well, you might be lucky. He claims it is owned by two brothers and their sister. Are you sure you want to pursue this, Mimi?"

"Yes."

Only Wendy was upset. She stomped along—a futile gesture in bare feet—and climbed over the stone wall back to the beach. "I *won't* come every summer and leave my friends. I won't!" She glared at me defiantly.

We took a long last look at our sandcastle as we headed back to the village. Had building it been prophetic? The "people path" up to the village was steeper than the "donkey path" down, but the world was alight with the vibrant gold of sunset. Once we paused for Yorgo to show us one of the tiny chapels by our path. It had seven icons. A cotton print curtain hung before the altar, a narrow satin ribbon stitched on the curtain to form a cross.

Back on the yacht there was no time to think. Yorgo Drakos soon arrived with one of the brothers who owned the land. We all descended to the salon where we sat, straight-backed and formal, to discuss the land, the ownership, and the price. When Tom expressed concern that this owner's brother and sister might not want to sell, we were assured that he had received a letter only that week from his sister in Athens, agreeing on the price. And as for his brother, he assured us, "My brother and I are so close that we even drink from the same wine glass."

"*En daxi*" (O.K.), I said in Greek, feeling cheered by our negotiations. Tom shook his head. He thought I was mad, "stark raving" mad. I thought it best to ignore his youthful judgment.

"We will meet you on the land tomorrow morning to measure it," I said, concluding our preliminary conversation. We shook hands all around and raced to dress for Helen's birthday celebration.

It is hard to recall how quiet Ios harbor was in those days. Just a few fishing boats and one lovely navy blue schooner were anchored there that June evening. Yorgo Frangakis's taverna was eerily lit by a bright gas lantern, a pressurized gadget which hissed so loudly that I could hear it from the yacht as I pulled on my best cotton dress for the celebration. I remember asking myself what exactly had happened to me that afternoon. *Was* I crazy? How could I have spoken without thinking, not even for a split second?

Yet I knew something really mystical had happened. I had felt, in beautiful Milopotas Bay, as if it were the "first day of creation." I had belonged to that land even before it was mine. It was "my place."

"Now, how can you tell anybody that?" my sensible self said, one last time. "Come on, Miriam, finish dressing." I picked up the small gifts for Helen which we had bought in Ios village that morning and joined my family on shore.

Our dinner table had been set out in front of the Akteion Taverna in the balmy June air. The Captain, all in white, was our guest as was our new friend Otto. The only other guests in the taverna that evening were an attractive middle-aged French couple from a navy blue schooner named MACAO. Told it was a birthday party, they presented Helen with a bouquet of geraniums, their stems wrapped in aluminum foil.

After some time Captain Antonio left the table and a moment later Richard yelled, "The yacht is one fire!" Panic seized us as we all sprinted toward the *Eva*. Almost immediately, however, we straggled back to the table somewhat abashed. The fire had been a red flare set off by the Captain in honor of Helen's birthday. Undaunted by our panic, the Captain set off nine sky rockets, then reappeared with the rocket gun so that Helen could shoot the last rocket herself.

After the main course was cleared away, Yorgo approached Helen and placed before her the *pièce de résistance,* a monumental cake. The seven women responsible for the creation hovered nearby — one, a little stooped grandmother who beamed a toothless smile; another, a young woman with a baby on her hip. But the cake . . . it was simply unforgettable. It arrived in a round, heavy aluminum pan about four inches deep, the kind used for roasting a chicken and potatoes at the village bakery. The cake was about half the height of the pan and resembled unraised bread. Covering the top was a layer of chocolate pudding decorated with citrus peel cut in zig-zag shapes. Around the outer rim of the pan, tied on with two strips of heavy cord, were nineteen thick white candles, each about seven inches in height. Everyone gathered around, and sixty-three matches later all the candles were burning. With assistance and exclamations of pleasure from all sides, Helen blew them out. Then every Greek child in the square came to gaze in awe and to share the cake which, alas, was basically inedible.

Rocked gently in my bunk that night and thinking back over the longest day of the year, it seemed to me it had been the longest day of my life, and perhaps the most important. Birthdays always seem to reunite a family. Maybe the birthday had made me particularly susceptible and open to — whatever! The decision to buy land eight thousand miles from home had seemed perfectly natural. Had the building of the castle inspired me? My decision certainly hadn't been rational. It felt almost dream-like and at the same time comfortable. Ios seemed to personify all the simple country values that had sustained me as a child.

"What a chance it was," I thought, "that Helen's pre-birthday revels led us to the windmill and my encounter with wheat — the smell of it, the feel of it and the taste of it."

All the strands of the day wove gently together in my sleepy mind as I wondered vaguely if we would accomplish the actual purchase of "my" beanfield.

⋆ *13* ⋆

Anyone Got A Check?

It was *proee-proee* (early-early) and my sons and Tom were already up and headed for the village. They were to arrange for the notary public, a most important man in Greek towns, to come that evening and meet with the landowners and us in the office of the Port Police.

"Buy some fresh bread in the village," I shouted at their retreating figures. Had I been simple-minded the night before when we talked price with the land owners? Would they think me a pushover? I knew that one always offered and counter-offered when buying real estate, any place in the world. Yet six thousand dollars for that wonderful nine *stremata* seemed so reasonable, especially as Jorgo Drakos assured us it had fresh water because of the small river which bordered the land. A stone well on the land adjoining "ours" was only fifteen feet deep — a good sign for us.

As Ann and I broke open a dozen Ios eggs for a breakfast omelette we talked about the spontaneous actions of the day before. The whole day had a rhythm as if spirit and time were united in ideal harmony.

I said what I thought: "I just don't want to sit around dickering for the land when the whole thing feels right. Even if we decide not to build a house I will own *land.*" My father and my grandfather had implanted in my deepest consciousness the value of "land." Land meant a place to live, land meant food, land was real. I suppose it was my heritage from pioneer days in the far west. "Let's just let it happen. We have the whole morning to measure the land and explore Milopotas Bay." In Greece "having the morning" meant many hours as morning lasted until lunch and lunch would never be before 2:00 p.m.

The *meltemi* had moved on so we used our Volvo for the 20 minute trip around the point of Ios harbor into the broad horseshoe bay of Milopotas. The *Eva* took her anchorage near the end of the beach where the path from the village terminated, and Jorgo shuttled us into shore. At the bottom of the donkey path stood a motorcycle, large, and black, and ugly. How on earth had it ever come down the stony path? The male motorcyclist, like a sentinel guarding treasure, stood silent and grotesque, dressed in a white, one-piece Danskin suit. That pair, motorcycle and driver, were so incongruous in the pastoral scene of Milopotas that I spoke to the cyclist — to be sure he existed. "Hello," I said. "Hello," he said. He did exist.

As we got out of earshot Wendy asked, "Did you get the view?" We all had! "Golly," she continued, "he should wear *two* of those things boys wear."

Andreas and his goats restored normality to the scene and we joined the others who were busy measuring, shouting, now and then taking a sip of *ouzo*. At noon we shared bread, olives, tomatoes and wine with the Greek men who had completed the measuring and the land calculations. Ann rode back to the village by donkey, calling, "See you in port."

As the *Eva* chugged back to Ios harbor everyone went below. Bill wanted to visit the burial place of Homer which Ios claimed. There is an *apochryphal* life of Homer which relates that, during a voyage from Samos to Athens, the poet was driven ashore on Ios, died there, and was buried by the seashore. We had all become so involved in *our land* that exploration for Homer's grave had been forgotten.

"I would really like to see that burial cave, mother. Ever since I read the part about Ios in that book by Manatt I've been determined to go."

"What book? What part?" Bill descended to the salon and returned with *The Aegean,* by Irving Manatt, published in 1916 about Mr. Manatt's years at the end of the nineteenth century as U.S. Counsel General in Greece.

Opening the book to Mr. Manatt's short description of Ios, Bill read about "the famous Dutch traveler, Paasch van

Krienen's," who claimed — in 1770 — to have excavated the tomb of Homer in the northern tip of Ios. He found the poet, "sitting bolt upright, pen in hand." Bill got laughing so hard at the vision of the Dutch traveler of two hundred years ago I was afraid he would fall into the sea.

"It is obvious our adventures are mild compared to Mr. van Krienen's," I commented to Bill. "Perhaps we'll stay on Ios again tomorrow and ride donkeys to Homer's grave."

As we re-entered Ios harbor I looked long at the dry brown hills trying to imagine them "completely forested by oak trees." It must have been many centuries past as most of Ios appeared to be terraced, the stone walls of terraces crumbling from neglect. These walls, which would have grown wheat and vegetables and fruit for the population, would not have existed if the island were forested. "Do you suppose it will be *our* island? Our *topo?*" (place), I wondered aloud to Bill as I headed to my bunk.

It was dusk when we gathered in the office of the Port Police just opposite the *Eva*. Once whitewashed clean, the room was streaked from winter rain, the stone floor thick with dust except a path from door to desk. One photograph, of King Constantine, hung behind the desk so high on the wall it almost touched the ceiling.

We sat solemn and straight, eight of us around the edge of the room on our taverna chairs. The notary public arrived to take his place at the only desk in the room. But first there were introductions and *metrios* coffee (Turkish coffee medium sweet) served with a glass of water each. On the notary's desk was an ancient typewriter. One kerosene lamp cast long shadows throughout the room.

The discussion seemed endless. I could not follow the Greek although the ebb and flow and the volume were fascinating. "Whatever are they talking about that the voices have to be at battle pitch?" I had not learned that the friendliest conversation in Greek may sound as if World War III were about to commence.

Sometimes Tom would turn to me and translate, things I had to know, questions that had to be answered. At one point we discussed, for at least fifteen minutes, the problem of my maiden name being also my middle name!

Two hours later, when all appeared settled, I was told that Jorgo Drakos would go to Santorini, the eparchy of Ios, to arrange things. Then he would go to Syros, the capital of the Cycladic islands. Jorgo Drakos was now my agent. Would I please get a check and pay for the land?

Panic. I had no checks. Someone said: "But no *man* would be without a check." I was not a man and I was checkless . . . except for travelers checks to pay our summer expenses. "Could I borrow a check?," someone suggested. "Yes, I'll gladly borrow a check" (it seemed such a ridiculous suggestion), "but from whom can I borrow?" Rick answered, "Remember the yacht that looked like an ocean liner that arrived this afternoon? It was flying an American flag. Maybe you could borrow a check from them."

The sleek white yacht was anchored in the middle of Ios harbor so Jorgo took down the Albatross and I went to call. It was the most dazzling yacht I had ever seen *and* the largest. We approached cautiously. The ship's officers were all dressed à la Cunard Line. There was a real "bridge." "Ah, well, nothing ventured, nothing gained." Bravely I mounted the hanging steps to find myself face to face with Mr. Fleischmann (of Cincinnati and yeast and gin) who asked most courteously, "May I be of help?"

By the end of my story he was laughing heartily and proffered me a Fleischmann Industries check, and a drink, and told me how he kept their yacht in Rhodes — with a captain from Maine. They came every summer to sail. Ios was their favorite island and he was totally intrigued that we were buying land in that remote place.

So I crossed off everything about Fleischmann Industries on the check, changed the bank name to Wells Fargo in San Francisco, and Jorgo Drakos was launched on his legal adventure to transfer the property to me.

By now the French couple on the navy blue schooner nearby were following our purchase and they asked us to have a celebration drink on their yacht, the *Macao*. As powerful and sleek as the Fleischmann yacht was, so was the schooner *Macao* elegant and aristocratic. We were all envious of our new friends' Italian cook who set out frosted glasses and poured our drinks. Richard and Bill could stand easily in the salon of the *Macao* and even in the staterooms they could be at full height. On the *Eva* they could only stand straight up in the salon and the doorways were a real hazard.

The Italians were intrigued: "Are you really going to build a house on Ios?" "Yes, I hope we will. We talked with Jorgo a little and he says he can build a good stone house — with his cousins."

We decided to buy graph paper the next time we were in a large town and to draw some plans. We would build a large, simple home, around a courtyard, with all the beds and benches built of stone — just like the Palace of the Minoans 5,000 years before.

"Can it have a fireplace and a place in front to sit?" Wendy loved our California kitchen fireplace with its raised hearth.

"Yes, darling, it can have anything you want. You can plan your own room."

So we started dreaming — if only there would be no problem with that damned check. *How* could I have come 8,000 miles from home without a check book? But I recall no feeling of amazement or doubt at buying a large piece of land on the beautiful distant island of Ios.

❧ 14 ❧

Into the Volcano

We could see Santorini as soon as we cleared Ios harbor, and within two hours we were sailing into a lagoon, which we suddenly realized must be the mouth of a volcano—a caldera. What a strange feeling to sail on a sea 208 fathoms deep and know that underneath the cauldron is still boiling. Passing Oia, the northernmost village of Santorini, we proceeded into the giant maw directly below menacing cliffs.

The cliff walls, which towered a thousand feet above us, were patterned in stripes whose colors were like those of a Navajo Indian rug. And like a rug, the change from one color to another was abrupt. The cream-colored stripe along the top was pumice, or so I assumed, since I had read that the island is famous for its pumice mines. The next stripe down, black and denser in texture, was lava; while the narrow, rust-colored stripe at the bottom probably took its color from iron ore in the rock. Down near the sea, the cliffs were crumbling in some places, and here and there we could see whole sections pock-marked with fortifications of past centuries.

Portside along the rim of the cliff ahead of us, I could see the modern town of Thera, looking for all the world like a white jasmine vine with tendrils hanging over a rooftop. Two massive buoys floated near the tiny dock, but against the background of the cliffs they seemed no larger than nickel pieces. No wonder all ships race for Ios's safe little harbor if there is any wind at all around Santorini.

"How unbelievably different each island is," I said, remembering the gentle beauty of Ios only 12 miles away. As we had sailed along the western coast of "our island," we had passed a dozen bays, each with a white sandy beach. Only one of these inlets had houses; the others were totally deserted, with steep mountains rising behind them. Now here we were looking up at an island whose history of human habitation was long and well-documented, yet still shrouded in mystery and contradictions.

We joined the ranks of scholars, poets, and romantic travelers who have wondered if ancient Thera was, in fact, the mythical lost continent of Atlantis. No one has ever been able to prove or disprove this enticing theory. What is certain is that this island civilization was destroyed some fifteen hundred years before Christ by an eruption five times larger than that of Krakatoa in the South Pacific in 1883. Details of the destruction seem to have been carried by word of mouth to Egyptian priests and thence to the Greek legislator Solon. Plato perpetuated and enshrined the legend in two of his dialogues.

We put all thoughts of Atlantis our of our minds, however, as we applied ourselves to the more immediate problem of getting to the modern village from the harbor at the foot of the cliff. So far as we could see, the only way was a steep stone path, which snaked up seven hundred feet or more to the gleaming white village on top. No wheeled vehicle could possibly manipulate the course, so the only alternative seemed to be to walk, or. . . .

"Do you think those scroungy-looking donkeys are waiting for us?" I asked, not sure at this point whether I wanted to tackle the cliff at all. But of course I did, bringing up the rear of our mounted group. Richard and Tom opted for feet — their own — and went on ahead.

As the rest of us started up the face of the sinister cliff, I recalled a *Life* magazine article printed at the time of the Santorini earthquake in 1956, in which the island was described as "A Purgatory for Donkeys." Indeed it was! Ann sat on the tiniest donkey I had ever seen — about the size of a Great Dane — which looked more like a stuffed toy animal than a beast of burden. Bill's old, slow donkey, with its head hanging low, barely made it around each curve. Robert's animal constantly cut Bill's off at every turn in the path by walking directly in front. Bill yelled at Robert every time their donkeys collided and finally got so discouraged that he offered to get off and walk. "Maybe *I* should carry *it,*" he muttered indignantly. I laughed so hard that I could barely stay astride my own little burro, whose flanks were beaten constantly by the donkey driver bringing up the rear.

Even purgatory comes to an end and eventually we crossed the last of the *750* steps leading to the village. For hours we wandered the streets of Thera, passing a massive Catholic monastery built in the Venetian period, dozens of ruined houses, and neat rows of modern pre-fabs provided the earthquake victims a decade later. Eventually we left the village to explore the countryside. What a strange island, with steep cliffs on one side and gentle sloping land descending seaward on the other! Soon we were walking among grapevines whose trunks had been trained to grow in complete circles, rather like large coiled snakes. Because of summer droughts and strong winds, we learned later, Santorini farmers train their vines to grow close to the earth in this manner.

"How about returning to the village and drinking some of the famous Santorini wine from these grapes?" I urged. I was thirsty, hot, and hungry.

At the southern end of the town, the Atlantis Hotel stood like a sentinel, each of its balconies shaded by a masonry arch. A mosaic of the legendary phoenix was set into the wall of the hotel porch. Inside, the high windows were flanked by handwoven, white drapes, which had been printed with motifs of Greek wildflowers. "Oh, how lovely," I exclaimed.

"You can buy the material here," the desk clerk told me. I took a square meter's worth, thinking about how it would look framed on the wall of our yet-to-be-built home on Ios.

With a simple lunch of moussaka and salad, we managed to consume two bottles of local wine: one, called *Atlantis,* was light and served icy cold; the other was slightly resinated and came straight from the barrel. Both were excellent, and we decided to buy a case of *Atlantis* for the yacht.

We wanted to see the sunset from the village, yet none of us was willing to walk the 700 steps down to the sea and back up again. So we decided to stay on top of the island and walk north along a path which followed the rim of the volcano. Somewhere along the way we hoped to find a spot for our *mesimera,* as the Greeks call their siesta time.

At the highest point of the village we came upon a home which had been destroyed during the '56 earthquake. The house must have been very large and substantial, as the two stories which remained still suggested an atmosphere of elegance. All the rooms facing the sea were in rubble but others which had been built into the cliff itself were in fairly good shape with nary a crack in their arched ceilings. Even remnants of wallpaper hung here and there. It was in this cool interior that each of us found a spot for a quiet time.

Robert was a little nervous as we had joked a good deal during the morning's sail about the possibility of vampires haunting such an infernal landscape. He wondered if perhaps some of them lived in the darker rooms at the back of the house we had borrowed for a siesta.

After allaying Robert's fears, I looked over at Wendy who had fallen asleep with her head in Richard's lap. Rick was running his fingers through her curls and gazing south toward Crete.

Quietly he asked: "Do you suppose this was really the location of Atlantis, Mother? It's a wild thought, isn't it? I try to imagine a two-hundred-foot tidal wave, which would have started here and traveled all the way to Crete to destroy an entire civilization."

"It must have done terrible damage on Ios as well," I replied.

We lapsed into silence and I thought how incredible it is that people keep rebuilding their homes in the same place after a major catstrophe. People who live near volcanoes have to believe totally in life . . . life on a day-by-day basis, life to be lived in spite of tragedies. There's a grim beauty about that sort of spirit.

Was it Churchill who defined courage as "grace under pressure?" Maybe courage is also not asking why things don't work out, accepting what does happen, and going forward.

And yet . . . one does hope to learn at least a little something along the road. I think I have learned the most when life was most difficult . . .. in the aftermath of my own personal volcanoes.

Rick interrupted my mental wandering by drawing my attention to the distant grapevines. "They say volcanic soil is good for growing wine grapes . . . that it retains moisture and is extremely fertile."

"You're right, Rick," I replied. "And I think the soil must have flavored our Atlantis wine in a subtle way. Didn't you detect the slightest smoky aftertaste?"

"Yes. Just a hint of the fiery furnace."

The cool of late afternoon saw us back at the Atlantis Hotel sitting on the terrace, sipping ouzo, and watching the sky turn from brilliant azure to pastel blue to gray. Below us — far, far below — the *Eva Maria* bobbed about, looking like a toy. In the twilight Santorini had lost its frightening quality and retained only its magic and mystery.

"Come, my loves," I entreated, "we must wend our way down that infernal path before it is completely dark."

We walked, two by two, hand in hand, to our floating home.

✶ 15 ✶

Cretan Interlude

For days we had woven our way through the Cycladic islands, never completely out of sight of land. Finally the time had come to point the *Eva's* prow in the direction of Crete. Tracing our course on the map, I realized what a long sail it would be. As we left the Aegean for the mother sea — the Mediterranean — we would be passing through open waters for the first time.

For nearly nine hours we rode the waves, using both sails and motor. Although we had left Santorini at four in the morning, it was afternoon by the time we pulled into the nearly circular harbor of Iraklion on the northern shore of Crete.

I awakened at eight that morning but lay in my berth lulled by the *Eva's* roll. The sea was rough enough to make reading unwise, so after munching two crackers — always a reminder for me of early pregnancy — that turned my thoughts to Robert and Wendy. My "babies."

Three weeks into our Greek summer Robert had already lost five pounds of baby fat and gained a few hundred new freckles. With long, sun-bleached hair hanging over his eyebrows and a nose that peeled every second day, he looked like central casting's idea of the all-American ten-year-old boy. And for a ten-year-old, life aboard the *Eva* was a dream come true. Not once in two weeks had he said, "What shall I do, Mother?" With not a whine nor whimper, he spent long hours in his rowboat nest watching sails billow, sailors bustle, and seagulls glide.

He became upset when I said that it was difficult to communicate with the crew without Tom's help. "I talk to Yorgo all the time!" he said accusingly. I nodded, sure that he did indeed bridge the language gap that confounded the rest of us. He was always by Yorgo's side in the "Albatross" while the older children and Ann water skied. He, too, had learned to water ski quite well because Richard forced him to try.

Like most of my offspring, Robert was an accident. Born just after Christmas, he weighed in at twelve pounds nine ounces, breaking the record at the Stanford Hospital. "Why didn't you bring a baby buggy?" the nurse teased. "He is too heavy for us."

What delight I took from Robert's ability to swim when he was only a year old. Waddling over to the pool with tiny fins on his plump feet, and with his baby's belly hanging over his bathing trunks, he would flop into the pool. He would swim underwater with his hands working like fins at his sides and his little body undulating like a dolphin. His eyes would be wide open as he came up for breath and reached for the side of the pool. It took five years more to persuade our water baby that it was all right to swim on top of the water like everyone else.

One of the dividends of our Greek summer was a chance for Robert to be with males. He had many women in his life: his mother; his "junior mother," Ann; our housekeeper, Vicki; and two older sisters. But father figures were scarce. Richard and Bill were in and out with school and summer jobs, but they spent as much time as possible with their young brother. I chuckled recalling the day I came home from work to find Richard and Robert skipping round and round our patio. "What are you doing, Richard?" I inquired. "Don't you have football practice today?" (He was captain of his high school team.)

"Don't you remember, Mother? I went to Robert's school conference today because you couldn't. His teacher said Rob was the only one in class who couldn't skip, so I'm teaching him."

Mothering he had! Now, I thought, this summer he is getting plenty of fathering, too, with the male crew members and our own young men.

Wendy and Robert spent much of their childhood together but now Wendy was becoming a young woman and she often felt that playing with her little brother was beneath her new-found dignity. Besides, our Wendy had become obsessed with a new phenomenon in her life: she had fallen in love with Tom Singer!

At every meal, she arranged to sit by her idol. She started putting her hair up in rollers, though it was naturally so curly that she could barely comb it after the rollers were removed. Just the night before, as we sat on the deck of the *Eva*, Tom told Wendy what fun it was for him to have a little sister. She beamed and after we had all retired she came into our stateroom and climbed into my berth to cuddle. "Mother, remember the note I wrote Tom?" she said.

"Yes, I remember."

"Well, Tom said it was nice to get a note from a girl after spending a whole year teaching at a boys' boarding school." She reached out and pressed a neatly folded piece of paper in my hand.

"Look, Mother, he wrote me a poem. Will you tell me what it means?"

Her first love letter, I thought to myself. I hoped to heaven Tom had handled this one right. I read aloud to her:

"Wendy, someone once said:

There is no secret unless one keeps it,
No wisdom unless one acts upon it,
No grown-ups unless one grows up,
No magic words unless one speaks them,
No comforter unless one comforts,
And, most importantly, no love unless one loves.

Sincerely, and with love,
Tom"

"What a lovely poem, Wendy," I said. "A treasure. Just think about it a bit, and you'll understand."

Ah me, growing up! It occurred to me that Wendy needed this summer interlude as much as any of us. Puberty had been doubly difficult for her because it came so early. She looked like a young, attractive woman so men were naturally attracted to her. But when she voiced her thoughts it became evident that she was still very much a little girl.

Crete, we discovered the next day, is very large — the largest of all the Greek islands. We realized that to do it justice and to explore it properly we would have to visit it again someday, without a yacht and with plenty of time. We decided to limit our homage to archaeology to just one day, with a guide and a rented car.

But first things first. We needed to replenish our supplies and, even more urgently, needed to get our hair washed. Sun, salt water, and low water pressure had joined forces to turn our coiffures into parodies of Halloween fright wigs.

The women and girls headed for a beauty parlor while Bill and Robert set off to find a barber. Our *kommoterion* was filled with shy, eager young women, all training to be hairdressers. We were the only customers in their three spacious, marble-floored rooms, and in half an hour our hair was shiny clean. We moved on to satisfy other feminine concerns. In a dressmaker's shop just under the beauty parlor the girls selected materials which the *modistra* promised to transform in just two days. Helen chose a soft white wool for a suit, while Wendy wanted a cotton sundress. As the girls were measured, the adults were offered *raki*, a strong, clear-colored liquor made from grapeskins. We never ceased to be surprised about what is possible in the name of dignity and courtesy . . . even drinking *raki* at nine in the morning! The *raki* was followed by a *gleeko* (sweet) of candied apricots served on a small glass plate, one each for Helen, Ann, and me. Robert and Wendy were served a child-oriented sweet called *vaneelia*. A teaspoon was dipped into the jar of gooey *vaneelia*, then transferred to a glass of water. The children removed the spoon, licked the candy off, and then drank the sweetened water. That is, they ate and drank after their mama spoke to them in stern tones and fixed them with the maternal eye that allows for no discussion.

When we returned to the dressmaker's later that day, we again sipped *raki* while the girls had their first fittings. The *modistra* pinned, snipped, and basted the garments right onto the girls, all the while using her small sister as a human pin-cushion. An assortment of female relatives were summoned to admire the girls' figures. Then they made me stand and turn around so they could admire my figure, which they claimed was remarkable considering the number of children I had produced. I was soon exhausted trying to hold my tummy flat and live up to my image. Finally, when the first fitting was over and we were about to leave, the *modistra's* grandmother presented each of us with a small bouquet of jasmine.

One of the most beguiling aspects of provincial Greek life is the personal touch. When we went grocery shopping in Iraklion, for example, we found a real concern about our satisfaction with the merchandise and the price we paid for it. A greengrocer would ask us to select the fruit and vegetables ourselves or he would carefully pick out the tastiest morsels for us. Shopkeepers generally would ask us to sit down, then enquire, "*Ena porta calatha* (orange juice)? A coffee?" As we sat and talked, experimenting with our meager Greek, the shopkeeper and other customers took delight in correcting us and nodding encouragement.

Selecting food while talking and drinking simultaneously was very time consuming, but *so* pleasant. They had time. We had time. Other customers came in, bought one or two items, looked at us, asked about us, then left. Finally, I would rise with determination and ask for the bill. A mad scurry would ensue as the shopkeeper would find he did not have a certain item — say, yogurt — and he would send the errand boy in haste to another shop to purchase it.

High noon in Iraklion found us, as planned, at the taverna in front of the Morosini Fountain near the open market. For an hour following lunch we roamed the open market. We had not seen anything like it, certainly not in Athens and most certainly not in the small island villages, where we were lucky to have a choice of two vegetables. Iraklion's market offered the usual tomatoes, onions, and potatoes, but also pineapples, bananas, apricots (tiny and tasty), cherries, plums, lemons, and even avocados. melons called *peponi*, a delicious cross between a cantalope and a honeydew, were in abundance. Deep purple eggplants were stacked in pyramids, zucchini came in every size and some were sold with their delicate yellow flowers intact (Yorgo had shown us how to dip the blossoms in batter and deep-fry them). We bought an assortment of all these vegetables, as well as a bag of red and green peppers — some sweet; others, long, skinny, and hot. No lettuce was available during the summer months, but there were lots of greens, or *horta* as the Greeks call this much-appreciated wild delicacy. Sometimes I recognized a particular variety, such as dandelions, but others were outside my horticultural experience: ruffly-edged, broad-leaved, skinny, and spikey — all were piled in great mounds on wooden tables.

While the others continued to shop for produce, I bought sausage to serve with our baked beans simmering back in the *Eva's* galley. I also ordered hamburger meat, which I watched being ground, and a leg of lamb. After a great deal of halting Greek and exaggerated body language, the butcher took the back of his white cigarette box and wrote down the amount I owed. I gratefully thanked whatever accident of history had given us common number symbols.

Wandering further up the market street I found booths in which only herbs were sold — the spicy kind and those used for making various kinds of tea. One elderly man sold buds of garlic which he plucked from long braided ropes made of garlic tops. Floating in large tins filled with brine were olives of a dozen different sizes and colors — black, purple, green, and "wartime camouflage." Other tins held shriveled black olives which looked dry but turned out to be juicy and especially tasty. In front of a store specializing in dairy products eggs in wire baskets hung at every level. I bought thirty eggs and the shopkeeper brought them down in their fragile basket with a long hooked pole.

Regrouping at the taverna we had a cool drink. Bill was discouraged in his attempt to have his hair washed at a barbershop.

"When I went in I pointed to the shampoo. The barber smiled, and said: *Nay, Nay* (Yes, yes), and motioned me into the chair where he tipped me back and shaved me! We played some more charades, and he finally made me understand that he doesn't wash hair. What can I do? The water pressure is so low on the yacht, I can't wash it there."

"I'll take you to *our* beauty parlor," I said. "I'm sure those girls would wash men's hair as well. Come on."

I returned to the *Kommotorion,* followed by all four males. Mounting the stairs, I heard a loud buzzing. We opened the door to find at least thirty women being washed, dyed, curled and styled. All conversation stopped at the sight of my brood of men. The operators began to giggle. Smiling sweetly at everyone, I quickly shut the door, and we all retreated to the taverna.

"Sorry, I guess it's Prell and low water pressure for you, gentlemen. But you'll have to wait until we leave the harbor. You don't want to wash your hair in *harbor* water."

Downhill we trudged, laden with our purchases, but managing to stop once more for bread and a plastic box of *zodziki* to serve with our pre-dinner drinks. We had all fallen for this middle-Eastern delight, served in most tavernas. It is made with grated cucumbers, yogurt, garlic, olive oil, lemon juice, and salt and pepper. "And I bought a surprise," Rick said. "In fact, tonight I will be in charge of hors d'oeuvres."

On the way back to the *Eva,* Rick and Bill went ahead as Ann, myself, and the two girls lingered over last-minute purchases. As we left the last shop, several boys started to follow us. Ann and I were becoming used to the situation. Whenever Helen and Wendy were along, boys followed us! That particular group, however, was especially persistent and, eventually, one of them came up to Wendy, took her bag of vegetables, and carried it proudly oblivious to her protests in English which to him, of course, were incomprehensible. Searching desperately for a way to get rid of him she spied Rick leaning over the *Eva's* railing.

"Rick, Oh, Rick, come here quickly!," she shouted. As he approached, she threw herself with passionate abandon into his arms, hugged him, and kissed him.

"See, I have a beau," she said to her would-be swain. Looking somewhat abashed, he returned the bag of groceries and along with his cohorts retreated hastily. From then on, both Helen and Wendy used this ruse and usually it worked. It would have taken an exceptionally ardent young man to tackle Bill or Rick considering their height — well over six feet — and weight — about two hundred pounds each.

That evening as we sat on deck enjoying the last golden rays of the sun we turned our backs on Iraklion and looked out to sea over the ancient harbor wall. Rick's treat was oysters and crab on crackers which we finished along with the whole container of *zodziki.* We watched two large motor cruisers back into the dock, one to each side of us. The yacht flying a Swedish flag made a smooth approach but the English boat was in trouble. An attractive young woman, a passenger, threw the mooring line five times to a man on the dock, but each time she missed and had to recoil the rope. Finally a crew member came to her rescue. We felt like applauding this little drama but managed to restrain ourselves. Yachtsmen cannot help watching these maneuvers

with a certain amount of interest. Being tied up within feet—
sometimes inches—of another boat creates an instant intimacy.
It also creates problems if your neighbor happens to snore
loudly!

Early the following morning a Volkswagon minibus picked us
up and our lovely guide, Irene, herded us all around Knossos.
Robert went ahead to point out special discoveries such as the
remains of ancient bathrooms which once had running water. He
and the boys walked the seven kilometers from Iraklion to
Knossos on our first day in Crete.

We all admired the excavation and controversial restoration
by Sir Arthur Evans. The restoration gives one an idea of how
such palaces really looked. We also visited the exquisite museum
in Iraklion where even the younger children were intrigued by
the ancient razor blades, a tablet inscribed with the first known
printing, and the golden jewelry.

Then on to Phaistos which failed to charm me in spite of our
excellent guide. In this case getting there was more than half the
fun. I adored the automobile ride across Crete, shooting around
corners, braking madly to miss hay-laden donkeys, our horn
blaring at frequent intervals to warn all bystanders of our approach. I was intrigued, but not comforted, to learn that the
numerous shrines by the roadside marked spots where fatal
accidents had once occurred. Along a road lined with prickly-
pear plants higher than our car we passed Kazantzakis's village
which he described in his novel *Zörba the Greek*. We skirted
towering mountains and watched stately cypress trees bow to us
as we passed. Olive trees from every century were changelings in
the wind. It was fun to be inland.

Afternoon found us sprawled on the beach of Matala near
Phaistos on the southern shore of Crete. A few years later Matala
gained a certain notoriety from the young Americans who lived
in the rock caves which surrounded the sandy beach. We ate
supper by the sea and experienced a night ride back to Iraklion.
Twenty years ago almost all Greeks turned off their car lights at
the approach of another car. That is, drivers of both cars turned
off their lights, claiming that it was safer to pass each other
without headlights. As far as I was concerned it was utter madness. I did not want to become another shrine.

Sailing east along the northern coast of Crete the following morning, Captain Antonio urged us to stop "just once more" in Crete. He was right—he always was. The village of Ayios Nikolaos had a splendid harbor and many old, charming homes. We anchored in front of the Minos Beach Hotel, and that decision was exactly right, too. The hotel was Greek down to the smallest detail. In fact, it looked like a small Greek village with each guest cottage an exact replica of a Cycladic village house.

"I want to look inside," I said. I knew instantly and instinctively that this architecture and decor would be the model for our dream house on Ios. When the hotel manager took me to see one of the cottages I concentrated on every detail. We would copy everything, I decided. The beds were built in the old island style: extensions of the wall made of stone which had been plastered and whitewashed. The headboards, which were also part of the bed, sloped gently for night reading. A shelf behind—still part of the bed—held a lamp. Above the shelf was a bookcase recessed into the wall. A round marble table rested on a built-in stone pedestal. Only the chairs were movable. Bright, handwoven rugs and curtains completed the effect. Perfect! I ran for my drawing pad and quickly sketched all aspects of the cottage interior. Later, after seeing the gracefully arched windows in the hotel lobby, I unobtrusively took their measurements and added them to my list. I felt giddy with excitement and the possibility of building a house seemed more like a reality than it ever had before.

Crete was not quite ready to release us. We had dinner at the hotel and over coffee in the salon fell into conversation with a French archaeologist. "You do not stay at all in Ayios Nikolaos?" he asked in amazement. "But you must stay, and you must visit Lato. It is a perfect example of a Minoan town. We, the French, did the excavations. You cannot leave Crete without understanding the Minoan people. Knossos is different. It is a palace. Come, I will draw you a map for the walking. But first you take a bus. . . ."

So early the next day we took the bus, said "Lato" to the driver, and in ten minutes were deposited near a church called Panayia Kera on the road to Kritsa. The bus driver pointed right towards a dirt road which meandered between old gnarled olives and repeated the word we had said to him. "Lato."

After half an hour of walking, arbitrarily choosing the right-hand fork, we began to feel discouraged. We were seeing a lot of very old olive trees of moderate interest but . . . trudging on in a ragged line behind Bill we were cheered when the track began to climb upward toward twin cone-shaped peaks. The Minoans, we knew, often built their villages in the saddle between two hills.

After an hour we found ourselves in the magnificent site of Lato. What style those ancient Minoans had! The town center, where we stood, spread out over the saddle on four terraces. A covered cistern and much of an exquisitely patterned mosaic floor remained. To the right were perfectly preserved walls and the remnants of two small temples. At the back of the town, and facing the interior of Crete, a steep street led down the mountain-side. The ancient shops of Lato opened off this road and it must have exhausted the Minoan housewife to climb up and down for her daily purchases. Homes fanned out in a broad arc on both sides of the saddle, curving around the mountain and overlook-ing a crater filled with lush greenery in the foreground.

I walked to the right over a narrow overgrown path and found . . . "my home." With a shock of recognition, I felt that this place might once have sheltered me. Even now, on nights when I cannot sleep, my mind goes to my home in Lato. It was about halfway to the fortress-like wall which hemmed in the crater-valley. In the corner of one of its clearly defined rooms sat an enormous amphora; along the wall of another room a bench remained. I sat on the bench and looked out over the crumbling homes on the other side of the crater to the agricultural valley far below. The bay of Ayios Nikolaos was as blue as the sky. It must have been the harbor of the Latoans, those mysterious, sophisti-cated Minoans who spoke a language other than Greek. Strange to think that they had exported their delicate arts and crafts to the warlike Greeks. I wondered if my house had been decorated with wall paintings.

Pulling ourselves away from Lato, we climbed down the steep incline to the rear of the town and a road older than three millennia! It snaked its way between walls of stone and was easily wide enough to have accommodated a chariot as well as a donkey. At the bottom, the rich soil testified to the source of Latoan foodstuff. Wending our way back around the base of the mountain we intersected the main road we had taken that morning. We hailed a bus and made it to the *Eva* by noon. Captain Antonio asked us to forego our swim and eat lunch while sailing as he was eager to get underway to the island of Karpathos.

I managed to stay out of my berth long enough to see the rest of Crete's northern shore. I tried to imagine the destruction to the mainland caused by the tidal wave from the eruption of Thera. A two-hundred foot wave! I was glad my house at Lato had been on such high ground.

⚡ 16 ⚡

Dolphins

"Dolphins! Dolphins!," Bill shouted from his perch on top of the cabin. "There to starboard, way out."

At first they appeared as mere flashes of silver, leaping high above the sea. Then they saw the *Eva* and streaked toward her. For a brief moment before beginning their ballet they swam alongside the yacht. Then they began to criss-cross in front of and under our bow. The first dancer entered from stage right with a flourish and at midpoint turned in one effortless swift pirouette, exposing his iridescent white stomach. At the same time, two ballerinas darted out from the opposite side to perform a pas de deux. Then under us, behind us, and to our sides, the whole corps de ballet appeared and disappeared, forming and reforming themselves in patterns worthy of a master choreographer.

"I think the adults are teaching the teenagers," Bill said, leaning perilously close to the water to observe the magnificent creatures. "I can definitely count eight different dolphins."

They leapt in perfect unison, using the *Eva* as a giant stage prop. Too soon they were gone, though a short time later three of them returned to play with us again. I wondered what they thought we were? A giant dolphin? I was reading Robert Graves' *Hercules, My Shipmate,* in which he writes that dolphins have figured in the earliest accounts of the sea, as well as on the wall paintings of the Minoans. And from earliest times their presence has been interpreted as an omen of good luck. Greek sailors still regard them as such.

"We could have used their good luck earlier this morning," Ann observed wryly. She was referring to the crisis that beset us as we had sailed out of the harbor at Ayios Nikolaus. No sooner had Helen gone down to the salon than we heard her shriek, "Help! Help! We're flooding!"

Pushing and shoving our way down, we discovered that Yorgo had forgotten to close the portholes of the salon. Great round spouts of seawater were drenching everything. The men wrenched the portholes closed and we all dragged mattresses and cushions up the hatchway to dry in the Mediterranean sun.

This mishap was forgotten in the excitement of spotting our first dolphins and soon we settled on deck to idle away the hours, each in his or her own fashion. Like our dolphin playmates, we presented ever-changing patterns, though our pace had slowed to that of lazy human beings on holiday. Ann and I settled into deck chairs with our books, I in a modest one-piece bathing suit after burning my virginal tummy in my Piraeus bikini the day before. Helen lounged resplendently in a French bikini, even briefer than my Greek version. As Wendy emerged from the hatch and spied her sister she wailed like an outraged Victorian, "Helen, I can see the crack in your bottom!"

"You mean my clovage?" Helen responded indolently, coining what has since become a fine family distinction: "cleavage" in front, "clovage" behind.

Rick played his guitar for a while. Robert and Wendy gossiped and giggled. Helen, Tom, and Bill kept reading. Eventually Ann put down her book to give me a back rub. Then I gave her a back rub. Rick and Robert climbed into the dinghy. Bill deserted his book to sit on the prow of the yacht facing the wind. Everything was deliciously lazy though my stomach had begun to urge my mind to think about lunch.

At two o'clock my dreams of food ended abruptly. The motor cut off and the Captain, shouting instructions in rapid Greek, raced below. He reappeared almost immediately wreathed in clouds of smoke which seemed to be pouring from the main stairwell in the direction of my stateroom. The Captain, still shouting, started the motor again and turned the *Eva*'s prow directly towards land. The crew raced this way and that. The Captain yelled something to Tom and Tom took the wheel. The Captain went below again. Tom yelled to us, "It may be a fire. Get ready to jump."

Rick and Bill found our foot-pump mattresses and blew them up. I shrieked to the girls to come above. "Take those damn bath-towel dresses off," I yelled. "If we have to swim stay near one of the mattresses."

As we stood poised to dive, Tom screamed over the confusion, "Don't jump! Don't jump! It's steam, not smoke." We were not particularly reassured. Captain Antonio kept yelling, "Mother of God, Mother of God," and gave instructions for everyone to gather in the stern of the ship. Bit by bit we began to piece the situation together. A gasket had blown, which flooded the motor, which in turn created the billowing smoke-like steam. Our hull, which drew eleven feet, was completely filled with water.

Tom kept the wheel and for more than an hour the crew formed a bucket brigade from the hold, through our stateroom, up the hatch, and over the side. Hundreds of buckets of black greasy water hit the sea. When it was finally over a jet-black Yorgo emerged from the engine room. He had been the first man in the brigade line.

We gave the crew a fifth of Scotch, canceled our dinner plans, and changed the oily sheets on our beds. Captain Antonio found anchorage by the village of Karpathos, and we dove happily into the sea. The emergency was over and our dear *Eva* still afloat.

As the evening progressed, we gathered on deck to talk about the day's adventures and to watch the brilliant night sky. While Tom read from his book on astronomy with a flashlight, Bill spotted our first satellite. It went so fast! The waning moon rose. Two young boys, dark shadows on the dock, fished with a light for bait. Captain Antonio came on deck to hang two miniature lamps of green glass above the deck table. Ann went below and returned with a tray of cups filled with rum-laced coffee.

Sleepy people sought beds and I was alone on deck. I felt restless and uneasy for the first time since we sailed. Was it because of the scare—the realization that, without warning, disaster can upset the best laid plans? One moment the dolphins had been sailing with us; the next, they had abandoned us to the vagaries of a blown gasket. . . .

I thought of the time six years earlier when my life—my luck—had suddenly changed. Abruptly I had found myself alone with five children, without money, starting a business I didn't want, living a single life in a world of couples.

I began to learn about another world that at that time was peopled mostly by men working in offices eight to twelve hours a day. I learned how exhausting office work can be. I learned how rare it is to find a real executive—someone willing to make decisions and risk being wrong.

I began to learn the hard truth about fair-weather friends, although individuals from my earlier life were endlessly compassionate and helpful in practical ways. But my heart ached with loneliness. I had not known until then that heartache is a real, palpable ache. Sometimes it drifted from the region between my rib cage and became a dull pain at the base of my neck.

Sanity and hope and laughter lay in the children who, more than ever, formed the core of my life. But I knew I must not use them to solve my own problems. More and more I turned to Ann and her husband, Jerry. After work I would drive to Ann's small house and hold her new baby. Some days Ann and I would deliver sandwiches to Jerry, a nuclear physicist, who spent endless hours on Stanford's nuclear reactor. Other days—the not-so-bright ones—Ann and I would drink brandy and talk . . . and talk and talk. Sometimes I cried as much as I talked. Then I would drive home, help the older children with their homework, bathe the little ones, read them stories aloud by the fire, and go lonesomely to bed, aching to be with a man I loved.

Those years did little to increase my tolerance for suburbia, although we all loved our home, three-quarters of an acre at the edge of San Francisquito Creek. We had a fine view beyond to the broad fields of Stanford University. Our rambling added-onto-four-times redwood house was shaded by old eucalyptus trees which rustled in the rain and filled our backyard with camphor smells. One of Bill's friends told me he loved our home because it was like a jungle.

No, the problems with suburbia were not those of place, but of people. We had a small cottage which stood next to Robert's tree-house in a part of the yard which had once been a pear and walnut orchard. Even in happier days, the cottage had been the focus of a clash between our upper middle-class neighbors and ourselves. We had once hired a black couple and they lived in the cottage. Soon a delegation of neighbors called on us to protest. "It's not that we mind the couple," one woman told me. "But it's obvious the wife is pregnant. What happens when she has the child and it begins to grow up and look for playmates?"

The neighbors managed to survive that black baby, and still another and gradually came to know and accept all of our family. A year later, after the black family had bought their own home, another unpleasant incident occurred. I rented the cottage to a Stanford student who came to us just before his lease expired and asked if friends could use it for the final month. I agreed. Two weeks later, a friend of Bill's dropped by on a Saturday morning and asked, "Have you read the *San Francisco Chronicle* this morning?"

"No," I replied.

"Well, you'd better." I picked up the paper and looked at the headlines on the front page: "Dope Pad in Upper Middle Class Neighborhood." The detailed story that followed gave our address but not our name. It recounted how a young girl had run away from home. The police, at her father's instigation, had found her with several young men and a stash of marijuana in our cottage the previous night.

After the young people were let out on bail they showed up to apologize for having caused problems. "We'd like to leave our food supply with you," they said.

"O.K.," I agreed, somewhat morosely. Sheepishly they handed me a small cardboard box full of wheat germ, molasses, and yogurt. I accepted the food and cleaned up the cottage, thinking to myself, "That's that." But it was only the beginning.

Wendy and Robert's friends were no longer allowed to come to our house to play. One of Helen's college friends from the neighborhood was forbidden to enter our house or to be seen in Helen's company. One of Bill's friends reported he had overheard several neighbors discussing how I had harbored a teenage marijuana ring . . . I who had never smoked a Camel and was not especially tolerant of others who smoked!

Some of this feeling against me softened in the months that followed, or so I thought. At Christmas Richard flew home from Princeton and as we turned into our property he noticed the two-feet-high white letters on our grapestake fence which proclaimed

"Give me a fix." Disliking vandalism of any kind, I had been annoyed by the graffiti, but had no idea what it meant. I was preoccupied with Christmas preparations and I had simply ignored it. Richard, however, was furious. He tried to scrub the paint off with a wire brush with no success. Finally he hammered the grapestakes off and turned them around.

As the months and the years went by I found that I had less and less in common with my neighbors. I could admire the aristocrat and I was at home with the farmer. But the great middle class (at least some of them) that preached one thing and practiced another was not to my liking.

Shortly after the cottage episode Ann encouraged me to build a swimming pool. The younger children loved to swim but I seldom was able to leave work early enough to take them swimming. I borrowed the money and we built the pool, shaped like a pie wedge with the tip eaten away. But when it was finished our backyard was devastated. It had become a construction site, not a home. I contacted a landscape gardener who estimated that it would cost approximately fifteen hundred dollars to plant a new lawn, build wooden benches, and so on. I did not have fifteen hundred dollars.

Our solution was to do it ourselves or, rather, to call up the community spirit that had inspired our pioneer ancestors! I had never quite lost my belief in the "house raisings" and "quilting bees" of my youth, and here was a perfect opportunity for the modern equivalent. Richard and Bill invited five friends to a work party. Jerry and Ann Pine helped by renting several huge wheelbarrows. I ordered a keg of beer. We all went to work early one Sunday morning and continued until after dark. Then we ordered more beer and made hamburgers for all the helpers who had broken dates and postponed studies in order to finish the job. After dinner, the exhausted bodies of our amateur work force lay in front of the kitchen fire as one of the boys played his guitar.

Five years later one of the boys returned to our house with his fiancée in tow. He wanted her to see the things he had built that Sunday: a strong bench in the tiny pool house and wooden benches around several trees. I told her how he arrived with his hammer and square and wouldn't let them out of his sight all day long. When they left, smiling and holding hands, I realized we

had built something worthwhile that day. In the middle of suburbia we had recreated the spirit of pioneer self-help and community caring.

Now on the dark deck of the *Eva Maria,* recalling those times, I
concluded that running through the fabric of luck and misfortune
there is a thread of personal choice. Or call it style . . . call it
spirit. From that elusive thread, the random elements of our lives
achieve some sort of personal consistency, some meaning beyond
the haphazard.

The velvet air had cooled, and I was tired of introspection. I
poured myself a large glass of Cretan wine and, after raising it in
the direction of our departed dolphins, I made my way to my
bunk.

⋆ 17 ⋆

Hello, Goodbye

It was an old-fashioned segregated sort of day. Males were directed to one type of activity, females to another. The boys struck out early to find, as Bill expressed it, "a place where we can swim naked and see if Karpathos has some redeeming features." Pigathis, the port village, certainly left something to be desired. It had none of the charm of the Cycladic islands we had visited. But then, we hadn't given it much chance.

We females headed for the market to replenish supplies . . . again! Soon we were joined by four eleven-year-old Greek girls: two named Anna, plus a Maria, and a Kiki. Now we had become a harem of eight. Together we visited the meat market where we bought a great frozen chunk of beef from Australia which the butcher ground into *kimas,* or hamburger meat. Then at the produce shop our harem expanded once again. I counted twenty-three girls and women acting as Ann's advisors as she picked out tomatoes, grapes, and plums. In perfect English one of them told us that plums were introduced to Karpathos twenty years earlier by a native who had returned from Australia. As we continued to get acquainted with our band of sisters, it appeared that half the island had lived in Australia or America at one time or another. We heard English spoken all around us for the first time in our weeks of sailing.

We were pleased to discover that eggplants had become plentiful. Yorgo taught us how to cut their shiny purple globes in half, fry them briefly on each side, squish the softened pulp with a spoon, fill the cavities with slightly fried onions, and then top the whole creation with a sprinkle of Parmesan cheese. After thirty

minutes in the oven, they were transferred into food extraordi-
naire called "papousakia" (little shoes).

Our chores completed, we retreated to a small table under a
plane tree in the village square where we licked ice cream cones
with Kiki, Maria, and the Annas. Then, good women that we
were, we whiled away the time by pursuing feminine themes:
children, clothes, and houses. We watched several dozen children swimming in the sea just below us. When that became
tedious, we examined the handsome native dresses worn by
women from another village who had come to shop in Pigathis.
When that too paled, we sketched ideas for our Ios house. We
talked, we swam, we ate, we napped. But we had become bored
without our men and *with* Karpathos.

In the late afternoon the boys returned to regale us with tales
of their morning's adventures. Robert and Yorgo washed down
the *Eva* by slowly circling her in the rowboat and scrubbing her
hull sparking white with soapy water from a large bucket. When
they had finished with the *Eva* they turned the rowboat upside
down and scrubbed *her* as well.

Helen manicured Bill's nails. We decided definitely that we
would try to find a new crewman in Rhodes and that Richard
would fly to Athens to interview cooks. Decisions!

But everything we did that day seemed tentative and insignificant. It was as if Karpathos were merely a transition point. With
the enchanted Cyclades behind us we were leaving the first part
of our summer behind. As we sailed on to Rhodes we would
enter the Dodecanese, a group of twelve islands strung along the
western coast of Turkey.

I wondered idly if Karpathos had been used as a stopover place
by crusaders on the way to their headquarters in Rhodes. Perhaps this island's fate was ever to be a stepping stone between
larger, more fascinating places. Never mind, she had served us
well. The *Eva's* gasket had been repaired, her larder restocked,
and her exterior cleaned. The next day we would begin a new
chapter.

⋆ 18 ⋎

Neighbors

It was our most beautiful backyard so far. The towering temple crowned the headland above a half-moon beach of white sand. The town of Lindos, an archeaological site, is protected by the Greek government which requires that every home be built or restored in traditional style. No half-built cement skeletons in Lindos!

Lindos was a Doric town and with two other Doric towns in 480 B.C. hired the finest architect of the time (a man from Asia Minor who introduced the grid system to city planning) to build the city of Rhodes. Rhodes became the main port of the island, a crossroad for many lands, and a principal refuge and domain for the Knights of St. John during the centuries of the Crusades.

When we sailed into Lindos harbor our yacht was alone but by evening we had acquired six neighbors. A quick consultation with our flag book informed us that one yacht flew the Belgian flag, one the South African, one the Canadian, one the Romanian, and the last and largest the American. We met the Americans on the beach after we swam ashore. They told us they were from San Francisco and invited us for cocktails on board. Together we gazed in wonder at the ruins of the Lindos temple against the setting sun — a massive stone acropolis between two perfect, natural bays.

As I savored the sight, my mind wandered back over the centuries. Who were the men and women who chose such an incredible location? Inhabited since the Stone Age, it had been invaded by the Minoans who built a shrine to the Moon here. They were displaced by the warlike Dorians who founded the three cities of Kamiros, Ialysos, and Lindos, and henceforth secured Rhodes' position on the trade route between the Middle East and the West. Led by the greatest of the three—Lindos— they founded colonies in several Italian locations, including what would eventually become Naples.

I wondered why the leaders of those three great naval towns decided to build yet another town. But they did exactly that and the "City of the Sun," Rhodes, was originally surrounded with fifteen kilometers of walls. It became one of the greatest and richest cities of antiquity, rivaling Athens and Corinth in their prime. The first naval code originated in Rhodes and its schools of law, rhetoric, and philosophy became famous throughout the then-known world.

I pulled my mind back to Lindos and tried to picture St. Paul visiting Lindos on his way to Rome. Surely he must have been moved by the sight of the acropolis, the temples, and the ever-changing sea. Did he go swimming?

In early morning, Yorgo beached the *Albatross* and deposited us ashore all properly attired. After a steep climb to Lindos town we emerged in front of the taverna with a roof of entwined grapevines and broad whitewashed walls broken by a series of arches. The waiter brought us fresh pears, a large omelette, bread, and honey. Fortified, we began our assault on the ruins of the temple, hoping to sort out the different periods in its history.

After a while, we girls returned to the yacht, as the boys, with Yorgo, went exploring watery caves on both sides of the temple's promontory. Back on board Robert wrote a description of his adventures and gave it to me for safekeeping:

"When we got to the big cave we tied up the boat and went in. It was very dark but we had some matches. There were two ways into this scary, scary cave. We went down one to the very end and found some wood. We tried to light it and make a torch but it wouldn't light. Everybody started back but Rick and me. The cave kept on going, but you had to crawl to get through, and I got really scared so we started back. Outside I saw a boy on a cliff, and he was very high but he dove. He came over and talked to us. He is from England and lives here all winter because his father is an artist. He goes to school in Greece. I wished I could have stayed and played with him. Sometimes I get lonesome for my friends."

A fresh wind pushed us along the rugged southern coast of Rhodes. All the bays seemed sandy and all were backed by groves of olives which had been planted by the Italians during their control of the island from 1912 to 1945. Rick played the guitar while Ann read Lawrence Durrell's *Reflections on a Marine Venus,* about Rhodes. Two sheeplike clouds appeared on the horizon . . . the wind! It was perfect sailing wind and we heeled over so far that our braced feet almost touched the sea. I felt as free as a bird. Robert held a black smooth stone which he had found on Lindos beach and rubbed it against his cheek over and over again. Wendy donned her "boy-watcher glasses" (solid blue plastic with small horizontal slits so she could see out but no one could see in). Then suddenly we were in Mandrak harbor and I pretended that the Colossus of Rhodes still stood arched high above the harbor's entrance.

Rhodes was our largest port so far. And what an anchorage! We were directly in front of the sprawling city market with the castle of the Grand Master to our left. When we backed into our berth there had been much shouted advice from bystanders as we wiggled our way into a narrow slot. "I hope we like our neighbors," I said, observing the yachts squashed together bumper to bumper. On our port side was a small sloop with two men busily repairing a sail. To starboard was a substantial motor yacht flying a British flag. But when we got up the next morning an enormous yacht named *Vagrant* had somehow slipped in between us and the British.

Ann and I discovered the new yacht when we arose at dawn. I had blown up at the older children when they came noisily on board at four in the morning and awakened the rest of us. Just as Ann and I were dropping off to sleep again the sloop next door came to life as it prepared to sail.

"Cast off!"

"Watch that bumper."

"Can you grab the wheel?"

It was as if they were inside our cabin and when I peeped out our porthole I discovered they damn near were. So what did we do — we made some tea, inspired by the large mugs we saw in the hands of the shouting, departing Australians.

Waving our neighbors away, we walked the plank into the broad promenade in front of the market square. This street area was blocked to traffic at night when hundreds of tables were set up for dining and drinking. But now inside the vast courtyard with all the food markets it was like midday as merchants yelled, donkeys plodded under constant whacks, and Ann I dodged three-wheeled pushcarts. We were the only women in a sea of male faces and we bravely joined a number of men who sat in front of the coffee house eating *souvlaki* and drinking Turkish coffee. We ordered a *metrio* (coffee served medium sweet) and soaked in the timeless scene around us. In the center of the marketplace stood a gazebo-like structure which now operated as a fish stall. Ann and I poked our way into every corner of the market and returned for more coffee and a souvlaki as well. It was a new variation of this dish. A cylinder of closely packed, boneless lamb had been slowly turning on an upright spit for hours. From this cylinder, the waiter sliced off thin pieces of meat and put them into an envelope-like piece of pita bread, along with tomato chunks, shredded lettuce, and onions.

"Delicious!" Ann said. "If the children discover this, we won't have to cook on Rhodes." She was right.

It was Tom's last day with us and we had agreed to spend it exploring the old walled City of Rhodes. Sleepily the rest of our group struggled ashore and, reinforced by souvlaki, we all began to climb through the lush foliage growing along the moat. We walked to the highest point of entrance through the stone walls. Fir trees were dwarfed by ancient maples and palms stood next to loquat. Hibiscus plants in many colors grew twenty feet high and the oleanders were as tall as trees.

"See, Wendy, there's Rapunzel hanging out of that tower window," Bill teased. I half believed him. The castle, seen from outside the walls, *did* have a fairytale quality.

Funny about a new place. I had heard and read much about Rhodes but none of the "feeling" of that old city — the spirit of the place — had touched me at all. Even now it was hard to take in the reality of a medieval walled city, bustling with modern enterprises, all housed in ancient, oft-repaired buildings.

As we walked across the wide road over the first moat, it was easy to believe that the city had never been conquered. It never had. Inside the first wall was a second moat and on the inside of the second wall was a *third* moat surrounding the palace proper.

Lying in the moats and under bushes everywhere were stone catapult balls—some in piles and some widely scattered like mammoth marbles. Each was at least two feet in diameter.

Wandering through the freshly swept streets we followed the map to the Street of the Knights. Cobblestoned and sloping slightly, the wide thoroughfare was lined with massive stone townhouses, each an inn for a different fraternity of Knights. Talk about neighbors! The Knights represented at least seven or eight different languages yet they lived close by for centuries. The coat-of-arms for each group was still emblazoned on the door or carved in marble above the door. Glimpsing these medieval homes (many with seductive inner gardens) it was easy to conjure up the ghosts of the sometimes devoted, sometimes rapacious men of God who built their Castello on the site of a temple to Apollo in Rhodes. Here they fulfilled their destiny for more than two hundred years until the Turks expelled them in 1523 and forced them to find a new headquarters on Malta.

We loved the ancient city. Our anchorage was so close that we could return to the city at will. One time we looked briefly at the museum ("we must return with more time") and the last visit that hot summer day took place at dusk when we walked on top of the outer wall from the old palace to the sea. It was more than three kilometers. In some places the wall was thirty meters wide. When we descended from the ramparts and tried to find a city gate we got totally lost. The maze of Mykonos was nothing compared to the medieval maze of Rhodes.

Next morning when I went to awaken everyone because Tom's plane was due shortly, people were pouring on to the cruise boat anchored not more than ten inches from our yacht. Helen, sleeping on deck in bikini underpants, was trapped under her blanket until the ship sailed. Rick was up, but said he awakened to find three ladies about six feet above him leaning over the rail, chattering in German and staring down at him with great interest.

Rick, Robert, and Wendy drove with Tom to the airport. We were all teary at Tom's departure—he was off on an African adventure. He had become "family" to us and to the crew. When our children returned they told me that while they waited for Tom's plane a beautiful woman came over to Richard and said her son would like to meet Wendy. "Is she your sister?" the woman asked. "You look so much alike." There were introductions all around. They were the Goulandris family—Dolly (the mother), her son Peter, a sister and nephew. They had a large painted sign and banners of welcome for their arriving relatives. Robert proudly held one of the banners and in the ensuing conversation the children discovered that they were our neighbors from the yacht *Vagrant*. Mrs. Goulandris said their youngsters had been hoping to meet some children their own age, hence *their* delight. When they parted company Mrs. Goulandris invited my children to "Come over for a drink at noontime and bring all your family. The boys play then." Richard accepted although he was mystified by what was meant by "the boys play then."

As we returned in late morning from yet another sortie in the Old Town, we found the answer. A large crowd had completely blocked the *Eva* from view by gathering on the quay around the stern of the *Vagrant*. The rhythmic beat of modern music resounded. On the stern of the *Vagrant:* Peter and group—all students at Groton Academy—playing electric guitars and drums. The amplifiers were turned up and the mob gathered around the yacht loved it. On board the *Vagrant* the sound was deafening. As we sipped our noontime drink and marveled at the concert, a steward from another yacht arrived with a note. Dolly read it aloud: an English couple on another yacht were complaining sarcastically about the "vulgar" music. We jointly composed a scathing reply which Dolly's steward delivered.

The children from our two families joined forces for an afternoon of swimming and Dolly Goulandris came over to the *Eva* for a drink. She asked us to go to a nightclub on the quay where "the boys" had been asked to play that evening—at eleven o'clock! It was the eve of the Fourth of July.

It took five cabs to get the fourteen of us, plus the piles of instruments and electronic equipment, to the nightclub. Robert was in heaven as he carried, arranged, and advised. During the afternoon practice sessions Peter had give Robert a drum stick which he had not let out of his hands since.

So we sat at our reserved table in the middle of the club, eating chunks of watermelon and drinking Scotch, while the young men played away. All our youth danced, Helen was the star. Wendy was different people, depending on her partner of the moment. With Rick and Bill she was serious and concentrated; with the young boys she became relaxed, laughing.

I loved listening to Nikos Goulandris, the father. He and his five brothers and one sister (she sat opposite me that night) had been shipowners for generations. I soaked up stories of the sea as well as the modern shipping business. I learned that to avoid sharks one should never swim near the entrance to caves and only when you can see the floor of the ocean. Nikos expressed approval of our Ios land purchase. "It is one of our loveliest islands," he said, "I like to fish there. Did you see my caïque? I go every morning before dawn with some of my crew to fish and I come back by lunch. It is the thing I love most in life."

On the way back to the yachts Nikos sat in the front seat with his arm around Robert, intently quizzing him on his knowledge of Greek. With a sudden pang I wished that Robert had a father.

Wendy had walked home with the boys. When she arrived she stomped in indignantly and reported that one of her new friends had tried to kiss her. I could only smile to myself and say to my young Puritan, "Well, my dear, there'll come a day. . . ."

At two the next morning the *Vagrant* sailed away in a blaze of rockets and firecrackers which they set off to celebrate the Fourth of July. We were sorry to lose our neighbors.

✴ 19 ✴

Apollo's Head

We had to make the Fourth of July special! We had a great breakfast in the marketplace in Rhodes. Afterwards we returned to the *Eva*, and although it was still morning, Helen fell fast asleep at my feet. She was happily exhausted, having written her own Declaration of Independence to her now ex-boyfriend. Filled with sudden joy and relief, she had rushed around planting kisses on various members of the family until, all emotion spent, she retreated into a cocoon of sleep.

Rick and the Captain had gone ashore to interview a new seaman. Yorgo and Robert sat cross-legged in the rowboat, playing cards and chattering away in their own synthesis of Greek and English. The giggles and chortles from the girls' stateroom intruded on my reading. Then Wendy handed me a letter she had written, with Bill's assistance, to a friend in summer camp back in the States:

"Dear Louise: Hi! Greece is very fun. We are swimming, skiing, singing and dancing almost every day. I have a new boy friend. He's been with us for three weeks and just left. He is very attractive to women (girls). He has blond hair (in the summer), green eyes, shiny teeth and a beard. But he is not the only boy I have met this summer. Last night my family went to a nightclub with another family to dance and listen to music. A boy from the other family started to get fresh. He tried to make me take a walk and he tried to kiss me. He did not succeed! My heart belongs to Tom, and Jerry shall not get it, try as he may. Enough of this hot stuff, now to something more cool. We are in Rhodes. Last night we went to see the "Sound and Light" in the old city next to a castle. The lighting, wind, and moon made the performance memorable. Well, anyway, what have you been doing? Having fun, I hope. Stay out of the woods unless you want to go in. I hope you will write and tell me about your camp. My address is: Wendy Wright, Eva Maria, Delmouzos and Louys, 4 Kriezlou St. Athens, Greece. Please write to this fantastic address. Love Wendy. P.S. Please don't take it seriously. Other people helped and told me things to say."

We were all so happy on Rhodes that we decided to spend a few more days. It would give us time for an excursion to Kamiros, give Richard a day in Athens interviewing prospective cooks, and give everyone more hours for the Old Town or whatever else.

After taking Rick to the airport, we went to the aquarium which Rick and Bill had visited earlier. "You won't believe it," was all they would say.

Entering at street level on a spit in the bay we found ourselves face to face with a display of dusty, shriveled stuffed animals, among them pickled animal fetuses and an eight-legged calf!

"It makes me think a bit of Sutro's in San Francisco," Ann said, looking pained. "But why call it an aquarium?" Where are the fish?"

Bill led us downstairs where we entered a series of grotto-like halls with exquisite black and white pebble mosaic floors in aquatic motifs. The fish tanks were set back into the rough-hewn stone walls. It was a bit scary because we were under the seas with all those sea creatures. I wandered into one cavern to find Ann and Robert sitting on the floor in front of an enormous tank watching a full grown tortoise moving slowly among darting fish.

"Now this is good TV, Robert," said Ann. "Please turn to Channel Six."

Leaving our cool grotto, we proceeded along the coast to the venerable Grand Hotel of Rhodes, a slightly down-at-the-heels relic of a more gracious era. We ordered tea . . . of course . . . and drank it on the wide veranda which was in a state of disrepair, redeemed only by the perfect view across the sea. One could easily imagine sitting and dreaming here in the days when English visitors came to Rhodes for months at a time.

With our taskmasters, Richard and Tom, gone and the well-stocked market enticing us, and the heady aroma of the souvlaki stand luring us, we felt ourselves rapidly sinking into the idle pursuit of whims. But remembering my maternal duties, I was determined to expose the young ones to a bit of culture.

"How about July Fifth in the palace or the museum?" I asked. The museum it was but a general lack of serious purpose persisted. Helen fondly kissed all the male marble statues and Bill followed suit with an occasional caress of a marble bosom. Then we came to a sculptured head of Apollo and I felt a shock of recognition. Bill could have posed for it — the wide, generous mouth, the mop of curls. I realized why Bill had been approached by women who asked if they could run their fingers through his hair! They must have felt that he was a modern version of the classic prototype. Bill always responded to their strange request with the sunny equanimity of a Greek god. He would shrug: "Sure. O.K. Why not?"

I found Bill's resemblance to a Greek statue more than superficial. Like a philosopher out of the Golden Age, he was, in his own way, a seeker after truth. His most effective quality had always been a total honesty which came easily and naturally. This guilelessness was totally disarming to everyone he met including his own family. Personally, I found it impossible to punish Bill when he was very young for he always seemed to take the wind out of my anger sails. Now for the past few weeks I loved watching him with this same openness and frankness as he played with or counselled the younger children. He would listen, laugh, tease, and make up songs for them on his guitar. With Richard his honesty remained a constant of their relationship. In fact, being together seemed to sharpen and hone the brothers' respective characteristics and talents.

A conscious pursuit of knowledge, however, had been a late-blooming passion with Bill. He always did everything in his own time and to his own rhythm. Until he was fifteen he made no pretense of enjoying books. Although he came from a book-reading family he read only when he was absolutely obliged to do so. Then suddenly he discovered *the* book which unlocked the door to all the rest. It was a first novel called *The Temple of Gold* by William Goldman. Someone had given it to me and I brought it along on a family picnic on the beach on Half Moon Bay in California. As I lay against a log reading I came to a passage which I realized should be shared with my teenage offspring.

Interrupting the conversation I asked: "Want to hear a great piece of dialogue?"

"Do we have any choice?," one of them asked.

"No," I laughed. "But you'll be glad you didn't."

So I read the scene in which the book's teenage hero asks a girl for a date. It was the first time he had asked a girl out and he was terrified. A friend helped him and together they wrote a script for the phone call. But when the conversation actually took place it went like this:

"Mary, this is Jim."

"Hello."

"Mary, where are you?"

"What do you mean, where am I? I'm home where you called."

"What I mean is where will you be tonight."

From that point on, the exercise became a shambles. Mary, alas, had not read the script!

The boys listened with fascination. They had tried the script idea once and with the same disastrous results. I had not known before my sons hit their teens how shy boys could be. I had always thought that boys were more sure of themselves because they were the ones who could initiate a relationship by calling and asking. Yet I learned that boys are wary of being turned down and will spend a whole evening working up the nerve to even ask a girl for a date.

Bill immediately laid claim to *The Temple of Gold,* read it over and over, and bought every paperback copy available in the local book store to give to friends. He pondered the book's theme which is a young man's search for "the handle to life." One night as I said good-night to Bill he asked if *I* thought there was a handle to life, a "way." I did not answer my son that night for I had never really thought about the problem as I bumbled along in my *own* way. But the next night I told him, "Yes, I do think there is a 'handle' to life, and that is in accepting that there is no handle."

After that maiden voyage in his quest for book knowledge, Bill continued to read, study, talk, write . . . and urge others to do the same. Indeed, aboard the *Eva* both Bill and Richard had encouraged the rest of us to become familiar with some of the lofty themes of the Greek tragedies by taking parts and reading the plays aloud. Bill would prepare us for our roles by recounting the classic myths in his own words and even Robert became fascinated.

All this is not to say that Bill was never caught with his laurel wreath askew. Or perhaps I should say that there were times when my Greek god reminded me more of Dionysius than Apollo. I chuckled inwardly as I recalled Bill's introduction to liquor back in Menlo Park. It was a Saturday night. I had tucked in the two younger children when the phone rang:

"Is this Davenport 2-1543?"

"Yes."

"Do you have a son named Bill?"

"Yes."

"Well, this is the Menlo Park Police Department. We have your son down here. He's drunk."

I couldn't believe my ears but I dressed hastily and drove to the police station. Four fathers and myself came upon a scene of utter bedlam. Each young boy, not one of them more than fourteen, was being walked round and round the outside of the station by a policeman. One boy had vomited in the station and two officers were cleaning *that* up. After repeated questioning the boys had confessed to taking a bottle of Scotch from one of the homes and sharing it with each other as they walked through the town.

After promising to return my son to the police station after school on Monday, I drove Bill home and put him to bed with a bucket next to him. Later Rick returned from a Stanford basketball game and burst into my room to announce, "Bill is drunk!" He told me he had gone into the room he shared with his younger brother who had straightened into a sitting position and tried to say something before collapsing into giggles. Poor Bill! He took a terrible ribbing the following day.

That Monday five chastened culprits reported to the police station, their parents hovering in the background. The police were cool, kind, firm, and impressive!

On the yacht I did not like it that Bill felt forlorn every time mail arrived. He got "friend" letters but none from Katie. As our group began to slow down in the pursuit of culture on Rhodes I suggested:

"Let's get back to the *Eva.* Rick may have arrived with our cook and the mail."

Rick was home with Eileen — the cook. There were letters but not the important one from Katie. "Bill, are you sure you gave her an address?"

"No, I can't remember."

"Well, have you sent it from Greece?"

"Yes, so I still hope." And he stopped to pick up his guitar and head for his favorite spot on the prow.

I poured an ouzo and took up my station in the stern to hear of Rick's adventures in Athens (awful, hot, crowded) and to watch the evening strollers. Rick went to join Bill with his guitar. Their music blended with the purr of passing motorcycles.

"How many things happen in one day," I thought. "Most are inconsequential but together they make for a rich, full day."

The cafes along the quay were packed and a six-piece band played in one. I watched a cruise ship dock and two yachts squiggle into slots. The men on the yacht to our port were sandpapering the hull of their boat. They'd been at it all day — beers in hand. A young boy came sculling down the middle of the harbor, a real live pelican riding on his prow. Dusk brought the spotlights and faint voices from the "Sound and Light" show in front of the Palace. Just then a call came from the galley:

"Don't anyone come down until we are ready. It gets too crowded and besides we are cooking a surprise." Helen and Wendy were celebrating cook Eileen's arrival with one last dinner by daughters.

I was glad for their call. I had been watching the town scene, yet I felt removed. I liked Rhodes. It was more civilized and lively than any other port so far. But I was not sure I liked it for too many days. Perhaps, I thought, one of the most important things about a private boat is the chance to go from a bustling town to a remote bay.

⊀ *20* ⊁

Meltemi

It was almost like being in a snowstorm dressed in bathing suits. The *meltemi* was whooping it up and the *Eva* raced along, sails up and motor running. We were all on deck, each of us holding tight to the boom — or something — as our bow went under and we rolled like a log. Gradually we all acquired a coating of salt. The men looked more interesting than the women as salt clung to their beard stubble. I wondered if I had discovered the derivation of the term "old salt." It was all wildly exhilarating, yet exhausting, when the wind reached gale force. When the Captain turned directly into a high brown cliff, we thought he might be seeking emergency shelter. But it turned out we had arrived in Simi, our original destination, and gratefully we sailed into the small opening neck of harbor and gazed with delight at the lone building — a sparkling white monastery sprawled along the sea.

In the harbor although the sea was calmer the wind was still so fierce that Yorgo could row us only to the nearest headland, three at a time. I was last in and was horrified to see two figures — undoubtedly sons from the first boatload — like slender bronze statues silhouetted against the sky, clinging to the side of a ruined windmill. Later they admitted they had been terrified by the ferocious wind which filled the whole bay with gray mist as it tore the tops from waves. We worked our way in toward the monastery, struggling around boulders, waiting for a pause between waves, and then dashing to the next patch of solid ground. All around us rosemary plants gave pungent odor to the air!

A priest was saying mass in a quiet droning voice as we entered the spacious church courtyard and sat under an ancient plane tree. The head priest then led us up to the big library in the Monastery of St. Michael. As we admired the ancient volumes a novice arrived with a tray of small glasses and a bottle of that potent liquor — raki. We had long since learned to swallow it with protestations of pleasure, and to quickly drink the accompanying glass of water.

As the Pappas, or Father, led us through the ornate church he told us stories of St. Michael's prowess including one tale of his own. In 1943 the Father, then sixteen, was returning with his mother to Simi from Kos. Their caïque was attacked by a German submarine and most of the passengers drowned. But our good Father and his mother were saved after four hours in the sea. While struggling to stay afloat the young man promised to dedicate his life to St. Michael if he were rescued.

"We used to have 30,000 inhabitants on our island," he told us philosophically. "They built many of the ships for Rhodes when it was a separate state. Now only a handful of people are left. Three thousand, I guess, and all the others are in Rhodes, Athens, or Tarpon Springs, Florida."

"In Tarpon Springs?" we echoed in disbelief.

"Yes, there are more Simians in Tarpon Springs than here, at least five thousand, and many of them still ply the trade of their forbears, sponge diving."

We left the quiet of the monastery and repaired to the tiny taverna next door for refreshments. Sadly the proprietor told us he had only beer as a group of Swedish tourists who had visited the Monastery the day before had drunk all his soft drinks.

The wind still howled as dusk fell. There would be no way for Yorgo to pick us up on the jagged rocks where he had left us. The Pappas offered to let us stay overnight in the Monastery. "We have guest rooms for those who come to worship," he explained.

Since the "meltemi" often calmed at night, we decided to have some supper and hope for its demise. The Pappas returned to the monastery and brought back his supper, three large pieces of fish, to share with us. In addition the taverna owner made cheese omelette.

"Why are eggs so much better in Greece than anywhere else?" Bill asked.

"Because eggs in villages are very fresh," the Father answered.

About ten o'clock the Pappas and two sponge fishermen who were playing tavali in the corner of the taverna decided that we should be taken back to our yacht in their sponge-diving boat. They assured us, "It is big and solid and you will be safe." A young man appeared with a lantern. We followed him single file, accompanied by the Pappas (and St. Michael we hoped) around the spray-filled arc of shore to the caïque. Just as we prepared to launch, Yorgo appeared in the Albatross. The wind had died down a good deal and the sailors decided it was safe for us to return to the *Eva* by our own small boat.

We moved out toward our graceful white yacht in the moonlight. The soft orange glow from her porthole lights welcomed us home. I gave everyone a dramamine — in case of seasickness — as the Captain announced, "Meltemi willing, we will sail for Kos at dawn."

Kneeling on my bunk I peered into the night through the porthole. I wanted to see the elegant simple monastery once more. What drama there can be in human life. A young man dedicates his life to a Saint. It seems beautiful and simple. But think of the thousands of days and nights achieving that goal. Was the Pappas often lonely? What determination it must have taken to stick to his promise. How much had been deep spiritual belief and how much simple human tenacity? Duty, character, responsibility — all those characteristics associated over the ages with "good" men and women. Why in the last half of the twentieth century had so many negated those qualities in pursuit of "self"?

What about me, I thought, as I knelt there in the dark listening to Ann's gentle breathing. Had I fulfilled my duties? Had I not, in the end, after more than twenty years, walked away from my husband and his illness? Yet I knew that my action — in divorcing a mentally ill man who was hospitalized — had to do with absolute reality. *If* Dick had come home *I* would not have survived. I could stand still for the children emotionally. I could earn their living and mine, but the years of supporting the ups and downs in the life of a manic-depressive had taken their toll. In the last analysis the children's and my health had come first.

My heart ached in the soft Greek night for the handsome young Dick of twenty-five years ago. I gradually learned to think

of Dick's manic-depressive bouts as just part of my life. That
disease can best be related to an electric oven which does not
have an automatic cut-off. After all, we all go up and down in
mood. Some of us more than others. But something inside—the
automatic cut-off—keeps us from going too far one way or the
other. Manic-depressives know when they are going into a bad
period, but cannot control it. It would only take five days for
Dick—in a depression—to be completely catatonic. He couldn't
work, felt he had caused all evil in the world (including wars) and
was often suicidal. Thank God, before his death, doctors came
to the conclusion that much of a manic-depressive illness was
chemical lack, and with lithium Dick eventually was out of the
hospital.

Once when Dick was hospitalized a young hospital psychologist sat me down and was asking a thousand questions about
family, children, etc. when the doctor walked in and said, "Oh,
leave her alone. She could write the book."

Not *that* book, although I did know more than I wanted to.
Fortunately I was so busy I don't ever remember feeling sorry for
myself. It was hard though, and once—as we rode horses together across a Wyoming ranch where the boys were working for
the summer—Richard, with keen perception, said to me,
"Mother, you have to be three people, don't you? One when dad
is well, another when he is depressed and the third when he is
manic. That's the hardest one, isn't it? I guess it's lucky he is
mostly depressed. He's such a good father when he is well. I
wish. . . ."

And so did I. The hardest time had been right at the beginning
with a war on, in Texas, far from home and family and I was so
terribly vulnerable. I can remember thinking it would be easier
to hear that my young husband had been killed in action on the
battlefield, than to spend months visiting a mental hospital.
Mental illness is so gray—nothing to hold on to or go away from.
It doesn't have the decisiveness of something like the Pappas
almost drowning. And I had learned that love can only exist
between two mature and healthy adults. Perhaps, if I had been
stronger, I could have kept caring for Dick even though I no
longer loved him as a woman. If American families stayed close,
as in Greece or in the "old days" in America, I suppose I could

have stayed with Dick no matter what. I had needed support — a mother, aunt, cousin — someone with whom to share the burden and on a daily basis.

You have to "get" from somewhere — if you are to stay healthy. My few years with Charles made my burden much more bearable. Without his support I am sure my marriage would have dissolved earlier.

Now my duty and pleasure was all centered on the children — as well as myself. I knew it had pitfalls, I must never, never "use" the children, I must give and let go. It would be in watching me and how I lived my life that they would gain their values and attitudes. They must learn to accept the miracle of life and not to waste it. I wished I had the Pappas' faith and a St. Michael to guide me.

Taking one last look at the monastery in the moonlight I went above to look at the sleeping children. Tomorrow we would be on Kos — the island of Hippocrates — and I wondered, as I crept into my bunk, about the ancient Greeks and citizens who were depressed or manic. How much had they relied on dream interpretation, on priests and oracles? How far had we really come in the practice of medicine? "Oh, well, I'll think about that tomorrow," I thought and smiled to myself knowing that if Ann were awake and I had said that phrase aloud she would have mocked me again.

"O.K., Scarlett" . . . referring to Scarlett O'Hara's penchant for thinking about problems — often unsolvable ones — tomorrow.

⋊ 21 ⋌

Hippocrates

"Mother, Mother," Richard was gently shaking my berth-bound form. "Can you come ashore and have breakfast with me?"

"What time is it?"

"Oh, about six."

Six o'clock is early even in July, yet there was something in Richard's tone that said, "Let's talk — it's important," so dutifully I pulled on a sun dress, slipped into sandals, and quietly followed Richard into the golden dawn on Kos. They claim Hippocrates taught his medical students beneath the shade of *the* plane tree of Kos. Gnarled and scarred, it spread out over nearly a block and looked like a banyan tree with marble columns holding up its spreading branches. Whether or not it shaded Hippocrates, it was a very impressive tree. Richard let me exclaim over it, but impatiently, and soon I found myself sitting in a seaside cafeneon across from my worried son.

"What is it, Rick?"

"Well, Mom, Helen is pregnant and she doesn't want to have the baby."

"Whew!" I gasped and thought immediately of the irony of learning this medical fact on Hippocrates' island. "Tell me, Richard."

"Last night we went ashore alone and she told me she suspected for a while but until she missed her second period she wasn't sure." Suddenly a Greek island, Hippocrates notwithstanding, seemed a very remote place. My Greek friends were limited to those we'd met during the summer.

"She's sure Richard, sure she doesn't want to marry" Sure she's pregnant?"

I was grasping at solutions, but actually I had talked enough with Helen in the past weeks to know that she was completely "over" boyfriend Chuck and eager to get on with the next phase of life. But what to do? how? where? Children!!

The blue of the sea deepened as the sun rose. Richard and I walked to a bakery and bought warm bread. At the end of the pier, in the shadow of stone walls centuries old, we ate bread and tried to think of solutions. I had never had an abortion myself. One of my sons had "fathered" a child (at an early age) and the girl's parents and I split an enormous bill for an abortion involving psychiatrists and gynecologists. It was all very hush hush. The whole thing was phony and expensive, but at least there *had* been a solution.

"Mom, I wonder about the Andersons. Maybe they could help."

We *did* have friends in Athens. Peter Anderson was head of British Airways. His wife Simone, half Romanian and half French, had recently entered medical school in Athens. I met the Andersons a few years before when I made a boat trip up the Nile River to visit Abu Simbel before it was dismantled and moved. We had become friends and seen each other—surrounded by our collective nine children—several times since. Richard's idea was good and I decided to act upon it immediately.

In every Greek village there is an OTE office—the phone company. A few minutes' walk brought Rick and me to the OTE of Kos and in moments we awakened the Andersons.

Simone listened to our dilemma, "Don't worry. Come to Athens. In Greece abortion is a means of birth control. I will arrange everything at the maternity hospital. Let us know which ferry you will come on and Peter will meet you."

I was stunned, relieved, but confused. It was only an hour since I innocently left my berth. "Rick, let's get a shot of brandy. I need some reinforcement before I talk with Helen and make a plan. I suppose there is not a terrible rush but we certainly don't want to have to go back to Athens from Turkey and *that* means Helen and I should leave soon. Besides, it will be better when the 'event' is behind us rather than in front of us."

We decided to tell the Captain and crew that I needed to see a doctor, to tell Bill the truth, and to tell Wendy and Robert nothing.

"Come on, Mom, it's all going to work out. Let's have an adventurous day on Kos."

In Kos's Mandraki harbor, the night before, we had had trouble berthing. Even though it was fun to anchor in the middle of a harbor so the children could water ski and we could all swim, I really preferred to dock the *Eva* in port. But on small islands there was seldom room for more than three or four yachts to dock. If we waited until the morning, after an evening arrival, a slot would usually open up and Captain Antonio would slide the long sleek hull of the *Eva* skillfully to the dock. The crew would immediately get hoses and wash the deck and sides clear of salt water. Next came the hoses to fill our tanks with drinking water and to replenish our supply of gasoline. Some ports offered the additional luxury of ice.

Our first evening in Kos we all wandered ashore long before the cleaning of the *Eva* was completed. The town of Kos had handsome sturdy Italian buildings along the waterfront as well as ancient ramparts, a castle, hundreds of substantial shade trees, oleander and hibiscus bushes. We meandered past partially excavated ruins to the museum. It was closed but next door was the foundation of a classical home where we discovered pipes for radiant floor heat. Richard was delighted to add this fact to his growing store of knowledge about antique plumbing systems.

It was still early morning, that "pregnancy day," when we all mounted our rented bicycles and headed for the Asclepion, a medical center of antiquity with mineral springs and a shrine to the site's patron God, Asclepius. When we rented our bicycles the shopkeeper had scoffed, "You'll never make it. Too far and all uphill." He probably wanted us to rent motor scooters instead! We girded ourselves for the long ride but after half an hour of peddling inland through fine agricultural land and, just at the point where the road began to climb, we found ourselves at our destination.

Hippocrates chose well. The first known medical center in the western world was magnificently located. We sat near the ruins in the lush grass beside a spring, under a spreading plane tree.

Richard read to us from a guide book. Then we climbed up the broad marble steps to see the hospital, partly reconstructed, and up more marble stairs, at least fifty, to nowhere! To the left of the stairs was a charming fountain which spilled its water into a pool surrounded by maidenhair ferns and eventually coursed on down the mountain. We all drank from the dank pool, and secretly echoed Wendy's dire observation: "Well, if we die, we'll all die together!"

Back on the *Eva* Bill followed me into my stateroom and gave me a letter he had just written to Katie. There I was, trying to bring some order into my Helen thoughts, and there was Bill— concerned about his sister, yes, but still for him, his own life and loves came first. Putting aside Helen's problem, I concentrated for a few moments on the outpourings of my son to his love in America. The letter revealed a side of Bill I seldom saw.

"The days flow by with the rhythm of the rich: island to island, ruin to ruin, people talking and drinking. I shan't write details. Perhaps one windy night I'll whisper Greek into your ear, or I may edit it all into a kiss.

"I will tell you about last night on Kos. Mail arrived, and I didn't get a letter. Did I give you an address? Last night I treated myself to a martini—my first. A night for a drink, thought I, and as the moments passed, I explored in depth the mysteries of my new companion. So, off to dinner. In a chain we marched, arms linked, and sang 'Mr. Tamborine Man'. I knew the infinite beauty and freedom of the moment and at dinner I found my wit. There was laughter. Good. . . ."

"It's a wonderful letter Bill. Katie will love it. Thank you for sharing it with me."

"Mom, I wish I could help about Helen. Would you like me to go to Athens with you?"

"No, darling, I think it might be good for Helen and me to have time alone, but thank you for offering. Go take a swim. I'll see you at dinner."

All day I had put off talking with Helen, needing time to think more and feel less. She knew Richard and I had talked—but now, before the day ended, I must show her my concern and love. I had not seriously thought about abortion before. Maybe a woman doesn't—until she or her daughter is faced with an unplanned pregnancy. Off and on all day my thoughts fled to Helen, to youth, to sex and babies. No wonder girls had been protected over the centuries, protected by fathers and brothers and mothers. If a girl became pregnant before marriage she had to resort to back street doctors, knitting needles and — we saw this in Ethiopia — drinking kerosene hoping to abort. Now here was my lovely fresh daughter, still so terribly innocent of the world, pregnant by a young man she thought she loved. The choices in such situations are definitely limited. Marry, have the baby as an unwed mother, or have an abortion. During the long hours of that full day on Kos I *had* decided that I harbored no moral objection to abortion. After all, every egg a woman produced was also a potential child. So it came down to an abortion under legal and appropriate medical conditions. Well, at least for me that seemed to be the practical thing to do, but what about Helen? How did she really still feel about Chuck? Did she have any feeling about the growing baby in her womb?

Arm in arm we walked to Hippocrates' tree and under its canopy (how many secrets had been whispered there?) we sat for a while. Pretty soon Helen asked, "Mother, are you angry?" "Oh, darling, anger is the last emotion I would be feeling. Upset, yes, very, because I don't know what's right or what to do. I guess it comes down to *your* wants. Either you fly home and marry Chuck or you go into Athens with me and have an abortion. How do you feel, Helen, about the baby growing inside your body?"

"Oh, Mother, I've felt so many things this last month when I really knew from the changes in my body that I *was* pregnant. Sometimes I felt evil, sometimes singled out or very special and sort of soft and most of the time I felt isolation. Now it all seems simple because you've made the choices very clear. I don't want the baby. I don't love Chuck. I want to get on with my life. I guess I never should have slept with him, but I thought I was in love. I guess I'm very fertile — like you, Mom."

Like me!! I managed to get pregnant using all known birth control methods at the same time — with nursing added. I had known Helen had an IUD which had seemed important during those two years when Chuck was so much in her life. Suddenly a giant wave of doubt threatened to submerge me. Maybe I, mother, should have held a much stronger position against premarital sex. No girl was ever hurt by abstaining. What a sharp turn sexual attitudes had taken in the last two decades! Helen knew I had been a virgin at marriage. We'd talked about it many times, but in her peer group that was archaic. But it was certainly practical!

"Mother, I am really more pregnant than I told Rick. I must be ten or twelve weeks. Oh Mom, I just want to be cared for. Can we go to Athens soon? You will take care of me?"

And I knew the enormity of being a Mother.

⋆ 22 ⋆

The Man Who Came For Dinner

It was eleven in the morning and we were sailing north and slightly west from Kos. Ann and I were stuck in our stateroom because the dresser had slid across and blocked the doorway. I peeked up through the transom and saw a wild scene topside with slippery wet decks and the crew all in slickers. But it was pleasant in the cabin, cool air rushing in through the ventilators.

I wanted to write John during the day's sail—and post the letter in Patmos. But it was far too rough to write and I had to content myself with thinking about him. On Rhodes, when Richard had returned from Athens with a cook and a sack of mail, I had received two wondrous long "John" letters. My life was so happy on the *Eva* that I couldn't be sad, yet I missed John terribly and knew he should be sharing those precious days with us, and selfishly I wanted to share my concern over Helen with him.

We had been in love for more than two years—a long time when you are no longer young. It began one day in my office near the Stanford University campus. My secretary poked her head into my office and said: "There's a Mr. Summerskill here to see you."

"I don't know anyone named Summerskill. Is he from an airline?"

"I didn't ask."

"Oh, well. . . ."

As I walked toward the waiting room I remembered that Ann often talked about a friend, John Summerskill, from Cornell University. "You don't suppose. . . . ?" I muttered to myself.

On the red upholstered bench in my small, chic waiting room sat a curly haired, Irish-looking, young man. I instantly concluded that he couldn't be Ann's friend. Much too young! A large black and very wet umbrella rested against his legs. "Hello, Mimi," said my visitor. "Who says it never rains in California in April. It's pouring."

"You *are* John Summerskill!"

He came into my office and we talked about Ann and her husband Jerry, friends in common. They had all been young teachers at Cornell.

"I am sorry that Ann and Jerry are in London this year. I'd looked forward to seeing them. You're the next best thing. Ann has talked so much about you on her trips east that I knew I should meet you. I trust her judgment."

"What are you doing at Stanford?"

"I'm doing a study of freshman dropouts for the Carnegie Corporation. I had an interview canceled this afternoon, so. . . ."

We chatted a while longer and I invited John for dinner.

"I don't want to put you out," he said.

"It's all right. I have a maid and only the two younger children are at home now. We'd love to have you."

"O.K. I'll bring some wine."

I did not know for years that John went back to his hotel and postponed a previous dinner engagement with the Dean of Women at Stanford in order to come to our house. Fate, set in motion by a little human determination.

In front of the fire in our old fashioned kitchen, John helped Robert with his homework, and shared our tough roast beef. I tucked the children in bed and we talked and talked and talked. He did not leave for ten days.

John visited every college within fifty miles to gather information for his study. We played square ball with the children, went to the high school performance of "The Music Man," picnicked on the beach at Half Moon Bay, and fell hopelessly and forever in love.

Hopeless because it was impossible. It was ridiculous. John had a family. He lived three thousand miles away. He had a highly visible position as Vice-President of Cornell University.

At the time it was "Spring Weekend" at Cornell and John kept calling the campus to see if there were any problems graver than the usual seasonal panty raids. I learned that he had been made Vice-President when he was only thirty-three years old. John was the first clinical (medical) psychologist Cornell had ever hired in Ithaca and he was a professor there since finishing his graduate work at the University of Pennsylvania. A Canadian, John had grown up in Montreal, attended McGill University, served in the Canadian army (as a "Leftenant") and become an American citizen in order to vote for Adlai Stevenson.

"It seems so long ago already—that April," I mused as I rolled backwards and forwards in my bunk on the yacht. I felt as if John had always been in my life. And yet he wasn't *really* in it. We had managed a fair amount of time together, but could see no solution. John had two beloved teen-aged daughters and a very young son.

I knew already the perils of being a mistress, yet loving and being loved is not to be given up casually by two mature adults. You can't *think* life. You have to *live* it.

I turned my thoughts to more frivolous aspects of our relationship. "What are you giggling about?" Ann asked, reminding me of her presence, "I thought you were still asleep."

"No, I'm dreaming. Mostly about John. I was just remembering last fall and that room mix-up at the Algonquin Hotel."

I had arrived in New York from Europe and by prearrangement went to the Algonquin where I told the desk clerk, "I believe my husband has already checked in."

"Yes, Madam, he arrived this morning. Take Mrs. Summerskill to room 304."

I bathed, washed some undies, read a bit, and then—terribly tired from the long plane trip—I slept. Waking around nine in the evening I was terribly disturbed to find that John had not arrived. Had he gone to Washington for the day and missed his plane? I wondered. I called my home in Menlo Park to ask if they had heard from him. In a few moments my room phone rang. It was the hotel operator. "Oh, Mrs. Summerskill," she said, "there has been a terrible mistake. Your husband is in room 452. He didn't like the first room and we moved him and the desk clerk who came on later didn't. . . . Oh, dear. I only found out when *he* called and asked me for the same number in California you requested."

So we were reunited in room 452, a record of "Hello Dolly" propped on a bouquet of flowers to greet me and every employee in the hotel alerted to our illicit presence.

❧ 23 ❧

One Beautiful Thing Each Day

We were ticking off the islands of the Dodecanese. Bypassing Kalymnos, famous for its sponge diving industry, and Leros, famous in Italian days as a naval base and more recently as an exile for political dissidents, we arrived mid-afternoon in Patmos.

The children went ashore immediately while Ann and I lingered a bit on the *Eva* before walking the plank and finding a small kafenion in the square. The uppermost thing on our agenda was to find out ferry schedules. When was the next boat to Athens. Since it was siesta time we would have to wait until evening to find schedules and buy tickets. At the kafenion we sat at a tiny metal table in the shade of an ironwood tree looking at the arched facades of the buildings. A small inter-island ferry entered the harbor and anchored close to a pair of fishing boats, one painted red and blue, the other pink and green. Next to us on one side there was a sturdy fishing trawler from Scotland and on the other side a caïque flying a French flag. A boy pulling a flat wagon loaded with grapes and green peppers passed by. We bought some of each. Nearby eight little boys gathered around an elderly blind man who was telling a story. In a corner taverna I could see my own children playing cards.

"Will you ever forget the scene this morning when Richard cut Robert's hair?" Ann asked. We both laughed remembering how we had spread an old sheet on the floor of our cabin and Rick attacked Robert with my sewing shears. Robert had been wide-eyed and worried, clutching a towel around his shoulders, giving Richard detailed advice about how much hair to cut off, and where. Various other family members poked their heads through the transom to offer advice. After Richard finished, the rest of the males asked to have a small amount of hair cut off as they all looked a big ragged and were unwilling to trust themselves to the ministrations of Greek barbers who were still cutting hair in the style of the 1930s.

A man from the bakery came out carrying a large tray filled with fried bread pieces dipped in sugar. He went around the square and offered each of us a piece. Five cars — the island's entire fleet — were lined up near the dock. It was nearing five o'clock and one taverna keeper had already begun to put out his tables along the quay for the diners who would arrive later on. Just to the left of the *Eva* on a rough, rocky point a tiny chapel looked like a huge white snowball sitting on a base of brown. Behind the snowball the crest of the hill was covered by a Byzantine monastery. Clustered around its walls were blinding white houses from the same period.

And more churches! Patmos claims 2,700 people, and 360 chapels all with bells. But I had learned that most of these buildings are not working churches with a priest on duty. Instead, they are monuments built by families or individuals, especially sailors, to win the favor of a favorite saint, to keep a promise made at a time of personal crisis, or to express thanks for the successful outcome of an endeavor. Almost all these little chapels have only one service a year on the name day of a patron saint. At that time the village women polish the brass candlesticks and dust off the icons. The men whitewash the walls (the women clean up behind the men) and after the service everyone joins in the Panayieri feasting and dancing. I suspected that on Patmos, with all its churches and chapels, such celebrations must take place practically every day of the year.

Halfway up the monastery hill, just below the village Chora, we could see a church in front of the cave where St. John lived while writing the Book of Revelations. "Let's take the whole day tomorrow and ride donkeys up that lovely stone road to the monastery," I proposed. Ann agreed, "And we'll walk back to the beach. . . ." That was about as much as we ever planned ahead.

"Look, Mimi," Ann pointed, "the Practorian is opening." We hurried over to the agent's office to find that the next Athens ferry—a night boat—was not for two days. Buying first class tickets with berths, I was determined to put my upcoming journey with Helen out of my mind and enjoy exquisite Patmos.

The next day we *did* hire donkeys, first cousins to those on Santorini, and rode the two kilometers to the Monastery of St. Joannes Theologos, prodding our little beasts, crowding each other and laughing. Below us the exquisite island of Patmos looked like a starfish with its fingers of land spread in every direction. Some of the bays thrust so deeply into the island that they almost met the bays thrusting in from the other side.

In contrast to its forbidding castle-like exterior, the inside of the eleventh century monastery was elegant in its simplicity. It was a maze of nine white-washed courtyards, all adorned with balconies, chapels, and roof tops. There were nine wells for water, all very much in use by the many monks in residence. Several monks stood high on the walls and gazed out through the ramparts, their black robes and beards billowing against the white walls. Mounting the many flights of stairs to the top, we joined them and discovered that they were looking northward to a hidden rock island where a freighter had gone aground. When we tired of watching that distant drama we descended to exclaim over the fine library and the chapel with its ancient icons. One monk gave such a graphic explanation of "what is an icon" that Wendy exclaimed, "Now I really understand!" Actually I was amazed at how attentively Wendy and Robert listened to guides or to one of us reading history aloud.

Later, in the Holy Cave of St. John, Robert insistently asked the guide, "But how do you *know* St. John slept with his head there?" as the poor man showed us the niche now framed in silver.

When we returned to the *Eva* we met one of our neighbors in the harbor. They were off the sturdy Scottish trawler which turned out to be a brand new yacht built for John Burgess, the manager of the Cyprus Copper Mines. He and his American wife and a couple of Scots named Thoms were sailing the yacht home to Cyprus. We joined company for a beach picnic and their men and ours had a two-hour rock-skipping contest with dozens of small Greek boys and girls gathered to watch and help find good "skippers." Rick again won the children's hearts with his "international squeegy bug." He would pretend to find a bug in a child's hair or sweater, then having captured the phantom bug he would stick it between his clasped hands and make it squeak by pressing his palms together. The children adored this antic and followed him as if he were the Pied Piper. Envying son Richard, I practiced this palm squeezing technique, *and* blowing between the thumbs of clasped fists to make a whistle, all summer. Finally I could do both. They remain among my more important accomplishments.

Bill won the rock-skipping contest. Back on our yachts, Mrs. Thoms called to the children, "Would you like a peanut butter sandwich?" She won their affection forever by offering such a rare delicacy.

We dined ashore — to the great relief of Eileen Barclay, our new cook. She was settling in, had been wonderful in her understanding of the problems of cooking in a tiny galley. She and her husband — now divorced — had run a charter yacht in Greece for many years so she was experienced. Her cooking uniform was a pair of pink cotton pajamas — novel but practical. She gradually made friends with the crew. Her Greek was excellent and after dinner that night she, a female, even stayed ashore with the Greek sailors playing tavli. Unbelievable, but true!

After dinner, the families from both yachts gathered on the *Eva* to talk long about Cyprus, Scotland, and genes. Helen, whose father was Scots, and Colin Thoms looked very much alike. Both had dark skin and black hair and eyes — "Black Scots." When our visitors returned to their yacht, Mr. Thoms fell off the gangplank into the harbor amid much mirth. My children later claimed his wife pushed him as he paid too much attention to Ann during the evening.

After everyone else retired I lingered on deck beneath a full moon. Its brilliance fired the whitewashed buildings and the meltemi blew lace-bordered waves.

The seductive indolence that overtook me that night seemed to infect all of us next day. For years Ann and I had teased about "doing one beautiful thing a day." But is was so easy just to *sit* on Patmos, or watch, or read, or stroll. By late afternoon in real disgust with ourselves, Ann and I pulled on jeans and sweaters, took ice from the tiny fridge along with some Scotch, and started for the "snowball" chapel. Walking past the local shipyard we saw six caïques under construction, one still a skeleton and the other being painted. "My favorite is that one," I said, pointing to a graceful boat painted salmon with yellow trim.

We climbed through winding streets and soon found ourselves above the chapel. We called to a young girl standing on a balcony and asked her how we could reach our destination. She motioned us to her and took us to the patio of her home. There she picked a tiny carnation and some basil for each of us and called one of her six brothers to escort us to the chapel. After climbing over the boulders on a rocky angular path we emerged at the gate of the blue-doored chapel. Inside were two little girls, Maria and Sophie, each with an incense burner. Standing in front of each icon in turn, they made the sign of the cross with their burners. Then Maria picked a piece of lemon geranium for us, but when she tried to retrieve her burner the chains became tangled. When the young boy finally untangled them, the girls locked the church, shyly bid us farewell, and, arms around each other's waists, disappeared.

Ann and I salvaged the melting ice, and feeling slightly sacrilegious, found a place to sit while we sipped our drinks. The boy took his leave and all the way down the cliff he did tricks for our pleasure, catching our attention by constantly calling, "Anna, Mimi."

We stayed on our rocky perch until the flaming sunball set. Only minutes later the moon rose, full and pink, on the opposite side of the starfish island.

We had done our "beautiful thing" that day. . . .

⊁ *24* ⊱

Unchartered Time

From the very first day on the *Eva* I kept a Log . . . parallel to the Captain's. But mine was about *us and Eva*. No one paid much attention to my writing as they all wrote their own letters and poems and songs. Because Helen and I were going to be in Athens for a couple of days I fretted about "The Log." "Stop worrying," Ann reassured me, "we'll keep notes and not forget a detail."

Still I was upset. Of course, it wasn't really about the Log. We had established a contained world of our own and I was loath to leave it and "them" and face an unchartered time.

With tiny canvas bags in hand, Helen and I took a launch from the port of Patmos across the water to the overnight ferry to Athens. The hulking inter-island ferry proudly bore the name *Aphroditi* across her white bosom. All was mad confusion on the dock — a crush of goodbyes, luggage, tears, fish, wine, butchered goats, flowers and the inevitable shouting. Our family had stayed on the yacht and as the launch chugged past the *Eva* Helen and I could see them clustered on the prow waving like mad. An ache went through me as I looked at that beloved group silhouetted against the rocky hill with the monastery looming behind and the whole scene bathed in moonlight. We had become so close, living on our eighty feet of teakwood, that I suddenly felt incomplete. Helen and I hugged each other. At least there were two of us.

A flimsy looking hanging stairway led up the side of the *Aphroditi,* which was bucking wildly in the wind. We exercised great caution as we pulled ourselves up from the launch to the stairs, watching an enormous Greek lady as she was pulled and hoisted up by no less than five men. Greeks *are* patient. Inside the ship our cabin was clean and after HOT SHOWERS we fell into bed.

"Mother, are you vibrating?"

"Yes, isn't it wild. Just like those awful motel beds where you put in a quarter. It must be the engine." But in the end it soothed us to sleep on our unwanted journey to Athens. Meanwhile the family sailed for Samos.

As the *Aphroditi* passengers poured onto the dock I could see Peter Anderson's tall form, arms crossed on his chest. He stood immovable in all that confused noisy dock scene, firm and sure, awaiting us. How glad I was to see him! By nine o'clock Helen and I were in the maternity hospital, not far from the Andersons' home. Helen was taken to a doctor's office and I was ushered to a hospital room. Soon Helen and the doctor arrived together. "Yes, Madam, your daughter is pregnant and we will perform the abortion immediately." He said a number of things—in perfect English—to reassure us both and then he left. Helen left, too, in her short hospital gown, wheeled away in a chair. I waited. In a very short time Helen reappeared, on a gurney, pushed by a nurse. She was slightly groggy and the nurse tucked her in bed saying that it would be best if she slept a bit and remained in the hospital a few hours. Pulling my chair up to the bed, I took Helen's hand and watched over her. When Helen awakened she held my hand tight and rambled on in a free floating monologue. . . . "It's all so fuzzy, Mom; it didn't hurt at all, and all the nurses seem like nuns to me . . . or angels . . . and they are so kind. . . . I'm glad I can speak some Greek. . . . I'm glad you're here . . . I'm glad it's over . . . what will we do now. . . .?"

Soon a nurse reappeared and gave Helen pills to "shrink the uterus" and some antibiotics. Then she put her arm around Helen and said, *"Despenis* (young lady) you mustn't be *sten-ihorimeni* (sad). You are young and you will have many babies. Go with your mother and be careful."

So out into the sunshine we walked and hailed a cab and spent the rest of the day in the Andersons' garden. We stayed within each other's sight all that important day.

Because Helen and I were to have a couple of days in the "city," we were given a list by everyone in the family *and* the

Captain too. Tearing myself away from the peace of Filothei and my daughter, I went into Athens the next morning.

Athens was hot, crowded, and confused. Two prime ministers resigned that day and as I went about my business in town groups of people were constantly marching, changing, and shouting. There were trade union rallies with huge banners, and marches up the boulevards, and yet, in and around and through it all, trod the tourists. One book on Greece claims that tourists are not even aware there *is* a modern Greece. Well, maybe, but it would have been hard to ignore modern Greece *that* July day!

And then we were "home" again. Back on an island. Back on the sea. At 3:45 a.m. the ferry blasted its whistle approaching Chios. Helen and I scurried into our clothes, grabbed our precious purchases (peanut butter, margarine, ground coffee, ice bucket, and chewing gum) and raced for the gangplank. No hanging stairs on Chios. Even at four in the morning a large crowd milled about on the dock. Instantly we spotted our family. Bill and Eileen had never gone to bed, because they had a "hot" chess game going in a nearby taverna. The others had slept briefly. Our embraces and tears indicated a separation of years!

As we hugged and kissed and laughed, I thought sadly of all those families who never hug at all. There must be a lot of them, if Wendy's instructions to me over the years were any indication. She would come home with a friend and get me aside: "Mother, hug her. No one does at her house."

At sunrise on the deck of the *Eva*, sipping fresh coffee, there was still much rejoicing while we exchanged three days of adventures. Rick and Bill and Ann and I had snuck a few minutes alone in my stateroom to tell of Helen's medical experience.

Helen and I had talked far into the summer night as we sailed around the tip of Attica the night before. We talked about Helen's college major. "I'm going to become a classicist, Mom. I know this is the most important time in my life. I *know* a direction." And she talked about having the time alone with me. "It's been like a vacation, a spree, and Mom, thank you, thank you for helping me. You made my decision easy. You offered two choices and that was simple for me. Oh, I'm sooooo happy." And I thought how easy it is to lose track of the truth that all children need time alone with their mother — their father. Group time has its place, but nothing is as important as those times when a husband and wife, a child and parent, steal minutes or hours or days to be alone together.

But now was group time—family time. Robert and Wendy clamored for their books. As I unwrapped seven paperbacks I took deep pleasure. Only six weeks ago life was TV, radio, record player, and movies. Now *Little Women, The Little Prince, Swiss Family Robinson, The Fifth Chinese Daughter,* were exciting. New worlds, new patterns of living, and *time.*

I think that perhaps time is the most important. Even grocery shopping takes on a new dimension when there is time. In Greece it was a "people" time, totally different from racing around a supermarket with that damn wobbly basket, throwing things in before taking everything out at the check-out stand.

Our shopping never involved less than seven stores where we were questioned, advised, sent to other shops, led to a desired source by a child, given coffee or soft drink. It took much of a morning.

"Stop wool-gathering, Mom!" My cherished family was gathered around, reporting on Samos and the sail to Chios. "You mustn't feel you were even gone." Ann leaned over to kiss Helen, "We missed you so much that on Samos we even met the early morning plane yesterday just on the chance you'd be on board."

"You should have seen that airport, Mom," Robert interrupted. "It had big chains lying across the runway and we took the *Albatross,* just Yorgo and Ann and me, and landed right by it."

"I know Robert, but remember how we couldn't find a gate into the field and thought we might have to walk miles around?"

"A little boy found us a gate and then we crossed over the runway, and I was scared if a plane would come."

"And when they got back, that's when I called you in Athens from the telephone office." It was Richard's turn. "We all really missed you both and just had to know exactly when you'd be home."

Home. Home is where the heart is, they claim, and it was clear as the Greek morning that as long as we were together we were home. That particular morning Helen's joy and relief made every hour glow a little brighter.

"How did you like Samos?"

"Not so much," Ann answered. "It was the first island where people seemed sort of unfriendly."

Robert bristled, "I liked it there. We went to a movie and I liked that tunnel."

"You went to a movie?"

"Yes, well, you see," Ann began, "the Captain took us to an ancient village port named Tigarie because he said the main port of Samos is exposed to the meltemi. The town wasn't very attractive and we all wandered along the waterfront wondering about you and Helen when Rick spotted a poster announcing, GREGORY PECK IN CAPTAIN NEWMAN M.D. . . also with Tony Curtis. It would be shown that evening. We immediately decided to go because then we wouldn't be so lonesome for you."

"Mother, you should have seen the theater. I loved it," said Wendy. "It was a 'walk-in'! We just walked in through a gate and sat in straight chairs on the ground."

"And," added Ann, "they showed the movie on a big whitewashed wall in this garden with the sky for a ceiling. The film was awful and kept breaking and we loved every minute of it."

Richard picked up the story. "You will be proud of us, Mom. We did some archaeological sightseeing. First we went to the Temple of Hera, and it was really a ruined ruin. We wandered around trying to figure what was what. It is a beautiful location right in the middle of farm country and a bunch of men were sickling the high grass for donkey feed. They carted it off on their backs."

"It is reversing the burden when man carries for donkeys!" Ann added. "When I visit ruins like those on Samos I find myself being particularly grateful to Sir Arthur Evans. He may have taken liberties at Knossos, but his reconstruction work there has really helped me at all the other ruins we've seen."

"But the best part, Mom, was the big tunnel Rick took us to," said Robert.

"Dragged us to," Ann insisted. "I hated it, all those slimy walls and the feeling of being closed in."

Rick quickly rose to the defense of the Tyrant of Samos, Polycrates, who, some 500 years before Christ, built that huge aqueduct through an enormous mountain on Samos. "It is an engineering marvel. I really thought our visit there was worth it."

"That's because you're a frustrated water-works engineer." Ann said she and Wendy had stayed in the sun while the men went into the mountain as far as they could and were disappointed not to find the whole 1,000 feet accessible.

We all felt lazy and decided to "idle" the day. On a people's bus to a nearby village four of us sat on the very back seat with an elderly Greek lady who presented Robert with an orange. At her feet struggled a trussed up chicken. *Einai doro yia to agori mou.* (It is a present for my son.) We chatted in our halting Greek and she told us how the island of Chios, besides being famous for its captains and ship-owning families, was known for centuries for its mastika. I knew that mastika had been chewed for years before artificial gum was invented. "Where does mastika come from? Is it a plant?"

Our Greek friend looked at me patiently, "There," she pointed to the brush along the road, "They are all mastika."

As we walked down to the beach we picked some mastika and painfully chewed and chewed trying to get a wad. Hard, and not too successful. But it happily made me think of chewing pine pitch as a child.

On the lovely shady beach we swam. There were two little hotels with vacationing Greek families and a taverna. After lunch we played one of our favorite games. You build a neat wet mound of sand and you put a stick in the middle of the top. Going from one person to the next, in a circle, using a knife-like stick, each person takes a turn at cutting away sand, slicing as much as he likes. His cut must be straight, top to bottom. The trick is not to topple the stick on top. The suspense and the shrieking rise and rise before the stick finally falls.

Our other beach game is a substitute for horseshoes. We plant a large rock in the sand. Players stand in a line about 20 feet back from the rock. Each selects three small stones which he holds for his turn. The closest stone wins. Much of our time was spent fighting over whose stone was whose!

Before dinner, back in Chios town, we bought a large bottle of what I thought was grapefruit juice to mix with rum. It turned out to be concentrated almond extract. Ugh!

When I finally climbed into my bunk that night I found another Wendy note: "Dear Mom, I didn't like you to be gone. Thank you ever so much for letting me wear your shell blouse. It's a bit dirty but I wore it with love. Thanks again. Love you." Wendy.

I turned to Ann who was already deep in her book. "How did Wendy get to be so empathetic? She always seems to sense when someone wants attention. She's such a beautiful child — inside and out. I hope people will realize that her beauty is for real."

"I think it is very hard to be physically developed at twelve *and* so beautiful." Ann was thoughtful. "She is going to attract men like mad. I can see it already — they all want some of her shining quality, her warmth and humor. I'll bet it's going to be hard for her until she feels secure. God, growing up can be painful."

So we lay in our pristine bunks as Ann told me of the sail from Samos to Chios. "Once we knew you and Helen would be on the ferry to Chios, we set off with the Captain's assurance that it would be a perfect sailing day. The Captain shamed Rick and me into staying above. We stored away all the mats and deck chairs and gathered by the wheel. First we practiced new Greek words with the crew. My favorite is *apeesholeemeni,* which means "busy." How did you do with your Greek in Athens?"

"Well, some is better than none. It helped in taxis, but I suspect that we all have a flavorsome peasant accent. It is the old problem of speaking a bit and the other guy taking off in a stream of words which I do not understand. Tom was really right when he said we should get down pat the phrase, *then katalaveno* (I don't understand) and *seega, seega* (slowly). Sometimes the second time around I can at least get the gist.

"Were you able to sail the whole time?"

"Clear into Chios harbor. The wind died about half way there and the sea had lovely lazy swells. The kids drifted up on deck toward sunset. It was magnificent with a riotous orange-red sky and those big Chios mountains a deep purple. Wendy and I went below and took cheese and salami and bread up to everyone and we huddled together on two mats. It was fun to sail in the dark with zillions of stars above and our bodies all entwined. We just stayed there quietly as we came into harbor. I loved looking up at all the lines and stays from the mast and at the crew scurrying about lowering sails. Their bodies were like black paper cutouts silhouetted against the sky. But most of all I liked knowing that you and Helen would be back before dawn. It's no good when we are not all together."

"What will we ever do in September?"

"Tomorrow we'll be in Turkey!"

✷ 25 ✷

In Another Country

"Who lives in Turkey?" Robert asked.

"Turks," replied Bill.

"You mean turkeys?" Robert was wide-eyed and somewhat skeptical.

There was no doubt in the crew's mind who lived in Turkey. They had determinedly fought our desire to spend part of the summer in Asia Minor with the Terrible Turks. All four men were convinced they would lose their heads or worse, and they laid in twenty loaves of bread before our sail from Chios in anticipation of being starved or poisoned by the Turkish populace. In spite of their fears we won the argument. After all, it *was* in our contract.

It was a heavenly morning for sailing with a fresh breeze blowing. We bounded along the Turkish coast and adjusted our eyes to the red-tiled roofs on the houses. They looked strange to us after weeks of exposure to the flat-topped white buildings of the Cyclades and Dodecanese islands.

The Captain had donned his whites and wore his captain's hat—a rare occurrence. He brought out a pair of particularly strong binoculars and he kept scanning the shoreline. With our weaker glasses we took turns looking at the rugged but fertile countryside. Then we rounded a point, and spread before us was the large city of Izmir, known to the Greeks as Old Smyrna.

Izmir reminded me a little of San Francisco. Thousands of houses tumbled down hills to an enormous bay. The crew raised our yellow flag indicating that we needed help in docking. Help never arrived, which only confirmed our crew's opinion of the

Turks! Captain Antonio then approached a Greek freighter anchored in the bay, and amid much shouting as we circled the freighter four times, he received instructions on where we should dock.

As we backed into our berth, Eileen called out, "Lunch!" Captain Antonio had told us it would take quite a bit of time to clear customs and that we might as well eat since we could not go ashore until the paperwork was finished. We had one of our favorite lunch dishes, a fake cheese souffle, i.e., cheese sandwiches over which we poured a milk and egg mixture before baking.

Papers and lunch completed, we eagerly raced ashore to explore our first Turkish city. It was Sunday and we assumed the shops would be open since Friday was the Moslem holy day. We were wrong. Turkey is a "secular" Moslem state and they have adopted many western customs and social institutions such as the Saturday-Sunday weekend. In short, the stores were closed. But the shoeshine boys were out in full force. I couldn't believe the sheer beauty of Asia Minor shoeshine boxes. They were made of highly polished wood and beaten brass, and contained a double row of shoeshine polish — sixteen bottles in all — each capped in brass. Magnificent!

Bill had his shoes shined. The young shoeshine boy rang a pushbutton bell on the side of the box every time he wanted Bill to change feet. Helen was so intrigued that she followed suit and got a shine. The shoes of both shone like mirrors. Since the rest of us wore sandals we remained shineless but a boy who was hosing down the sidewalks washed our feet, sandals and all.

At the Izmir market we bought some oranges and peaches and I was "picked up" by a nice-looking young Turk who spoke English. (Perhaps motherly types appealed to him.) He helped us by asking various shoeshine boys how much they wanted for their boxes. We envisioned Robert shining all shoes for the remainder of the summer.

"Twenty dollars," one boy offered. "No, too expensive," I replied deciding to abandon the project. Then my young admirer pointed us toward the Castle we could see high on the mountain behind the town, and we started up. Up! We always seemed to be hiking up. And that day the "up" was at least five kilometers.

As usual, Richard collected a troop of children, all of whom were delighted with his "squeegy bug" routine. I decided that Rick's bug might be a bigger boon to international understanding than the United Nations.

Halfway up to the Castle we stopped at a fountain to drink, splash water on our faces, and wash our feet. I began to understand the reason for all the feet washing in the Bible. It is sheer delight to encounter water when your sandled feet are hot and dusty.

Passing a tinsmith's tiny shop, we watched a young boy coat small bowls with a liquid solution and pass them on to his father. The older man stood over a hot, hot fire built in a depressed part of a solid, waist-high cement table. After heating the bowl he threw some sort of silvery metal onto it. As it went into flux he spread it quickly with a rag. Hot work on a hot day.

Up, still up, passing donkeys laden on either side with ice. Families sat on stoops and leaned out of windows. Children played games in the steep, narrow streets. Everyone pointed us on and up to the "Castello" that crowned the summit.

When we finally arrived at our destination we sat in front of a tiny shop gazing at the ruins and drinking flat warm beer. "Where was the City of Alexander the Great?" Bill addressed his question to the world at large.

"Impossible to tell," replied Ann. "You can't work back from modern terrain to ancient sites simply by reading historical descriptions."

As we climbed along the ruined walls I fretted over Robert's propensity for always climbing to the highest, most dangerous point. Bill gave me a well-deserved lecture. "Let Robert climb," he advised. I decided the only solution was to stay as far away as possible from my youngest son when we reached the heights.

By the time the taxi deposited us at the dock, it was already evening. "Why didn't we take a taxi up and walk back?" I asked, but no one answered my question. It was pointless after the fact. The sun, like a child's red beach ball, had set and the sky still glowed pink. Bill, Wendy, and Robert sat on the prow singing and giggling. The Captain joined us for whiskey which he insisted on serving prohibition-style, in tea cups. He recounted his lengthy negotiations with the Turkish Customs. He had "oiled the gates" with ouzo and cigarettes, but had told them we had no whiskey. "So that," he explained, "is why we must drink our whiskey from teacups!"

✶ 26 ✶

Ephesus

Years after the summer cruise, John and I were having dinner in Delphi and gazing down at the river of olive trees below. Glancing up from that awesome view, I noticed a couple we had seen on Ios the week before. Both husband and wife were small, neat, and appealing. Around his neck the man wore a leather thong knotted with a piece of turquoise, which to me suggested residence in either the American Southwest or Mexico. After dinner we approached the couple's table, introduced ourselves, and joined them for coffee. We asked them how they had found Ios and where they were going next.

"We loved Ios," the woman replied, "and now we're on our way to Turkey."

"You're going to Turkey!" I said. "Then you must read *The Loom of History* by Herbert Muller. It's history written as if it were happening today to real flesh-and-blood people. I just wish I had a copy to give you."

On and on I talked, determined to persuade our new-found friends to read my favorite book about Asia Minor.

The little man looked uncomfortable and flustered. Finally he penetrated my soliloquy about the merits of the book. "Hmmm, ah hmmm . . ." he mumbled. "Well, you see, I wrote it."

From this unlikely beginning, we became friends with the Herbert Mullers. I learned that he was an English professor turned historian, a fact which convinced me that more historians should preface their careers by first teaching English.

Back in 1965 aboard the *Eva,* however, I knew nothing of the man behind the book. I only knew that I had found a

LISTENING TO A PIN DROP (WHAT ACCOUSTICS!) AT EPIDAURUS

RIDING DONKEYS TO THE MONASTERY
CROWNING THE ISLE OF PATMOS

THE *EVA MARIA* IN FULL SAIL

ON THASSOS. RICHARD, HELEN, MIMI, ROBERT, WENDY, BILL.
ANN IN BACK.

THE FAMILY ABOARD THE *EVA MARIA*:
WENDY (CURLY HAIR IN CURLERS),MIMI, RICHARD,
ANN IN FRONT, ROBERT, HELEN, BILL.

HAIR-CUTTING TIME IN MIMI'S STATEROOM. ROBERT, RICHARD

MEASURING THE LAND ON MILOPOTAS BAY

JORGO DRAKOS WHO BUILT OUR HOUSE

IOS WINDMILL AND MILLER'S HOME ON MOUNTAIN S.E. OF VILLAGE

ANN, WENDY, MIMI, HELEN

THE GATE TO OUR BEAN PATCH AND MILOPOTAS BEACH

FRONT TERRACE

THE HOUSE ON IOS

LIVINGROOM

VILLAGE OF IOS

MIMI AND JOHN SUMMERSKILL

modern classic which could make Turkey's past come alive for me.

Muller's intriguing chapter on Ephesus, the great city dedicated to Diana (Artemis), important from a thousand years before Christ until a thousand years after, inspired us to pay a visit. In a minibus which we rented in Izmir, we sallied forth. It seemed strange to be traveling on land after spending so much time at sea.

Even Mr. Muller had not been able to prepare us for the magnificence and magnitude of the ruins at Ephesus: the long, broad marble streets; the vast theater located on the side of the mountain; the sheer number of civic buildings and private dwellings; and the agora that looked as if merchants might arrive at any moment to lay out their wares. We sought shade under pillars to read more and study our map. We were alone, just one family, in the middle of that once bustling metropolis. We found a hand water pump near the agora which we returned to time after time during the course of our explorations in order to draw water for drinking and to splash our heads and feet. It was delicious, cool well water. Richard, as usual, found extensive remains of plumbing installations.

Surveying Ephesus from the top of a hill where one of the main roads began, we easily imagined the city at its zenith in the first century after Christ with a population of over a million.

"I would like to have lived here when this was the New York of Asia Minor," Richard said wistfully.

"You'd have been minister of water-works," I teased, but knew that in any century Richard would have been a leader . . . and a good one. He was strong enough to be gentle.

A few storks had built nests on the top of columns but they obviously preferred the area of St. John's tomb where we spent the morning. Almost every chimney, on the old houses in the nearby village, boasted a stork's nest with a stork standing over it on one leg. I expected to see a baby slung in a diaper below the low-flying birds.

The Orthodox Church claims that the Virgin Mary came to Ephesus with John the Baptist, died there, and was buried in a small house at the very top of a mountain behind the city. "Is it far?" I asked our minibus driver.

"A steep climb but not far. It should only take half an hour. You will go?"

"We will go." So the driver began the long ascent up the winding mountain road that cut through barren, rocky fields. Only an occasional dwarfed pine had survived the onslaught of weather and goats. It was exactly noon, still far from the summit, when our rented minibus balked. The driver let us out near a pine tree where we were left to huddle as he coasted back down hill to get water for the car.

By one o'clock he had not returned. Discouraged, hot, and frustrated, we decided to walk up (of course). Our party, strung out over a hundred meters, trudged doggedly on. At least the view of the ancient Ephesus with the plain and the sea beyond was magnificent. Bill led the way with Helen and Rick following closely behind. Farther back, but ahead of the rest of us, Wendy stalked alone. She was furious with Ann who had scolded her for constantly complaining about a stiff neck when no one could do anything about it. Later that day Wendy told me, "Mother, I was so angry at Ann that I decided to commit suicide and make you all sorry. I saw a good place to jump — right where Rick was. But then I held on to my wrist and I said to myself, 'Control yourself. Wendy. Gosh, if you jump, and halfway down you want to come back, you can't. Tonight I'm glad I didn't jump." At moments like that I realized how much I loved my twelve-year-old.

But as we plodded ever onward and upward I had no inkling of Wendy's brief flirtation with eternity. Ultimate reality at that moment was the sweat trickling down my back and chest in rivulets. "It's not fair," Robert began to grumble, "Girls have boobs to hold up their shirts." Robert was right. We females had tucked our shirts up under our arms where they remained happily supported.

Finally we reached the top where we discovered the shrine and a small taverna. The waiter, who spoke an isolated word or two of English, brought us pieces of ice, and showed us a fountain where we gulped down gallons of water. One waiter approached me asking, "You sved?"

"Yes, indeed," I replied firmly, turning to comment, to the children. "That's the first time I ever had anyone asked me if I was sweating. You wouldn't think he had to ask, though. It seems pretty obvious."

The children shouted with laughter. "Mother, he asked if you were a *Swede!*"

At the shrine the caretaker produced an extremely clever garment—a sort of wrap-around skirt of brightly printed cotton—to solve the problem of half-naked tourists wishing to enter a religious shrine. Boys and girls in shorts could wear it as sort of sarong, while bare-armed females could use it as a shawl. Clad thus, in a wild variety of patterns, we paid our respects to the Virgin Mother.

❧ 27 ❧

The Next Generation

Back in Izmir after our driver had revived the minibus and rescued us from the top of the hill, we found ourselves the center of action along the quay in the busy port area. Just before dusk our boys descended on the *Eva* with a man, a boy, and a fancy shoeshine box in tow. As they began to bargain near the gangplank, at least fifty people gathered around to watch, to advise, and to comment on the lengthy proceedings. Finally a price was agreed on, and amidst much handshaking and good will, we took possession of the box. Robert rushed to shine Captain Antonio's shoes. Now, in addition to Richard as our family barber, we had Robert as our official shoeshine boy. The only remaining problem seemed to be what we could possibly do with the numerous bottles of pink, purple, and orange shoe polish.

Robert spent the rest of the evening playing on a rope that hung from the mast. Sometimes he would swing on it or practice climbing. When he tired of this he simply untied it and used it as a jumprope. Later he went ashore with the older boys and Helen to play billiards. "Rick said I was very good," he told me when he returned. Eventually the excitement of the day took its toll and, as I went to my berth, I could see his towhead snuggled near Yorgo on deck where he had fallen asleep.

The next day we pulled up anchor and once more crossed the invisible boundary between Turkey and Greece on our way to Lesbos, the island made famous by Sappho. I settled back in my deck chair, preparing to finish *The Loom of History,* and basked in the pleasant sensation of a return to the normal routine aboard our floating home.

I loved all our sailing days, but particularly those when the breeze was fresh and steady and we could spend hours reading and writing. I became used to Robert or Yorgo leaning across my prone and sleeping self in my berth as they closed the portholes on the days of early sailing: "Excuse me" . . . *"signomi,"* they would mutter as they bumped me about in their struggle to secure the portholes.

We could all get up and down the hatches with aplomb and, with time, we learned to stoop to avoid bumping heads on low doorways. We learned exactly when to relinquish and stow away deck chairs on sailing days. We knew the driest spots on deck and the best places to hold on in rough seas. Like any inhabitants of a home, we were becoming friends with our dwelling's secrets and learned to live with its idiosyncracies.

Richard had definitely taken over as the MALE which, in Greece, meant he ran things. All plans were filtered through him to me, which was fortunate because his Greek was definitely best. Rick's relationship with Bill was that of brother-friend, but with the other children he was older brother-father. Somehow he managed that role with grace and humor.

With Robert, for example, he inaugurated a four-point campaign: 1) Not to ask "buy me this"; 2) Not to fuss when something hurt; 3) Not to carry tales; and 4) Not to let a day go by without reading something. He used a firm hand when the occasion demanded.

I was fascinated by his insistence that Wendy and Robert learn to water ski. They really resisted. He persisted. And, of course, in the end, they adored it. There were many things he insisted they do or try. As I watched these events, I wondered, "Will he be the same with his own children someday?"

Though Richard's development into a strong and loving adult was especially significant to me, the relationships between the other children were also a source of delight and, sometimes, amusement. Helen taught Wendy every song from her own childhood, and they spent hours fussing over their nails and hair. The boys made a checkerboard of cardboard with stones serving as checkers and this homemade game became their favorite pastime.

We were forced to become interdependent and to learn the rewards, and to avoid the hazards, of intimate living. . . .

Later, as the older children went off to University, I began to think about my child-rearing philosophy. At first I did just what new mothers do—fed the baby, cuddled, loved, longed for a whole night's sleep, and delighted in every nuance of motherhood. And then there was another baby, and then another. . . .

I owned Dr. Spock's classic on child-rearing but only read the first chapter as there never seemed to be time to read about what I was doing. Nevertheless, I slowly came to understand that my actions and decisions were not totally accidental or spontaneous. Often I thought about my own parents and I did what I remembered their doing.

Education in California had deteriorated in the last few years, especially when Wendy and Robert started school. With the pressure exerted by tens of thousands of new Californians the schools proliferated and the quality went down. The "open classroom" system was big news—disastrous to my way of thinking. I knew it was important that the children all receive a good, solid base of knowledge to work from, but they weren't getting it in Menlo Park's public schools at that time. I didn't know how, nor did I have the time, to supplement their school work so I just tried to push reading. I have regretted that my children did not have the musical education that I and my brothers and sisters had had. Attention to music was one area where I did not follow my parents' example. My mother spent thousands of hours sitting on the piano bench with one or the other of us while encouraging another to practice the violin. . . .

But with this summer sailing I knew we were making progress. Everyone was reading and reading and reading. And we spent hours talking about what we had read.

We talked about professions and what each child wanted out of life. We decided that it didn't matter what profession or trade they would choose, but it did matter that they do it well.

We talked about excellence and the search for it. We related that quest to what we read about Alexander the Great and his brilliant ability to conquer and convert.

We talked about the importance of "rolling with the knocks." Perhaps this simple home truth came closest to Bill's "handle of life." You simply never knew what would happen, so you had to be prepared to cope. We decided a good education would help. So would the ability to get along with people. But most important was the opportunity to go forth from a strong, loving family. *That* was what life aboard the *Eva* was all about.

✦ 28 ✦

I Have Three Cucumbers
and Two Daughters

•

"Lesbian fruit, olives, and wine are famous in Athens today as well as in antiquity," Ann read aloud from a guide book.

" 'Lesbian,' 'Lesbos,'. . . yes, I guess it all makes sense," I said. "But when did the word 'Lesbian' change to mean a homosexual proclivity?"

"I looked it up in our Webster's this morning. It actually gives both definitions: '1. Pertaining to the island of Lesbos in the Aegean and 2. A woman who is sexually attracted to another woman.' "

"Doesn't it all go back to Sappho?" Richard interjected. "I'm sure it does. She ran a kind of special girls' boarding school on Lesbos and wrote passionate verses to some of her pupils. I've read somewhere that her literary leanings followed a long tradition. This island was famous for centuries for its musicians and poets and philosophers."

Well, I thought, Rick hadn't majored in religion and philosophy for nothing. Turning to Ann, he asked, "Wasn't Sappho from a noble family? And wasn't she married? I'm sure I heard that somewhere, too."

"It says here that Julius Caesar made his first mark as a soldier in Lesbos when he rescued some fellow soldiers under fire."

"O.K., O.K. But what about Sappho?"

"Well, it says Sapphic poetry can be compared to Homer in quality and that Sappho lived to a ripe old age. I wonder how old that was twenty-five hundred years ago?"

The island of Lesbos seemed to be as lush and lusty as the guidebook said. Some of us decided to go to a taverna at seven-thirty in the morning to eat a tasty pile of *loukoumathes* which look like doughnut holes, made with yogurt and flour deep fried and dribbled with honey. The harbor of Mytilini was humming with activity. Across the road the *Eva* was being hosed down and the tanks filled with water.

"We found bikes," Robert shouted as he raced out in front of Bill to report the news. "Did you save some *loukoumathes* for us?"

Everyone felt the need for exercise and the bicycles were the answer. Off we rode for miles along the shore of Lesbos, passing dozens of wooden Victorian mansions. Each house was shuttered and most of them looked forlorn and unkept. Our book explained that a number of wealthy English shipbuilders and Greek shipowners had summered on Lesbos before the turn of the century. World War I interrupted these holidays and after peace returned the former tenants forsook the island for other fashionable resorts.

Robert had a bad fall from his bike, adding several more bruises to his already colorful legs. Eventually we found a pebble beach and formed a 'human dressing room' to put on our suits. This highly mobile change room was made by six of us standing in a circle with our backs turned toward the middle. There was great hilarity as everyone teased the victim in the center about getting "the view," Wendy's term for peeking. "It's not fair, girls have two places where somebody can get the view," she complained. Bill got so disgusted with all the giggling that he broke the circle and walked to the edge of the sea, turned his back on everyone, undressed, and pulled on his trunks with a minimum of fuss and bother.

When Bill's bike broke down on the way back to Mytilini we paused at a tiny wayside store for help. As usual the questions from the local clientele came hot and heavy:

"Who are you?"

"How old are you?"

"How many children do you have?"

"How did you get here?"

"You have a yacht?"

"How much did it cost?"

I was used to the questions and had my answers, albeit in halting Greek. Yes, the yacht was rented. Yes, we were Americans. I was the "mama" and I had three sons and two daughters . . . "See . . ." and I would point to them with pride.

As we peddled down a peaceful road between olive trees that seemed older than time, Rick came alongside me and said, "Mom, you have to be careful. You know, when you answer that question about how many children you have. . . ." His voice trailed off, and he stared down at his handlebars with an expression somewhere between a frown and a giggle.

"Well?"

"Well," he repeated, "you always say in Greek that you have three cucumbers and two daughters."

"Three cucumbers! Oh, Richard, did I say that? No wonder they all smile so sweetly at me. Damn this language! Only in Greece would the word for boy be practically identical to the word for cucumber. What exactly is the difference?"

" 'Boy' is *agori*. And 'cucumber' is *aggouri*. The double 'g' sounds sort of like an 'n'."

"Well, I'll retreat to some remote spot and say both of them over and over. In the meantime I'll let you answer all questions."

Richard chided me and said that only by practice, with silly mistakes, would my Greek get better. I knew he was right but the grammar was terribly difficult. All those long new words seemed so isolated. Making sentences was totally confusing.

"Ah, well, *seega seega,*" I said. "Let's storm the castle of Mytilini after siesta."

In the cool of evening we headed for the grove of pines which surrounded the Genoese Castle high on a headland. "Let's see if we can 'take' the castle," said Helen. So we imagined climbing the steep slope with bows and arrows on our shoulders. Helen hid behind a rock and pretended to shoot each of us as we passed her. Bill executed a dramatic fall to the ground.

A man, with wind billowing his shirt, came through the pines. He herded four goats whose heavy udders swung rhythmically from side to side.

Helen came up behind me, grabbed me in a bear hug and whispered, "I'm so happy Mom. I feel just like a little girl."

We explored for over an hour while the sunset provided an extravagant backdrop. The winds were warm and heavy. My sons and daughters, lingering behind, were silhouettes against the castle. Ann and I reached the road along the sea just as a wagon streaked by, like a runaway in a Western movie. The sides of this wagon were painted with flowers. "I don't want today to end," I turned to Ann. "We do so little each day, yet they just slip away."

"Don't be sad," Ann chided. "We have tomorrow. Aren't we going to sail to Gera Bay?"

Captain Antonio wanted us to spend that day in one of the two famous, deep bays of Lesbos. He had chosen Gera and there we went by sail to spend a second perfect day while the children water skied and I read and explored the shoreline. At sunset we sailed back to Mytilini in the fresh cool air with the Castle as our landmark.

Helen's happiness of the day before held and she coaxed Wendy into taking a long walk along the dock to see what "talent" had arrived aboard two naval ships anchored near us. They were back in an hour.

"We sang softly as we walked along," she reported. "The Mytilini males looked boldly at us but they didn't daunt us. After we exhausted our English repertoire we switched to Greek musical rounds. The later it got the more active the males became. We came home to safety."

The following day we were market bound as we stocked up for the long trip through the Dardanelles to Istanbul. Richard and I stayed in one store the entire time, buying most of our staples there. Wendy, Ann, and Robert took trips for items that couldn't be located in the center. Rick acted mainly as an observer, trying to keep a reasonable running account of what was being purchased and at what price. "Come on, Mom, *you* ask for it," he urged me. "You *have* to practice your Greek."

But I was still embarrassed over my three cucumber sons. "Rick," I complained, "how am I going to ask for cooking fat?"

"With your usual versatility and imagination." My oldest son grinned reassuringly as I went into pantomime.

Our "runners" kept reappearing with messages such as, "Oh, they were so nice and made us sit down and have a lemonade." An hour later we returned to the *Eva* laden with supplies for the long sail to Istanbul, the city of Constantine, the Byzantine kings, the Ottoman sultans, and Ataturk the Father of modern Turkey.

⚹ 29 ⚹

Helen of Troy

". . . And when Helen was only a child the famous prince, Theseus, carried her away to his own city of Athens, meaning to marry her when she grew up, and even at that time there was a war for her sake, for her brothers followed Theseus with an army, fought him and brought her home. Helen had fairy gifts. She had a great red jewel and when she wore it, red drops seemed to fall from it and vanished before they touched and stained her white breast."

Helen was reading aloud to us from a children's book about her namesake, Helen of Troy. We were to spend the following day at the site of Troy and had all been boning up on Helen, Menelaus, Achilles, Paris, King Tendarus. At meals Richard would quiz us on the events leading up to the ten-year siege of Troy as well as those endless years of war. Even Robert entered into this historic game, so captivated was he by the story of the wooden horse filled with soldiers.

Early the next morning I took my camera up on deck, destination Helen.

"Mother!" Helen was furious. "Why are you taking a picture of me before I even brush my teeth?" She was still snuggled in her sleeping bag on deck and I had called her name to get her attention.

"Because this is *your* day and I intend to record it from beginning to end."

"Mother." This time there was *some* tolerance for my behavior in her tone of voice, "I'm *not* Marilyn Monroe!" she grimaced at the camera, muttering, "Mothers."

We had sailed into Canakkale the evening before after slowly passing through the entrance to the Dardanelles. Captain Antonio told us that his charts showed many hidden rocks so we had reduced our speed. But the scenery was fascinating as all along the north shore of the Dardanelles were spectacular monuments erected by various countries in honor of their dead. One monument looked like the Arc d'Triumphe, another was a grouping of columns which could have been lifted from Luxor. They were wildly incongrous standing on those remote shores — as if some God had flung his building toys haphazardly about.

The older children had a big discussion as to whether they should swim the Hellespont. Bill said, "What Byron could do, I can do."

"I thought it was the Bosphorus which Byron swam." Richard spoke.

"Why," asked Ann, "do you want to swim either? *You* don't have to prove anything — Byron had a clubfoot."

"*And* he was incestuous," Rick added.

"*And* he wrote miserable poetry," Helen was not to be outdone.

"Besides," cautioned Bill, "did you see the size of those freighters passing us? I'd want traffic controlled before I launched myself across this channel."

So much for Byron and the Hellespont. We continued placidly on to Canakkale, found an anchorage and proceeded ashore to make arrangements to rent a minibus the following day. Herbert Muller in *The Loom of History* suggests that the ancient Trojans were pirates because they extorted payment from ships going through the Hellespont. We decided that the descendants of the Trojans were latter day pirates as we struggled with them over the price of our minibus. Our side won and in high spirits we looked forward to a full day at the site of ancient Troy.

We were so steeped in the several books we had read about the excavations at Troy that there was no way *not* to enjoy our time there. We speculated about the relationship of land to sea and where the Schleimans had lived, and tried to separate out all the levels down to the earliest, number nine, which was the famous city. I had to let my imagination run rampant in order to re-create Homer's Troy, a walled town which withstood a ten-year assault by Menelaus, the King of Sparta. But the location of

"The Troys" is lovely and the countryside around fertile and peaceful, so we explored and rested, to explore again.

Strangely—was it because of a name—it really was a very special day for our Helen; we all felt it and decided a bit of action was in order. In front of the main gate of Troy the older children clowned out Paris taking Helen from Menelaus. Bill played the wronged husband and Rick the Judge of the three Goddesses. Helen, of course, played Helen in spite of the lack of blond tresses.

As I watched my tall slender daughter happily laughing with her big brothers, I thought of a long ago day in Palo Alto when the three of them had entered the children's May Day parade. Helen was exactly three years old. Rick and Bill had built a canopy on their wooden wagon and decorated it with garlands of flowers. Helen was dressed in her favorite pale yellow ruffley dress, wore a fresh flower crown and was seated on a small wooden Mexican chair in the wagon. "The brothers" donned their leather chaps and cowboy hats, strapped on their pistols, and took their places in the parade up University Avenue. With her brothers pulling the wagon, Helen was happy, and her father and I kept pace with the wagon, walking behind the admiring townsfolk lining the street. Several blocks later Helen climbed off her chair, sat down in the wagon, put her head on the chair and went to sleep. The boys kept glancing back at her, but seemed unperturbed as they pulled their tiny sleeping beauty on up the street. The spectators were delighted.

Helen adored her brothers, but sometimes they gave her a bad time. When she was a freshman in high school, Bill walked me down the tree-lined drive of our home for a private talk. "Mother, you must talk to Helen about some of the words she uses. She doesn't even know they have double meanings." I confessed to Bill, after he mentioned some of the words, that *I* did not know they had double meanings either and that either he or Rick would have to enlighten Helen.

When Helen was sixteen she went off to Lausanne to study French for a year. First she spent some time in Geneva with some Egyptian friends of ours who were summering there. Late the next spring, her studies completed, she flew to Athens, where she took a Russian boat to Alexandria. She was to proceed to Cairo and spend a month visiting the same Coptic Egyptian friends. No one had thought to tell her that one must have a visa *before* entering Egypt. Nassar was President of Egypt then and rules were rigged. One joke told of even the Sphinx being refused an exit visa. So my nearly-seventeen-year-old arrived in the famous old port of Alexandria, wearing a Mata Hari hat, and somehow wiled her way to a visa. However, all her mail was opened the month she spent in Cairo. Helen spent her mornings, while with the Kirollis family, riding horseback in the desert near the pyramids, accompanied by an elderly protector hired by Mr. Kirollis. One day Helen's trousers ripped from stem to stern and her Arab protector calmly removed his long white *gelibiyas* and, bowing, presented it to her. Fortunately he had his daily garb, cotton pajamas, underneath.

I had told Helen about the sugar treatment for superfluous hair which all Egyptian women subscribe to, and so one day she went with Mr. Kirollis to his barber, were she was led upstairs, seated in a room with a number of other females, immediately attacked by a husky Arab girl with a bowl of what appeared to be taffy. The concoction was made from sugar, water, and lemon juice. Spreading this warm candy in strips up the leg. The attendant then ripped it off, along with all hair; it hurt. Following this ordeal Helen was rushed home and into a bath so the flies wouldn't devour her.

The year following Helen's Egyptian adventure I was amazed and amused to have her read me a letter from a friend whom she had met at that time. He asked Helen if her "poor dear mother" had finally been able to get an exit visa from Egypt.

"Helen," I asked, "What on earth did you tell him?"

"Oh," she said blithely. "I told him I was a student from Egypt and just made up the story about you, Mom."

Well, with her black hair and eyes she *could* be Egyptian.

I came back to the present just as the children returned from a tour of the great gashes in the earth which were labeled "Troy I, Troy II," and so on. Our Greek princess Helen was still bubbling with delight as we headed back for Canakkale.

It was magnificent at sunset in the Dardanelles, our visit to Troy behind us. When darkness fell Richard read aloud to us from Muller, by the light of our tiny green lantern. "He looks like

Lorenzo," Ann whispered to me while Rick paused every sentence or two as someone would interrupt, questioning a date, asking about a century, or to recall some other author on the same subject.

"Why don't we sail up the Dardenelles tonight? Jason did." Bill was excited.

"Bill, we don't have any inkfish to dye our sails black. That's why," I answered.

"Oh, Mom, come on, why not?" They all joined the chorus. So we went ashore and found Captain Antonio and the crew who agreed to go along with our re-creation of myth-history and within the hour we had sailed.

✕ 30 ✕

Following Jason

The sky held a million stars against the velvet sky. The myriad stays and ropes from each mast creaked and strained in the wind. Sometimes, turning over on my air mattress on deck I would open my eyes and catch a glimpse of the shadowy shore, a long string of lights marking a village, or a passing vessel. Once we passed three freighters at the same time: one going up the Dardanelles and two going down. Our small running light on top of the main mast seemed desperately inadequate in all that traffic. Some freighters were so large they loomed like cliffs above us. We rode their swells and spray covered us and I slept again.

Silence woke me. Our motor, which had lulled us all during the night's sail, was quiet. It was mid-morning and we had docked at a village on the island of Marmara in the Sea of Marmara. We had all slept on deck, honoring Jason's passage, and gradually people drifted below to wash and dress. Poor Captain Antonio was off to do our papers again as we, of course, had reentered Turkey.

We all walked in a clump the dusty little road through the town to buy eggs, plums, and cucumbers. Talking with a shop-keeper we discovered that Marmara isle was a summer resort for Turks — mainly from Ankara. The shore was lined with grand spreading trees with dozens of small tables set beneath. Nearby cafes supplied food and drink and already many vacationers were sipping morning tea. Leaving our purchases at the *Eva,* we then walked the opposite direction along a pebbly beach. As we swam we got talking to a young Turkish girl who asked us to come back to her family's small beach cottage for tea. We accepted, met the family, and sat in a circle on the beach in straight-backed wooden chairs which her father brought out from their house. The father was a professor of math at the University of Ankara. He, the mother, and two daughters were vacationing to celebrate one daughter's graduation from law school. A cousin, who played the violin in the Ankara Symphony was with the family. We drank our tea in the charming fragile tea glasses used by all Turks; after awhile other families who lived along the beach came to see the foreigners and our circle became a center. Anyone who spoke six words of English joined the conversation.

Behind the beachfront homes were other much older private homes, some with lush gardens. Across the channel from Marmara two isles rose out of the mist, one the shape of an upside-down teaspoon. The rocky hills behind the village reminded me of the Big Sur coast in California — golden, with gray rocks and with live green trees climbing up their flanks.

Leaving our new friends we walked through the village to the other end of town and on out to a small boatyard. We found a beach log and sat to watch two men framing a large boat. My sons had a Turkish rock-skipping contest. I counted eleven boats moving in the Sea of Marmara, each painted a vivid color. Some carried tourists to other beaches or villages and these had gay fringed canopies; others were obviously fishing boats. In front of a small nearby cafe three men sat preparing eggplant for the evening meal and two others squatted by the sea, cleaning chickens.

The sight of all that food sent us scurrying back to the *Eva* for evening *mezethes* — our pre-dinner snacks. We had purchased three round watermelons from a huge pile under a village tree and the village policeman helped us carry our purchases back to the *Eva*. I sat on deck reading *Hercules, My Shipmate*, Robert Graves' story of Jason and the Argonauts. I wondered about the small island where we were anchored. Did Jason, having fled with Medea and killed his father and brother, stop, perhaps, on this island to rest his men? To hide on the back side and let his pursuers pass? What did the men of the Argonaut eat? Did they make *zodsiki* — they must have had yogurt, ever the staple food of the Middle East.

Yogurt had certainly become a staple for us. That evening on the island of Marmara, Bill was seated on a deck chair cautiously peeling nine *aggouri* (cucumbers), handing a slice of each to me to taste for bitterness. Robert sat on deck grating the foot-long cukes. Ann was peeling garlic to add along with the lemon juice when the ingredients were finally mixed. That night she used two whole garlic bulbs before she was satisfied with the taste. Helen was husking the corn we had bought from a man selling it, roasted on charcoal over an old oil barrel. Helen carefully saved the corn silk for Robert, who loved its feel. "Mother, grab my silk before it flies overboard!" Robert shouted as a gust of wind fanned us.

Wendy came out on deck. "Ann, may I borrow your blue sweater?"

"Yes, if you've got deodorant on — you're pretty good about that."

Wendy said, "*And* I write thank you notes."

Suddenly, an emergency. The crew had been trying to fill our empty water tanks from seventy-five yards of striped green, red, and yellow hose. There was not enough pressure so Captain Antonio suggested that we sail at once for Istanbul. We backed out of our mooring and joined the other boats bobbing along on each other's waves. Everyone in these small boats was in a holiday mood and they sang, clapped, and waved merrily to us as we passed.

We seldom ate while sailing, but the Sea of Marmara was smooth — once we escaped the vacationers — so we devoured our cheese soufflé sandwiches, corn, tomatoes, and watermelon as we churned over the dusky waters. The evening star appeared and soon the sky was awash with stars. Wendy lay quietly with her head in my lap.

Bill said, "It is a summer we'll treasure. We are all together."

Robert said, "Why should *I* put on a sweater? You are cold, Mom, not me."

Climbing into bed later, Ann and I each discovered a Wendy note. Ann's was about the blue sweater and mine read, "Mom — thanks a lot for the bathing suit. I looked pretty sexy and I'm sure everyone thought I was crazy. But I know I'm not. Love you, Wendy XXXXXXX OOOOOOOO."

I was glad I was I and not Jason.

❧ 31 ❧

We Conquer the City of Constantine

No wonder it is called the Golden Horn! Everything was bathed in the golden light of dawn; Topkapi perched on its massive walls; St. Sophia and the Blue Mosque with their graceful minarets. From these old and glorious monuments Istanbul spread endlessly, the Golden Horn its foreground.

Richard had awakened Ann and me at first light and we sat huddled in the cool morning air, gazing raptly.

"The only way to approach Constantinople is by sea," Ann voiced my thought. "Rick, do you know when the name was officially changed to Istanbul?"

"In the fifteenth century, but have you noticed that all the Greeks we've spoken to about coming here . . . they still call it Constantinople, even after five hundred years."

"A city straddling two continents," I mused. "It looks as if it could have more than the sixty miles of waterfront the Guide Blue gives it. Aren't the hundreds of minarets piercing the sky exotic? Oh, I can barely wait until we dock."

Hoisting our yellow flag, we anchored in front of an elegant white marble building sprawled in the middle of formal gardens and which was surrounded by an intricate wrought-iron fence. Jorgo rowed Robert, Richard, and me ashore; our mission, to find help. No one had answered the call of the yellow flag. I was first out of the rowboat, and as my feet touched the marble step, a soldier, gun pointing, came running toward me shouting "No! No! No!" Pushing me back into the dinghy, he pointed to the right, where there appeared to be a landing dock. We soon found that we had attempted to land at the main gate of the Dolma

Bachi Palace, built in 1853 to replace Topkapi as the home of the Sultan. A couple of days later we explored the palace and found it to be the most palacelike palace any of us had ever seen: its furnishings unbelievably rich, each room having a fireplace made of colored crystal, or of cut glass. All had been made in Czechoslovakia. Most impressive was the furniture in the Sultan's suite; everything was made of cut glass and a double bedstead of glass is impressive indeed!

But all we knew at our landing was that we had to have water and help. High above the palace on the brow of a hill we saw the Hilton. Rick and Robert and I started a long hot hike up to it. Looking back to see the *Eva,* I shouted, "Where is she?" as just then the *Eva* emerged from a cloud of smoke—looking for all the world like one of Medea's miracles. We had mistakenly anchored in the path of the ferries that cross and criss-cross the mouth of the Bosphorous. Each time a ferry passed, the *Eva* rocked madly and was completely enveloped in smoke.

Eventually we found an entrance to the gardens of the Hilton and, feeling definitely underdressed, the boys in jeans and me in a wrinkled sundress, we entered the cool, high-ceilinged lobby with its grass-green carpets and its splendid view out over a strip of vegetable gardens, the Palace, and the Bosphorous.

"When a concierge is good he has to be the most important person in the hotel." We were sitting on soft Turkish cushions sipping tea in the lobby of the Hilton letting the concierge manage our lives. I was happy. Within an hour he had found us a broker—"he is on his way over, Madame"—and brought the manager, who offered to let us have the penthouse suite for a few nights (the travel business paying off!!). We were all eager to luxuriate in hot baths and be central to a couple of days' sightseeing.

However, we were destined to spend at least one more night on the *Eva* as the yacht agent, upon arrival at the Hilton, informed us that no boat supplies were offered on Sunday and he suggested that we sail off for a visit to one of the Prince's Islands for the day. "They are charming." His English was perfect (as were his French and Greek). "It will make a lovely introduction to our country, and then your Captain can begin tomorrow having the yacht serviced and you will be free to explore Istanbul."

As the boys and I walked back down to the *Eva,* I wondered about the crew and how they would survive for the next few days. The agent had told us they would find that most of the Turks living along the waterfront spoke Greek. That would help.

So an hour and a half later we pulled into an exquisite bay on the Prince's Isle called Buyuk Ada (Big Island) with cool-looking pine woods covering the hills behind. Hundreds of people were swimming, picnicking, and playing games. At the dock were anchored two large cargolike boats, which apparently had brought the mob. One friendly member of the mob found us two carriages for a trip around the island while we waited for our ham dinner to bake. Carriages were the only means of transport on the island and each carriage was more luxurious than the other. They had wicker and velvet seats, and surrey tops. It was such fun, bouncing along in our carriages with enchanting views in every direction, the wind making patterns on the sea. Driving through town, we found ourselves in Victorian England, or so all the wooden houses made it seem. The gardens were formal and even the grass was English green. The streets were of stone and I silently thanked the Istanbul agent for pointing us to that lovely island in the Sea of Marmara.

Back in the bay where the *Eva* floated, we tried for an hour to signal the crew. No luck, so Bill and Rick stripped to undershorts and swam out. There was a light breeze and our gasoline supply was very low, so, hoisting sails, we left behind the vacationing Turks and set off in a red sunset. The older children had a singing contest. Later Robert had a reading lesson with Richard. Wendy looked down the hatch and called, "Ann, that's neat, those x's you're putting on top of the ham." Ann was finishing up dinner cooking, gently mocking Eileen, the cook, who was putting on "eyes" and fixing her hair against the evening in Istanbul.

᚛ 32 ᚜

Turkey Yes, Customs No

We had moved into the Sultan's suite. We were almost in heaven. The decor was that of a harem with deep turkish cushions abounding. Fortunately, the suite had three bathrooms and tubs were seldom empty. The children kept saying, "Thank you, Mother." Helen raved, "Imagine going to the loo and not having to pump!"

"I'm going to marry a man rich enough to build me a house as beautiful as this suite," Wendy had decided!

The first morning we spent in the Hilton saw me up at dawn. I simply had to write to an old friend who had written some weeks before and proposed marriage. I could no longer delay and so I seated myself in front of the dining room table in our suite (there was no other use for it) with my pen and paper. I sat and sat trying to think of the words to put on paper that would tell Jim how much I cared for him, but that I felt we should not marry. Maybe I was crazy. He was a fine man, a friend since Stanford days. My children liked him, and adored his ranch in northern California. I was sure we could make a good and interesting home, but I loved John Summerskill. I didn't say that to Jim, but of course it was the real reason. An agonizing hour later I sealed the letter and took the elevator down to post it before I could change my mind. Relieved to have at last made a decision, I awakened the family — I think they would happily have slept through the day — and we set off to "do" Istanbul.

First Topkapi, a warm, rambling, many-gardened old palace, in an incomparable location. As a museum, it contains not only the now famous jeweled sword of the movie *Topkapi,* but an impressive collection of china and jewels. We were even shown jars of powdered rhinoceros horns — an aphrodisaic used by the sultans. "How do we know if it works?" Helen asked. "What is an aphrodisiac?" responded Robert, at which Rick put his arm around Rob and walked him off through the garden for a lesson.

Recovering my equilibrium, I answered Helen's query, "Why not ask the rhinoceros?"

Just as we came out from a visit to the newly restored harem quarters we encountered a prince from Saudi Arabia who was visiting Topkapi along with his four wives, all dressed in black, one with child. A bevy of servants flowed around them. When we encountered the entourage later, on the stone balcony of Topkapi that overlooked the Golden Horn, one of the servants sat breast-feeding what we assumed to be a royal baby. Robert was intrigued.

Then to St. Sophia, so impressive in size; and the Blue Mosque with its handsome windows, but most of all we enjoyed a small mosque built by a sultan's daughter — built with her pocket money.

Some members of the family could hardly wait to visit the justly famous Istanbul bazaar with its 3,000 shops under one roof. So off we went with mama constantly harping at the girls to "stay close to your brothers." Richard had a real horror story about this bazaar. One of his Princeton friends, on his honeymoon in Turkey, had lost his wife there. She had been lingering a little behind him. A year later the young bridegroom had still not found her.

It was a delicious time — those hours in the bazaar. Everywhere people were good to us. In many shops we were given a squirt of glycerin and lemon to rub on face and hands. It was deliciously aromatic and cooling.

None of us had ever seen so much gold, all stamped 22 carat. Turkish people, quite rightly, do not trust their banks so invest their savings in gold jewelry. Ann had wanted a gold ring for as long as I could remember, a special gold ring. In an antique shop she found her dream ring — carved white jade set in gold. The bargaining began. Ann, Rick, and the owner dickered to and fro, with a dollar off here and a dollar added at the other end, when suddenly Robert called out, "Sixty-five dollars." Everyone laughed and soon a price was fixed upon and the ring purchased.

That day at the bazaar we ate at *Pandelis,* a Turkish business-man's restaurant that is above the spice bazaar. The restaurant has several domed rooms with beautifully tiled walls and is famous for its Black Sea fish.

In fact, one of the delights of Turkey is the food, subtle and unique to us. For three days we enjoyed everything we ate — having been briefed a bit by that wonderful Hilton concierge. We had mussels chopped up and served with rice, pine nuts, and currants and exotic seasonings. This delicious concoction was served in mussel shells. The eggplant salad, tasting of charcoal and garlic, was served with a sauce made from crushed walnuts, bread, garlic, and oil. We learned always to order eggplant with yogurt dressing, and one day we had large bowls of fresh rasp-berries served with whipped goat cream.

Our other favorite restaurant, Caruj, was on the Bosphorous. Because of it, we decided we had to sail the channel. We wan-dered down to our yacht on the third day at the Hilton, and asked Captain Antonio if he would take us up the Bosphorous and into the Black Sea. "Yes," he said to the first query, but to the second, "I don't want to sail the Black Sea. It is called black because it has such sudden winds and could be dangerous for us." So we compromised and set off up the Bosphorous. My dream to explore the mysteries of the unpredictable Black Sea and to visit Trebson and Samson (where Marco Polo set off on his journeys) would have to wait.

The Bosphorous turned out to be a gently winding channel between wooded hills, but it had fierce currents. Its banks were lined with charming wooden houses, a few castles interspersed! "And there," Bill pointed, "That must be the place where Darius sat on his chair carved out of rock and watched his armies cross on a floating bridge from Asia Minor to Europe." It did seem the narrowest spot. We had to dodge countless ferryboats which shuttled back and forth across the channel delivering people from one continent to the other.

We had become so incensed at Turkish customs procedures — having to re-do papers at each port with the additional problem of having to give gifts of liquor and cigarettes — that Ann and I decided to visit the offices of a well-known newspaper in Istanbul, the *Milliyet*. There we told our story to one of their foreign correspondents, who was attentive and helpful. I personally thought it was his attraction to Ann, but in any event following the interview he carried groceries with us to the *Eva,* which we were stocking against our next-day departure. A charming man in his mid-thirties, he talked to each of us, took pictures of Robert shining the shoes, and promised he'd write something about our problems for the next day's paper.

That he did!

With our tea and biscuit tray, the following morning at the Hilton, was delivered the mornings *Milliyet*. A huge picture of Robert and his shoeshine box, with everyone standing around as he polished Bill's shoes.

There were two headlines. The larger informed the citizens of Istanbul: AMERICAN MILLIONAIRESS AND HER CHILDREN (now smaller headlines) Say Turkey Yes, Customs No (meaning customs procedures). Oh, dear. I rushed down to the concierge to get the whole article translated. It turned out to be not too bad. The concierge explained to me that anyone on a yacht would be considered a millionaire and, "You must remember that they are talking about our currency, not yours, and there are nine lira to the dollar." We sounded colorful if slightly eccentric but if the article had not carried our names we would have failed to recognize our own adventure.

✶ 33 ✶

Home to Greece

"Mother, you and Ann have hearts born in Europe." Wendy and I were standing by the main mast with the *Eva* anchored in front of good old Canakkale. By the time we had cleared Turkish customs one last time, it was too late to sail for Limnos as the Captain did not want to arrive at night in an unfamiliar harbor. So we would begin the eight-hour sail just after dark.

Wendy and I were watching the very active harbor life when past the forward mast a sliver of a moon appeared and then Venus against the blue-green and rose of the last tinge of sunset.

"What do you mean Wendy, our hearts were born in Europe?"

"Well, Mom, I don't know really what I mean, but you seem to like so many things here."

Wendy was absolutely right and standing there in the dusk, with the huge monuments of World War I looming against the sky on one side of us, and the dimly seen plains of Troy on the other, I tried to explain to myself and Wendy why I "liked so many things here."

"I feel at home in small European towns, Wendy, and in Greece too. I guess even in Turkey. Maybe it has to do with growing up in a small Western town. I don't know. But I do like that people take time to sit and talk, to care about the other person, to help us. I guess hearts are funny. Maybe it's even genes. Who knows where our ancestors came from?"

"Is that why you bought land in Ios? Did you think you had an ancestor who was Greek?"

"I didn't actually stop and think about it, darling, but maybe that is the reason."

"Mom, I've decided on the perfect life. I would like to have a month in Menlo Park every summer and then two months in Greece at our new house. Will we really build it?"

"Funny, isn't it," Helen had come to stand between Wendy and me with an arm around each of us, "I feel as if we are going home tonight, just knowing we'll be in Greece in the morning."

"As property owners, I guess we can now consider that we have two homes. I'm glad of that, darling daughters, because I want you to grow up at home anywhere in the world. People aren't that different anywhere. It's just the damn languages that make it so hard to communicate!"

"My French is pretty good, Mom, and I've decided that at the university this year I'll major in classics and take both Greek and Latin."

"Bravo, Eleni!" Ah, I thought, already the effects of the summer are beginning to show.

Ann came above and quietly we four women stood in the twilight. I thought how intrigued I was with the fact that familiarity breeds respect. I knew the saying said the opposite, but we were living proof of it, being the way I *knew* was right. My respect for all of the children grew by the day as they learned to give and take, fight and laugh, and forgive. As if she could read my thoughts, Helen interrupted them. "Living together gets easier every day—and there is no place to hide."

I didn't particularly enjoy traveling at night. The motor—just under Ann's and my stateroom—was bothersome and I hated to miss passing any island or ship. But it was good to be back in Greek waters, and when I came above in the first flush of light it was to find us deep in the Thracian Sea, anchored in a perfect small bay surrounded by craggy mountains. We had arrived at Limnos island and the port of Myrina.

Directly above us was a massive cliff, topped by a Genoese fort and castle. Its ramparts were so similar in contour to the natural rock that, in the dim light of dawn, I could barely tell one from the other. A small patch of earth on one slope boasted a cypress grove.

Limnos is rich in myth and particularly famous for one story. Zeus was the patron God of Limnos in ancient times. When his wife, Aphrodite, committed adultery with Ares, the Limnian women (according to Fodor's *Greece*) "neglected her worship. In revenge, Aphrodite afflicted them with halitosis [now *really*] and their husbands neglected *them*—in consequence of this, every man on the island was massacred." I remembered the rest of the tale—that Jason and the men of the Argo, in their quest for the Golden Fleece, had put ashore at Limnos, and finding all those unattended women, they stayed two years happily repopulating the island. One could only assume that Aphrodite had removed the halitosis curse by then.

We took several long lovely days to sun and swim and restock the larder on that gentle agricultural island. The first day our group kept shopping and returning and shopping and returning as they discovered new sources. Rick returned from one foray dejected. He had visited every shoe store in every town for the last month to buy shoes, size 46, and Limnos had none, either. He had only a decrepit pair of Japanese go-aheads and longed for a real pair of shoes. Size 46 isn't even that big in America, but in Greece and Turkey it was another story.

I found a particularly neat grocery store that morning. Its huge ice chest had one panel inset with a fancy mirror. It had at least thirty gunny sacks filled with all sorts of meals, and beans, and pastas, and all kinds of salamis hung from the ceiling. There were hundreds of two-litre wine bottles covered in straw and the usual *denekes* of olives and cheeses.

Wendy and Ann returned from a late-afternoon expedition filled with praise for Myrina. Wendy had jeans on and Ann her long bath towel dress. Everyone loved their costumes and laughed and assisted them. "You're sure it was your costumes and not your smiling faces that pleased the populace?" I teased them.

"Well, the men were a bit too friendly," Ann was puzzled, "Why, at my age, I don't feel I can really cope."

Richard and Robert returned to the *Eva* with ice cream bars for everyone and we sat licking and watching a large caïque preparing to go out for the night. Great piles of net were on deck—yellow, olive green, deep red—and all with blue wooden floats. Eight men sat, examining the net; other men worked on the motor, coiled ropes, read newspapers. I counted nineteen men and two boys. And suddenly all was ready and with calm dignity the caïque motor chugged and she began her departure, almost bumping the *Eva* twice. Our Captain shouted wildly, our crew lined up with bumpers, and everyone pulled ropes and shouted. Then from shore came nine baby boats, each with two acetylene lanterns in its stern and each rowed by one man, standing, Venetian fashion.

The next day was for play. We walked a couple of miles to the loveliest beach we had seen since Ios. Serene and with white sand, the perfect beach lay between two dramatic headlands formed by huge boulders. As I swam in water so clear, I could watch my shadow and the sunbeams on the ripply sand of the ocean floor; I wondered if perhaps this was the beach where the women of Limnos chewed ivy leaves, and, crazed, killed all their men and boys three thousand years before. Was the story only myth? Was it rooted in fact? It was incredibly peaceful and with no one about we swam without suits and the boys found a diving rock.

Fortunately, we had donned our suits and were sunning when a young man galloped bareback down the beach on his horse. Calmly he dismounted, waded in the sea, leading the horse, and for nearly an hour he fascinated our group as he and the horse swam and played together in the ocean.

After a wonderful open-air late lunch under clusters of trellised grapes, we meandered back to the *Eva*. If being back in Greece felt like coming home, so did walking back to the *Eva*. We were totally settled in. Everyone knew that in Ann's and my top right-hand dresser drawer lived the fingernail set; in the middle drawer jewels, Scotch tape, and swimming kit; lower left-hand drawer medicine, paragoric, aspirin, alcohol, and tape. Writing paper had its home and everyone had strict orders to return finished books to the shelves in the salon. We had all finished with Muller, for the time being, and Robert Graves, as well as several books on Ataturk. Now Edith Hamilton came into the foreground and that evening on Limnos, Bill read aloud the chapter on "Why, while expounding democracy, Greece had slaves."

This weighty subject was soon interrupted by a shout from Robert, "Somebody come close this door." The bathroom sliding door often sticks and frequently people had to have help getting in or out. Wendy was holding her little transistor radio, hoping

Bill would soon finish reading, when suddenly over it came the Captain who was calling on his radio. When Captain Antonio heard himself on Wendy's small set, he started calling, "Wendy, Wendy, *ti kanies?*"—(How are you?) Limnians began to gather around the stern of the *Eva* to listen as the Captain kept chatting with Wendy. Suddenly she handed me her transistor saying, "Captain Antonio wants to talk to you, Mother." In a second I heard a voice—not the Captain, but Wendy saying, "Mother, I just want you to know how much I love you." Everyone on shore clapped and we all felt as though in a fish bowl.

That evening the sunset was blood red on the flanks of Mt. Athos fifty miles to our west. Mist shrouded her base and she looked like photos I'd seen of Mt. Fujiama.

On shore, the lovely village was framed in rugged purple tinted mountains and the Sunday night village band was playing a haunting off-key melody as hundreds of townspeople sauntered in the warm evening air. I looked forward to the next-day's sail to Thassos, the most northerly of the Greek islands.

It took us seven hours to motor to Thassos. There wasn't a breath of air and the sea was a looking glass. For the first time we didn't shut our portholes. For an hour two dolphins played with us, and then we encountered an enormous sea tortoise—it looked large enough to tow the *Eva*. We could see Mt. Athos beckoning for the whole day, until we began to sail up the east side of Thassos. Olive trees climbed the mountainsides on ancient broad terraces and then gave way to oak and plane and pine trees. "It looks like the Sierra Mountains, Mom." Helen had been in love with the Sierras ever since we had packed in and camped one summer.

Thassos town is built on top of the ruins of the ancient city, and since we all felt boat-bound, we headed for town and a visit to the remains of the great walls ending up deep in cool pine woods at the site of the ancient theater. Sadly, its "season" was over, but we had seen an ad for a movie that evening and decided to attend.

"Good water, all bathe, more water tomorrow." It was Jorgo and no one needed urging. For the next hour we took turns in the shower while Jorgo madly pumped, ran to man the heater, and to the pump again. Early egg-lemon soup dinner and by dusk we

were in our miserably uncomfortable wooden chairs at the outside movie house, watching ten-year-old *War and Peace*. The film
broke five times, the sound was scratchy, the film was four hours
long, and we all adored it, munching dried pumpkin seeds
through the whole film.

As we sauntered home after midnight we told Rick and Bill the
story of Robert and the mountain oysters. A month before we left
for Greece, we had spent the weekend at Jim's ranch north of San
Francisco. It was round-up weekend and all new born calves
were shot with a vaccine, dehorned, and castrated. Robert had
assisted, being assigned the job of painting the wounds, following
castration, with a black tarlike substance which helped the heal-
ing. He was fascinated, and not at all happy with our dinner that
night. One of the cowboys turned cook and took all the day's
harvest of testicles, called "mountain oysters" in the Western
U.S., and fried them with onions, tomatoes, and garlic for our
dinner. After dinner, as all the men were sitting around talking
over the day's work, I approached. "Time for bed, Robert."

"O.K." He was willing but reluctant. "Tomorrow at the round-
up will we get some more of those country clams?" The men
howled at the new and even more descriptive name, and the
cowboy cook actually rolled on the ground laughing.

We had found that the best means of travel on most islands
was by people's bus or by foot. Cycling was fun if, like Limnos or
Chios, the terrain was gentle. Thassos, one huge mountain of
white marble, encouraged us to walk one of our days there. We
had heard that a particularly lovely beach was Macrin Ammo,
just a two-kilometer walk from the port. Setting out in early
morning with one of our string shopping bags filled with tuna
sandwiches and hard-boiled eggs, we passed through town to
pick up a large bottle of wine and orange drink. Just at the edge
of town two elderly ladies stopped us to marvel at Rick's serapi—
I had made each boy one by sewing two colorful bath towels
together. They admired the two-towel idea, Richard himself—
whom they called Agemmemnon—and then launched into the
usual run of questions. The children were usually patient with
me and my pride!

Macrin Ammo was indeed a remarkable beach, the sand
almost whitewash white, having been ground out of white marble. The waves were ideal for easy body surfing and we played,

ate our sandwiches, and promised ourselves to return to that particular beach. Three young Greek men, playing handball on the sand, spoke to Helen. "When the French see you they ooh-la-la. We Greeks just whistle, whit-whit—o.k.?"

Walking back to port, we took a detour through a pasture to a taverna at the edge of a pine woods, where we ate cool *karpuzi* (watermelon) under a four-hundred-year-old chestnut tree. "What about tomorrow?" I asked. "Who has been most involved with the *Guide Bleu?*"

Helen, now completely turned on to the classical world, said she had read all about Thassos and intended to visit all the ruins but would join the family on a trip to "the most interesting of the mountain villages on Thassos—Panaghia. We have to take the bus though."

The bus it was, at mid-morning, but we almost missed it as a funeral was winding through the center of town. Everyone stopped as the mourners passed, led by a man carrying the coffin cover. He was followed by two young girls with wreaths of fresh flowers, and behind them the professional chanter chanted. Then came the tiny coffin, and one could see on all faces, Greek islanders as well as tourists in bathing costumes and straw hats, a look of universal sadness at the death of a child.

Crushed into the bus, holding our watermelon to keep it from rolling on a dead chicken, we began the snakelike assent through the woods, on a narrow road paved with white marble gravel. All through the woods were beehives—thousands of them. Many beekeepers come from the mainland in May and stay on Thassos until late September. It seemed an ideal life, with the keeper's little hut near his group of hives (each keeper had his hive boxes painted his particular color), and the bees doing all of the work.

Sometimes corners were so steep that our driver had to back and turn a couple of times in order to negotiate. But the village was worth the crowded trip. A real mountain village with spring water running through the village in open troughs. It was easy in Panaghia to imagine life being lived the same way for centuries. In the main square was a carved marble fountain with two large brass faucets gushing water. Several townspeople had placed watermelons in the fountain to cool. At one time the fountain had been painted the same deep reds, yellows, and blues of the ancient temples and much of the faded paint was visible. Around the fountain sat nine old gentlemen on the now familiar wooden chairs with cane bottoms. The streets of Panaghia were steep and lined with handsome old houses of Turkish design, that is, with stone bottoms and protruding wooden tops, and always the balconies looked about to collapse.

Catching the next bus down to a beach, we found it was not of sand, but of millions of stark white marble pebbles and rocks, which had been polished over the centuries by the sea. We collected dozens and eventually eliminated all but nine which we carried from the beach to the *Eva*, the *Eva* to the plane, and eventually home to Menlo Park for use as paperweights.

When we thought a beach might be crowded, we did not bring our "human dressing room" into play, but wore suits under our clothes, which made it even easier to be ready for the sea. We continued to be impressed with the modesty of Greeks. That day on Thassos we encountered a new wrinkle. A large middle-aged man donned a "changing garment." Like a large cotton sack, it was open at the bottom and had a drawstring around the neck. He put it on and we snuk peeks as the cotton tent wiggled from his struggling-inside. Nearby a grandfather puzzled over a two-year-old girl's bikini — which end was up? Before putting it on her, he protected her by carefully wrapping her in a towel.

Unfortunately, we chose to go back to the *Eva* at the very time everyone else was leaving the beach. All those nice bathers raced for the rickety old vehicle, pushed and shoved and yelled, and one pig-sized man shoved his way on before some of the arriving passengers could get off. Eventually we got on, taking the back seat and, amid great hilarity, managed to squash Bill and Richard each on to a camp stool (provided by the bus driver) in the aisle. Then there were so many passengers that each of us on the back seat held another person. Just then a second bus rolled in. The pig man was frantic. Trapped by all the people in the aisle, he couldn't get out. We sauntered to the new bus. When we were seated, Wendy, who had been fascinated by the whole scene, said, "I guess it's true that if you wait 'til last you sometimes get the best."

❧ 34 ❧

For Men Only

"The sea is usually very rough around the Mt. Athos peninsula," announced Richard. "Darius lost his whole fleet here."

That was no consolation to me. I was sick, as we pitched and rolled at the same time. Everyone looked green, but I alone gave way. "Please, would someone hold my dark glasses," I asked and leaned far out over the side of the *Eva* with Bill holding my legs. Later, somewhat recovered, I turned to Bill. "I think your reading aloud from Camus' *The Fall* didn't help the way I felt. I don't like that book."

But even a rocky tummy couldn't divert me for long from the grandeur of that great mountain peninsula called Athos, the only monk-ruled state in the world. We sailed down the east side of Mt. Athos, around its windswept end and up the west side of the Mountain to the tiny port of Daphne. From our small vessel we could see some of the monasteries. A particularly large one had vast retaining walls. Another spread out like a small village and we could see its gardens and orchards through our binoculars. Other monasteries were small and looked desperately lonely as they clung to a cliff rising nearly seven thousand feet from the sea. We spotted many caves, sometimes with little shacks beside them, the dwellings of hermit monks.

"How many monks live on Mt. Athos now?" Ann asked as she peered through the glasses at their rugged world.

"About three thousand," answered Bill. He and Rick had been boning up, as they were to spend a few days visiting some of the monasteries. Rick continued, "At its height the Greek Orthodox State of Mt. Athos had forty thousand monks. They were from everywhere in this part of the world—Russia, Serbia, Bulgaria, Greece. They were very rich, too, in ikons and church artifacts. Most of the important things have been taken away to museums or sold."

"Or stolen, perhaps." I'd been reading, too.

"We'll let you know," replied Rick, "After we research personally some of the thousand years of history here. Did you know the Mountain State just celebrated its one thousand and third birthday? How's that for a bit of esoteric information?"

"Pretty good, but not very impressive to a good Jewish girl," challenged Ann.

"*S'parakalo,* please" called Captain Antonio, "We are getting near to Daphne. The women should all put on clothes."

"We *have* on clothes," Helen protested.

"Bathing suits don't count," responded Richard, so, obedient to the Greek male—our beloved Captain—we complied, pulling on slacks and shirts.

"You know," Bill added fuel to our fire, "not only are women not allowed to touch the earth of Mt. Athos, but Robert can't go either, because he is too young to grow a beard. What's more, there aren't even any female animals on Athos."

"What do they do about birds and bees?" I was nonplussed, "Well, at least I have *some* satisfaction in knowing that every male in the whole damn state was born of woman!"

"Mail," Wendy shouted.

"Yes, male," I answered.

"No, Mother, not that kind of male. The word just made me think of letters. Don't we get them here?" As our most prolific writer, Wendy also never failed to reap her reward. And the boys' permits to visit Mt. Athos, applied for two months ago from the American Embassy in Athens, should be in our mail bag at Daphne.

Jorgo and the Captain made a quick run into port and returned with two weeks' worth of letters. A feast. Bill, thank goodness, had two letters from Katie. "You didn't leave me an address, so I couldn't write until a letter came from you."

"See, Bill, I told you so."

I had a letter from my secretary saying, "There is a strong rumor that you are married and on an extended honeymoon." With five children? And no husband?

We did not. "Many years ago," he spoke slowly, "an ikon was sent to Athos from across the sea and on the way it was ship-wrecked. The monks on the Mountain saw where it lay, as a stream of light from the heavens shone on it. They fetched the ikon [after some walking on water, I wondered?], taking it to Iviron, their monastery. The next morning they saw the ikon back in the sea. Again they took it to the monastery. The next two days were like the first. Finally the ikon spoke, "I came to protect you, not to be protected by you!"

None of us knew what to say and Bill intervened again, asking, "Why did God have to rest on the seventh day? Was he tired?"

I was beginning to feel sorry for the young priest, who answered, "No, of course not, but as God had just completed his task he had nothing to do but rest."

I quietly thanked God, as our call came through from Athens. Some kind soul at the American Embassy told Bill that, proba-bly, he could receive a permit in a few days. "What about the application sent two months ago?" The conversation dragged on, and when Bill hung up the manager gently suggested that *he* try to get permission for Bill. He snatched up the phone and dialed the police chief of Daphne. He spoke in Greek, but his face spoke too, and we knew the permit was granted. So, happy and re-lieved, we said, "Happy Birthday" again to the manager as we raced for the *Eva*. We had to deliver our "men" immediately to Daphne. After Helen made them egg sandwiches, off they rowed, and we sailed back to Ouranopolis.

Later that day, when the boys had been gone about five hours, Helen said, "I miss the boys. But it is sort of nice now. They take up so much room."

Having space was a new experience on the *Eva*. Captain Antonio let Robert swing on a large rope attached to the top of the main mast. What joy! He would stand on the middle beam and sail through the air to the main boom. "Rob, may I have a turn?" Helen pleaded.

"O.K., but you're sort of big."

In her red bikini, Helen was sensational and squealy. We nicknamed her "Jane" on the spot.

Ann dropped her headband in the water and Robert put on goggles and dove fifteen feet down to retrieve it from where it nestled amid sunbeams in the crystal water. "Are you glad I brung your band up Ann?"

"Brought, Robert."

"If Helen can say 'stauntered,' I can say 'brung.' "

Later that evening Robert, having come in to his own with the absence of the older males, informed us, "I'm keeping track of Wendy's gripes. Yesterday she had ten, but she is doing very well today."

And so we waited for our men to come back.

One whole day was spent at Ouranopolis in sunning and reading. A day filled with small-life things. Strange how even with all that time there was never enough time. A day would slip away with a book unfinished, a letter unwritten. But there was always time for people and for daydreaming and for silliness.

Helen and Wendy rowed on the calm pink sea at sunset. Just as the sun passed from view, the moon rose and the girls came back to the *Eva* for supper. We were conscious of space as we lolled around the salon. Robert resumed his role of entertaining the women and told us about a nine-year-old girl who weighed seven hundred pounds. "Oh, Robert," Wendy sounded disgusted, "You shouldn't listen to that kind of rumor!" We all shouted with laughter. And Helen asked, "Did I ever tell you the story about the two sisters I knew in Lausanne who were so prejudiced?" We chorused, "no."

"They were really cute, but they were prejudiced about absolutely everything, including race and religion, so one day I told them I was Jewish on my mother's side just to see how they'd react."

"Helen," I protested, "I know you've made me part Cherokee, then I find out a couple of weeks ago I'm an unhappy Egyptian mama awaiting my exit visa, and now you've given me to the Hebrews. Do you have any other revelations for me?"

"No, Mom," she answered blithely, "it's just that being a White Anglo Saxon American isn't very exciting." Standing and stretching in all our space, Helen announced she would sleep on deck again that night, "But I wish someone would help me identify some constellations. I'm really bored with the Big Dipper and Orion!"

And then it was the third day of awaiting our men and Captain Antonio moved the *Eva* and us from Ouranopolis to Daphne at noon — in anticipation of their return.

Robert and Jorgo rowed to a small village near Daphne and bought us fish for lunch. The Captain took Robert into Daphne to ask about Rick and Bill. Robert wore bermuda shorts and a T-shirt. The monks at port requested that "the boy wear long trousers next time." The Captain asked us not to swim, "because of decency," but when he rowed ashore I snuk a little swim, wearing my flesh-colored suit and keeping the *Eva* between me and shore. Wendy and I skipped six times around the deck to exercise and to escape waiting.

We were anchored at a buoy as the waters around Mt. Athos are very deep. Toward evening a small caïque came out from shore and tied up to "our" buoy. To have another vessel on the buoy meant that our crew would be up all night and with the motor running. We were low on gas, as well as water, and so Captain Antonio asked the Captain of the caïque to please move back to the Daphne dock, as "We cannot dock because we have women aboard."

"*Ohi,* no," bellowed the caïque Captain tossing his head back.

Captain Antonio rowed ashore and returned with the port officer, who asked the caïque Captain to move.

"*Ohi,*" and another toss of the head. Then much shouting and gesticulating and eventually the caïque moved off our buoy. It was a diversion, and through it all we women sat on deck in our long towel dresses trying to look like girl monks. Ann read the first volume of Carl Sandberg's books on Abraham Lincoln. I read *Marco Polo*. We kept reading aloud choice bits to each other and I became totally befuddled leaping from the thirteenth to the nineteenth century and back again. Suddenly it occurred to me that we were *in* the twentieth century . . . or were we? Were we actually awaiting our males, albeit impatiently, who were cohorting with monks and we women were behaving almost as if we also had taken the orders?

The moon crept over hulking Mt. Athos and its centuries of secrets. Though the mountains of the moon stood out clearly. The whereabouts of our men was not clear. Bravely we tackled the mounds of mousaka Eileen had baked anticipating the return of our pilgrims. Mousaka and Mt. Athos red wine, "made by the feet of monks." Ann was derisive.

In my bunk that night I confessed to Ann that I was worried about Richard and Bill. Not really worried, but I felt fretful. Ann chided me, "Think how long they've been away from home and you never knew whom they were with or what they were doing. They're all right. Hundreds of men visit Mt. Athos every year. Have you ever heard of one not returning?"

I had not. Somewhat comforted I feigned sleep. But long after Ann's regular breathing told me she slept, I thought about my two oldest sons. Two boys, so quickly young men. Ann always accused me of treating my male children differently from my female progeny. She was right. I did . . . because the girls were me. As I was my mother, they were me. I'd been all the girl places — at least a lot of them. Maybe there was some variation because of generations, but the fundamental life things didn't seem to change — no matter what country, no matter what century.

But with the boys it was different. I had learned a lot in raising sons and one thing was how instinctively different a male baby is from a female, different even in the way they attach the breast for their first meal. My only brother was five years younger than I, which meant I was too preoccupied with "self" to know anything of his psyche. And so, as my three males grew, I learned how gentle boys are, or can be, how sensitive, how loving and loyal, and definitely how physical! Like great romping animals Rick and Bill would wrestle, and I couldn't count the times the beds in their room had collapsed under the strain.

Bill and Richard were only twenty-one and twenty-two that summer on the yacht; it seemed to me they were already secure in their maleness and so at ease in the world. They'd had a lot of family responsibility thrust on them in their teens and sometimes that fact of life worried me. After all, they weren't husbands, they were sons and brothers, and I consciously tried not to "use" them as substitutes; tried not to take my own problems and concerns to them. I was not totally successful.

"To thine own self be true." As long as I could be true to myself, they could trust me and so learn to be true to themselves.

Thank God for Ann. How often she scolded me, interpreted the children to me, and explained me to them. So my mind played around with memory flashes of Cub Scouts and Little League, of football and basketball and the innumerable parent-teacher meetings. Cars washed, gardens tended, pack trips in the Sierras and in Canada, and gradually their turning on to the pursuit of knowledge. Thank God I'd been able to let go, and so they had come back to the family as men, young, but nevertheless men.

"I hope they are here tomorrow," I whispered to me—and slept.

"They *still* aren't here, and there is no way we can go and find them. Damn. They really have us." I complained uselessly to my breakfast companions. We had watched a number of men come down the road from the Mountain, we'd seen three boats dock bearing pilgrims, but our males were not abroad. We fumed, we read, we talked and went on rows to nowhere, and after dinner contemplated sneaking ashore just to say we'd been on Mt. Athos. I had a few daylight motherly qualms. "Were they really all right?"

On the morning of the sixth day, at eight o'clock, they arrived by boat. They came and we gathered them in—beards, dirt, bloody toes, blisters, mosquito welts—and fed them leftover mousaka, fried eggs, and strong coffee.

We were eating breakfast, leftover salmon made into pancakes, when we saw them coming. "Hurry," I admonished everyone, "Hurry and finish before the boys get here. There aren't enough pancakes." Even though the girls knew exactly what I meant, they teased me all day, "Mother! and they are your own children!"

My own children. Yes, my treasured, my beloved sons. I was so damned glad to see them that I wept and we got buckets of water to bathe their sore feet before they went to the quiet of the girls' stateroom to sleep, mumbling about telling their adventures later.

⋆ 35 ⋆

Stories

The bay was a perfect oval, its entrance small, almost hidden. The sail from the rugged hostility of Athos had taken three hours and Captain Antonio was happy as we anchored at the small dock in front of a farmhouse. It was a yacht refueling station — water and gas.

Porto Koufo is on the tip of the middle prong of the three lanky peninsulas hanging on the underbelly of Madcedonia. It was a jewel of a bay, its white sandy beach about two kilometers long. Helen, as boat-bored as I, leapt ashore and disappeared into fields of grapes and kalami. When she returned she had a long bamboo pole, "for fishing and I used it to polevault into a haystack. Hay is really soft." Having known many a haystack as a child, I smiled at her wonder.

"Just don't vault into a haystack with a black cashmere sweater on," Ann was actually teasing Bill, who had, last summer at Jim's ranch, returned from a romp in the hay with Katie. It took the whole family an hour to pick the hay out of that new black sweater.

Ann, Wendy, and I walked along the shore and gathered tiny periwinkles which we steamed and had as *mezes* with crispy french fries, courtesy of Robert. The boys spent the whole afternoon swimming, showering, sleeping, swimming again, and washing their hair. Rick brought a tiny crab aboard, and we all laughed watching it scurry sideways.

It was pastoral, peaceful, and remote from the action of the twentieth century and the vague hostility of Athos. A young farm boy, dressed in his pajamas, came down and sat on the dock listening to Richard strum idly on his guitar. A man tinkered with his small boat on shore. Three donkeys brayed in relay. A pig squealed as a farmer carried him from one pen to another. A boat slid silently past our stern, the two fishermen standing to row. Kerosene lanterns glowed from the windows and porches of the three farmhouses in the bay. The moon river made every-thing to starboard of the *Eva* glimmer; the haystacks, the pasture, the mountains were silver-washed. On our portside all was dark.

We sat silent, for the moment, conscious of the beauty and history of Porto Koufo. Finally Richard and Bill began to talk about their five days with the monks of Mt. Athos. Bill began.

"It's beautiful, really beautiful, except for the paths and their searing rocks. They may be okay for the donkey, but they plague the hiker."

"Start at the beginning," I entreated, "start when you left us in that small boat."

"Okay," answered Rick.

"Well, we went to Daphne where they took our passports and we stopped at a little taverna to have a beer and await the return of our passports, and ponder our fate. Two men approached our table, a slightly built German and a hulking American. They asked if we had any idea when passports would be returned. No, we told them, and then the overgrown middle-aged American boy — the big one — introduced himself. What did he say, Bill?"

"Bedford. Jimmy Bedford. Bed — what you sleep in; ford — what you ride in; Jimmy — what you do to a lock." The story returned to Richard.

"He had a handlebar mustache and a well-cared-for beard. He is a freelance reporter and wrote a book called *Around the World on a Nickle.*"

"I wonder about that book," Bill broke in. "He also told us he was off this week to swim the Hellespont. We saw him several times again. Jimmy is the kind of a guy you can like but wouldn't ever envy because Jimmy is a dream — not a reality."

"But what happened next?"

"They returned our passports and we got on a bus, bulging with humanity. Yes, males," Rick anticipated my question, "and started up a little dusty road to Keryea, where we checked with the police and bought passes for our room and board at the monasteries."

"It was a spooky, tiny village," added Bill, "with its few run-down buildings and bearded monks. I kept thinking about Kafka's *The Castle* — 'the authorities, the authorities, let me talk to the authorities.' We were in a tiny room. . . ." The boys were vying with each other now, and Rick raced on.

"With pictures of heroic Greeks, bloody Turks and religious pictures, all hanging ceiling high. Passports were checked by police and they pointed us to a building across the street to a monk-checking-station where two melancholy monks checked us over and finally we were free to go."

"Go where?" I asked.

"Anywhere on the Mountain," answered Richard, "but since the Monasteries usually close at sundown we set out at top pace for Iviron. We were walking with a couple of young Greek architects and we almost got eaten alive by tiny insects who swarmed us. Finally we put our jackets over our heads, got lost, headed straight uphill until we intersected the path. We were frantic as we didn't want to stay outdoors all night. When we got there and bolted our supper, Bill went into one of the large bedrooms, took a cot and slept. A large-bellied monk came and asked if I were Bill's brother — size I guess — and when I said yes, he began screaming at me something about Bill couldn't sleep in there as there were two Frenchmen and a Greek and you shouldn't mix up races. The Tower of Babel came into his railings, and America, which was the perfect example of the horrors of miscegenation. I tried to rouse Bill, couldn't, found myself a bed, fell asleep while the old monk still shouted his disapproval."

The stories went on and on. After I'd returned to my bed, Bill brought me the Katie letter he'd written during the afternoon. Again I was cast in the role of typist. I can't recall, nor can Bill, why those particular letters had to be typed. Having quoted the bit about the hotel manager earlier, I confess to lifting part of the Mt. Athos adventure for my log:

"The monasteries I saw were majestic. Made of stone, they towered big and stout in fairy tale settings, between lush ridges and looking over the sea. Rick commented, 'The esthetics are great, the ascetics stink.' Indeed, in thinking back, I can only curse the monks for not seeing God in their earthly surroundings. That they do not was confirmed on our last night. We had spent the day hiking and were exhausted. The monastery where we stopped for the night had a courtyard looking hundreds of feet down to the sea, while cliffs rose thousands of feet behind. The sun hovered on the horizon, coloring the sea and the mountains a gold red — the crowning of the day. Perched on the balcony, we were absorbed. But dinner was ready, and the monks guided us to the basement. In darkness we ate. I cursed their ignorance, why did they not serve food on tables in the courtyard? I pondered without conclusion."

As Bill kissed me goodnight, Wendy arrived to climb in bed, "Please, Mother, see if these two letters are okay. I wrote them today."

July 24, 1965

Dear Tom,

Hi, we all loved your letter, but me the most. Istanbul was gorgeous. It was very hard to talk in stores because you did not teach us Turkish. Now we are back in Greece and the crew are very happy. Tom, I am happy about Ios. I think it will be great. I just couldn't get up to admitting it. I know now I will miss Greece when I leave. This summer is going rapidly. Only six more weeks. Oh, God, please let it last. Tom, are you going to cut your beard? Please don't. I do so love it. Tom, I must tell you I haven't found another man. I'm good friends with Jorgo (sailor). I must go now. I do miss you because it's not like with Annie because I know I'll see her in five weeks, but with you maybe never again. I do love you.

Wendy

P.S. Annie says she doesn't miss me because she's too busy, but she does think about me. That's the way I feel too. I love you.

Dear Jim (my beau),

Hi, your letter was great. We are now back on our yacht I am glad, but I did like staying at the Hilton for three nights. Mom treated us so we could get clean! The first night we went to a night club where they had belly dancing. It was good for me and Robert as we had never seen it before. The girl was very pretty and she made eyes at Bill and at the end of the show her strap broke. What a scene! The next day we went to a palace, which had all its furnishings in it. It was the first palace I've ever been in that I'd really like to live in. It's name is Dolma Bachi. Please keep writing as we like to get your letters. I miss you and the ranch.

Love always,

Wendy

"They are wonderful letters, darling."

"Mother, I am glad that Rick and Bill are back. Now we are a family again."

⚕ *36* ⚕

The Fight

Leisurely we sailed south spending a memorable night on Skiathos after swimming at Koukounaries, a beach almost as beautiful as on Ios. The night was memorable, because at the disco in Skiathos village, Bill danced with three French girls at once. "All put together they aren't as big as Bill," was Helen's observation.

We chose to sail the inland sea, between the mountainous island of Evia and Attica on the mainland, waiting several hours for the tide to turn in Chalkis so we could navigate that narrow strip of sea with its powerful tides.

Richard decided we should anchor that night near the plains at Marathon and the next morning we sailed past Sounion again, doffing our caps in thanks, and by late afternoon, some eleven weeks after beginning our odyssey, we were briefly returning to Athens. No smelly Paselemani harbor this time. We would secure a birth in the new and elite yacht harbor at Voulagmeni Harbor just east of Athens. The sleek navy blue yacht belonging to Mr. Niarkos lay anchored in the harbor and, in the end, so were we. There was no berth, August being the biggest sailing month in Greece. No one cared and, with the possibility of big shopping on the morrow, we devoured all the rest of our canned delicacies such as crab and salmon. The wind was high and we ate below and stayed long in the salon as the children got telling stories of their younger years.

But we stayed too long, as in a moment I found myself disagreeing vehemently with Helen about some remembered event. The other children took Helen's side, and feeling totally frustrated and *knowing I was absolutely right,* I stood, drew myself to full height, pointed at the stairs to deck and bellowed in controlled tones, "GET OFF MY YACHT."

They didn't. They only laughed.

So *I* got off. Jorgo, thinking God knows what, lowered the rowboat for me and away I rowed. Fortunately the wind had calmed, so I rowed around the Niarkos yacht; I rowed into the yacht harbor and admired the variety and size of all yachts; and finally I rowed around in circles. Two hours is forever when you row to nowhere. The portholes of the *Eva* glowed and beckoned and, chastened, I slowly turned the boat toward home and my loving, teasing children.

✷ 37 ✲

Ulysses and John

We were sailing through the gigantic slice that is the Corinth Canal. I lay on my back looking up at the steep smooth walls, panicking slightly as we passed under the bridge and saw dozens of people gathered along its rails peering down at us. I could only hope they would control any urges to spit or pee. There is a curious optical illusion in going through the canal built and completed by the French in 1893. Looking forward it appeared that we were sailing uphill and looking back, downhill. After much discussion of how to spend our last three weeks on the *Eva:*

"Let's go to Sicily and visit the Hellenic ruins there."

"No, I opt for the Dalmation coast and in and out of Yugoslavian fjords."

"But why not sail around the Peloponnesus? No one seems to ever do it and I'm eager to at least touch Mani."

In the end we decided that we'd stay in Greece and, after visiting a couple of Ionian islands, sail around the Peloponnesus, which would put us in position to go back to Ios and discuss the "house."

The "house" began to seem an actual possibility as we had found the deed to the land awaiting us in Athens and Peter Antrum's lawyer (British Airways) had gone over it and found all to be in order. Hurray for Jorgo Drakos! And we bought graph paper and a meter ruler, to give reality to our ideas for the design of the house.

After two days in Athens, refurbishing the speedboat and buying supplies, we realized how spoiled we had become with the open sea and clean air our daily fare. We did have a couple of delights in our two days. The whole family saw Katina Paxinou in Euripedes ' "Hecuba." She was superb and the audience went wild. We loved watching Robert watch the dead bodies, and though fascinated by the whole production, in the end he voted against actually seeing Greek tragedies. "I think I'd rather just read them." But we all adored being in that magnificent ancient theater on the Acropolis, with its massive stone settings silhouetted against the sky.

The children all visited the Hilton Hotel to have "A Slow Boat to Corfu"—the Greek version of a banana split.

But no banana split would equal the delight I felt in being at sea again and headed for the island of Odysseus made poignant for me since my love, John, lived in the namesake of Ithaki—Ithaca, New York. We sailed all day, past islands and headlands and ferries from Italy. The winds were fresh and we were under full sail. We had stopped once during the day, early, because Captain Antonio wanted us to see the tiny elegant port at Nafpaktos on the northern shore of the Gulf of Corinth. We sailed into its miniature Venetian harbor, sought out the baker and, with our warm bread, climbed quickly up to the castle which topped the village. Men were at work repairing walls of the castro and women led donkeys who carried large cans of water for the cement mixing. Other women carried, slung over their shoulders in string shopping bags, stones for the wall. The cement mixer stopped his labors when we arrived at the castle and invited us to sit and share his sack of almonds, which he broke open with a heavy rock. We shared our warm bread with him. Following the great stone walls which descend steeply from the castle to the sea, we found a patch of mint and chewed the fragrant leaves all the way back, hurrying to be within the hour time limit the Captain had alloted us.

During the afternoon we read *Medea* aloud. I'm glad we didn't read it before the Dardanelles. Jason was such an unpleasant character that I was not at all sure I would have followed his lead! Once Wendy went below and came back bearing "a present for Mother." It was a gin and tonic, "The first I ever made. May I take a sip, Mom?"

She did—holding her nose.

Later in the day Robert and Richard climbed into the dinghy and Rick read a Salinger short story aloud to his brother. At the conclusion, when they wandered back to join the family I asked Robert how he liked the story. "Not much," he answered. "It's not really a story—it's only words hooked together, and most of the words are swear words and whenever people said anything they always said it twice."

It was six in the evening when we sailed into the Bay of Malo, that deep thrust of sea which divides Ithaki nearly in two. As we were wondering where to anchor (Captain Antonio had never visited Ithaki), a narrow inlet opened up on our portside. We turned in, passed several new moon beaches of white sand, and anchored at Port Vathi. What had been a sixteenth-century Venetian town until the 1958 earthquake was now a rather ordinary, modern one. After a delicious supper of cold veal, salad, and cut up fresh fruit, we all went ashore to explore our first Ionian settlement. It wasn't inspiring and after buying several lovely black and white blow-ups of Ithaki—physically a very beautiful island—for John, I wandered back to the *Eva.*

"Mother, how could you have sent the *Odyssey* home? And just when we need it?"

In Athens we had packaged up a lot of already finished books, the shoeshine box, rugs bought in Turkey and our air mattresses, braved the fancy new American Express offices at Constitution Square, and sent the whole lot back to Menlo Park. And now we couldn't use the *Odyssey* to help in exploring Ithaki. However, Ann remembered that the Nymph's Grotto (where Odysseus hid his treasures) was only an hour's walk from the harbor, "but which direction I have no idea." We tried asking a couple of local people at shops near the yacht; they all responded as if we were slightly balmy. "Well," I suggested "since town is to the left, let's start walking to the right."

"What am I doing to do for shoes, Mom," queried Richard, "now that one of my thong sandals is broken?" It was very early in the morning as the day promised to be August hot and we had decided to explore early and then take off for Corfu.

"I don't know, Rick, maybe you can actually buy some shoes, in Port Vathi when the stores open. Perhaps men in the Ionian have larger feet than in the Aegean."

"Oh, well, I'll just walk with one bare foot this morning." And so out we fanned, following a narrow gravel road beneath the endless terraces of olive trees. The views were wondrous with navy blue and turquoise seas off the rugged coastline. In no time Rick's feet were the focus of all concern. The road had ugly sharp rocks and off the road a prickly plant covered the earth. I found an empty cigarette box and we tried to improvise a shoe by placing it under Rick's foot and pulling one of Robert's socks over it. Totally unsuccessful. And as Rick hobbled along, the other ancient thong sandal gave way. Bill then gave Rick one of his canvas shoes, and though Rick had to wear it with the back broken down, they both made out with one shoe off and one shoe on. Walking behind them, I could barely contain myself. It was so ridiculous, a yacht filled with shoeless men. We would stay in Ithaki, if need be, an extra day and have a cobbler make Rick a pair of sandals out of old automobile tires.

Just an hour's walk from the town we found a steep path ascending to our left through a vineyard. Before long we saw a long perpendicular slit in a rock—large enough for a person to pass through—and sitting nearby, a wizened old lady. She couldn't seem to understand Rick's Greek, but urged us to pass through the crack. We had no flashlight. As we all crowded on a ledge inside, we found our matches of slight help. Waiting until our eyes adjusted to the dim inside, we could make out a large cave below us and finally, with the help of the matches, we slid and bumped and felt our way fifteen feet to the bottom. The tiny Greek lady tossed us some brush to light a torch, but we failed dismally, even with the help of my ever-present Kleenex. In disgust, and chatting away unintelligibly, the little lady slid down the steep embankment, wadded up some of the thorny branches into a tight ball and lit it. In seconds our cave was aglow. From above hung stalagmites, mystical in the smoke. The children became mysterious shadows as they explored the cavern. Bill gave an incantation over the pyre, Robert curled up on the primitive altar "to rest," while the old lady showed us the beginning of what is supposed to be the ancient underground passage from cave to sea.

The smoke, some of it, escaped through a tiny hole in the roof of the cave, but I began to fret. After all, Ithaki had had a terrible earthquake, and what if we got caught in one. "Why don't we begin to climb out?" I tried to sound casual. "If we don't leave soon we might become smoked tourists and *not* delicious to eat."

"Oh, Mom, not yet. Can't we explore the tunnel?" Robert implored.

"Not today. Someday you can return with a flashlight," I was firm as I led the ascent to fresh air.

Following the gesticulations of our Greek friend, we followed a pleasant dirt path which wound through the olive trees, and which would, we hoped, end us up at the *Eva.*

"I wish we had time to find the Raven's Rock," Helen said plaintively, "and I wonder where the crew put Odysseus ashore?"

"And I wish John were here to explore the original Ithaki," I said, "don't you think it would be fun to come back here with Homer's *Odyssey* in hand and a couple of weeks to spare?"

"Yes! Definitely! But never in August," panted Ann, "Homer is not high on my list right now. A cold beer is."

⚡ 38 ⚡

Friends

"What is your name?" I was facing the yacht which had just pulled in on our port side and suddenly I was sure I knew the yacht and the man on deck. That uniquely shaped boat could only be the *Yankee* and the man had to be Irving Johnson — both of *National Geographic* fame. "Oh, I'm terribly sorry. I didn't mean to be rude. I just had a sudden flash that I knew who you are." Mr. Johnson smiled and admitted his identity. What a marvelous face he had, weather-beaten from years at sea, and what splendid shape he was in!

During the next few days we spent a good deal of time with the Johnsons. Their lives — what little I knew — had always fascinated me. I'd known Sterling Hayden in San Francisco and knew he had been Captain Johnson's first mate for many of his sailing trips around the world in the 1930s. Now we learned that the Johnsons had raised their two sons aboard their yachts — the one next to us being *Yankee III* — and Mrs. Johnson spoke seven languages. Together the Johnsons could sail the *Yankee III* alone, their sons long since grown and gone. Captain Johnson told us that 500 people had designed the present *Yankee*. "Primarily she was built to travel the canals and rivers of Europe."

"Yes, I remember that article, and I've wanted to follow in your footsteps ever since."

"Careful, Mother, remember the Ios land?" Rick cautioned as he asked Captain Johnson if the yacht next to us was the one he'd taken up to Abu Simbel in Egypt the year before.

"Would you like to see inside the *Yankee?*"

Would we!! So for several hours we admired the mast, which went up and down electrically, her tank, which carried five tons of water, but most of all we admired her space and beauty below deck. "Imagine, a double bed, king size," and I was awed by the ceiling-to-floor bookcases that banked the bed.

"It's our home," Mrs. Johnson said, "at least for a great part of each year. Children, would you like some peanut butter?"

They were ecstatic as they munched peanut butter sandwiches and drank water. Suddenly Wendy exclaimed, "This is *Pindakaas* peanut butter, I can tell by the way it sticks to the roof of my mouth!"

"Right you are, Wendy," Mrs. Johnson laughed, "How do you happen to know *Pindakaas?*"

"Well, you see last summer we were on a barge in Holland and we rode bicycles all over and I ate *Pindakaas* every day."

As we headed the two feet back to the *Eva,* Mrs. Johnson presented Wendy with a whole jar of that delicious stick-to-the-roof-of-your-mouth delicacy.

Sometimes we shared a carriage with Mrs. Johnson into the handsome town of Corfu to do shopping. The yacht harbor on Corfu is dull, new, and very inconvenient, as town is a long walk. Strange that the most beautiful and handsome of all the towns we had visited during summer should have the dreariest harbor. Corfu town is European in flavor, for good reason since the Venetians were there for centuries, then the British. The town covers a broad peninsula and fits in between two acropoli. One of these stone masses was totally fortified, some parts in ruin, but other buildings and forts were in good shape. We spent nearly a day exploring the castro, returning now and again across the moats to sit in the Venetian arcade facing the park and sip cooling drinks.

It was in this esplanade that we met Mrs. Turner. She was having tea alone at one of the taverns under the arches. She was perfectly dressed, white gloves, hat, and printed sheer summer dress. As we noisily occupied the next table, she asked our identity and we were lost. That wonderful seventy-eight-year-old lady, a character from a drawing room scene in an Oscar Wilde play, had been living the past year in Corfu, having "lived on

most of the continents during my life including 'Frisco.' " She
took us home for dinner, later took the children to a movie, and
our last night in Corfu we invited her to have dinner with us
aboard the *Eva*.

It was a night none of us would ever forget as we listened to
Mrs. Turner's soliloquy on life. "I lived years in Shanghai . . .
I'm afraid everyone but everyone knew Mrs. Jeffrey Turner."
About England, "I'm afraid I never really lived there, was mostly
in Cannes. The only good thing left in England is the Hunt."
About Africa, "A third-rate country for third-rate people." About
her only daughter, "She had no guts, that one, and she married
an oaf, and his oldest girl is just like him — an oaf." About her
monocle, "It's not an affectation. I just can't see without it. In
Africa it is most useful; they think it is the evil eye and I can walk
about safely." About animals, "I love them. So much nicer than
people. One night in Africa I found a large worm under my
Louis XIV bed. After the servants all stopped thrashing about
my room breaking furniture, I got it out into the garden quite
easily — really quite a large snake it was." Robert's eyes were
fixed as he stared at this charming white-haired lady. Her last
remark had to do with Indo-China and Malaysia, "Such beautiful country. Now it is all ruined. The 'Reds' are in."

The children adored her. We all did. An original. A delicious,
feisty female perfectly at ease in her large garden hat and spotless
gloves on our crowded narrow deck. A vanishing breed.

We had our first fever on Corfu. Wendy, diagnosed by me,
had tonsillitis and was running quite a temperature, so I broke
open our supply of penicillin and read to her much of the day
while the others rented their first motorbikes of the summer to
explore the wonders of Corfu. I liked the day, just Wendy and
me on the *Eva* as we gave the crew the day off. Tiring of books, I
told Wendy stories about her grandmother, my mother Helen,
who had died two years previously. When I got married she had
told me of her wedding night with such charm and ease that I
wondered how a woman of such gentle rearing, who lost her own
mother when she was eighteen, who had never heard sex mentioned even during her four years at Berkeley, how this same
woman could tell her own children anything and everything that

she knew about loving and mating. We three girls and one boy always knew we could ask mother anything. Somehow, in the middle of raising four active young, being secretary to my father's law firm during the Depression years, she still always had time for us collectively and individually.

Then Wendy and I talked about Ann, who, a couple of nights before, had unsuspectingly become totally inebriated on ouzo. The younger children had been wide-eyed as Ann simply went berserk. We couldn't leave her for a moment and for hours took turns holding her. In the morning she did not recall one single thing about the evening. It frightened all of us and renewed our respect for ouzo. Wendy adored Ann and needed to talk about her worries. That beautiful, slim, laughing New York woman had become an integral part of our lives. In the past two years Ann had struggled with her own concern at leaving Jerry, her husband, and shared every moment of our family's life. She *was* family, and Wendy and I talked about Ann being the best salad-dressing maker in the world, as well as the best singer of Bessie Smith songs. Ann had a way of making every party joyous. Feeding friends was one of her big delights. We'd had wonderful Sunday evening suppers during the past two years. Every member of the family could ask one friend. Ann made soup — borscht, clam chowder, thick split pea soup — and I baked bread and pies. They were memorable evenings, and when you added them to our games of "steal the flag" in the Stanford amphitheater, and endless picnics at the ocean or the Santa Cruz mountains, we had quite a full life. A little heavy on women and children, but there *were* a few men in Ann's and my lives, beside the ones at work.

"Mother, do you think Ann was just born wise?" I had fallen silent as I thought about Ann and the past few years in our lives.

"What a good way of saying it, Wendy. Yes, in lots of ways I think Ann was always wise."

"Even when she was a little girl?"

"I wasn't there, darling, but Ann's Jewish heritage and all the stories she grew up with — the hardships and escape of her family from Russia, may have instilled wisdom."

"Tell me the story again about you and Ann in Moscow. . . ."

My company, Travel Desk, was not like most travel agencies. We did all the travel arrangements for seventeen electronic companies — we *were* their travel departments. In addition we did vacation arrangements for a few executives, and some twenty charters to Europe each year for KQED (San Francisco's Educational TV station). Also Ann and I had gotten a ten-week high school tour of Europe started, and the summer before, she and Richard and I had been the leaders. We had become intrigued with a lot of young Europeans whom we heard talking about spending a summer in Russia with "Sputnik." "Sputnik" was a youth travel organization under the Russian state, but try as we would, no information was available anywhere in the United States about it. We hoped to send some young Americans — the prices were a tenth those of regular tours to Russia (very popular in the sixties). In desperation, Ann and I, the winter before the *Eva Maria,* had used two of our precious airline passes and flown to Paris to connect with Aeroflot to Moscow.

We arrived, lunch having been home-cooked on the plane by a couple of broad-beamed Russian women, on December first. Running in the freezing cold from motel to office building, we soon accomplished our mission and took a couple of days to look at Moscow. No one had ever told me that the walls of the Kremlin, in my mind a stern gray, were painted daffodil yellow! But the most interesting day we spent was at GUM, the state-owned department store, which covers acres and is composed of tiny shops. We had just emerged from an awesome visit to the shop that handled brassieres only. They came in pink satin, blue satin, and white and navy polkadot satin and their sizes started off the American chart.

"And it was there that a lady asked Ann where the toilet was?" Wendy knew the story well. "But why did she think Ann was Russian?"

"She looks a little slavic, Wendy, with those high cheekbones, but she is much finer looking than most of the women we saw in Russia."

All too soon our motorbike family returned, full of the wonders of Paliocastrisa, "the most fantastic beach, Mother, it looks like Bali Hi," and of the millions — quite literally — of ancient, gnarled olive trees with great holes in their trunks which give Corfu the distinction of being called "The Green Island." Obviously, as on Crete, one would have to return to Corfu with at least a month to spend.

✶ 39 ✶

No Name

"Enough of that, Wendy," my stern voice was accompanied by a whack on her round twelve-year-old bottom as she had spoken to me in a rude manner. She raced to the other end of the *Eva* but within minutes she was back and, throwing herself into my arms, she sobbed, "Oh, Mom, I don't want to be like Karen Binkley!" At a complete loss as to her meaning, I just held her until the sobs petered out.

"Karen's so awful to her mother and I hate it!" Stroking Wendy's curls I prayed that she would always keep her oneness. When Wendy wandered off to play checkers in the salon with Helen, Ann turned to me, "There you go again, defying the quotation."

The year before, we had a heated argument over the saying, "Never strike a child in anger." I was convinced that it read, "Never strike a child *except* in anger." Ann won the argument, but I was still convinced that *my* interpretation was the right one. Obviously it would be better *not* to strike the child at all, but if a parent were *really* angry and the child *really* naughty, it would be best to administer the corporal punishment to the fanny at the time of the anger. Any child can understand *that* language and the action usually benefits both the giver and the receiver. On the other hand, to hit a child in reason — with calculation — seemed to me most harmful.

The fact is that I disagreed with many of the "sayings" of old. "Love is blind," seems exactly the opposite from reality. Love is all seeing, all accepting, and so it isn't blind! "Familiarity breeds contempt" again seemed reversed to my way of thinking. Familiarity breeds respect — that is, if there is anything to respect in the first place.

We were anchored in the bay of Lefkas town on Lefkas island, having entered through a canal. I was struck again by the wild contrast between islands. Four hours' sailing had changed our world from the timeless beauty of Pargo to the flat, dry, dreary-looking island of Lefkas.

Leaving Corfu, we had sailed four hours down the coast of that island, and then over and down the mainland. It was impossible to read, partly because the day was vivid clear with the mountains looking like rows of cutouts, and partly because we had large swells which rolled us around. I found that particular movement most unpleasant. And then we sailed into a fairy tale Pargo. Two small bays form the village of Pargo. On a headland between them are the remains of a fort. Built on many levels, it is overgrown with passion flowers, fig trees (one even grew in the middle of a cistern and we climbed the old crumbling walks and feasted), cypress, and pine trees. Many of the passages and rooms of the fort were intact though roofless. For centuries men fought, killed, and struggled, and now only rocks and trees reigned. At one time or another in its long history, Pargo was controlled by Russia, Turkey, England, France, and Venice. The Venetian influence showed the most, though a Turkish castle still brooded on a mountain top, two ancient cannons abandoned in the garden.

"Why is this place the most enchanted?" Rick had been urging me to consider at least one day more in Pargo, but our weeks were numbered and we still had the whole Peloponnesus to sail.

"I'm not sure, darling, perhaps because it has all the blessings of an island with its sandy beaches, variegated water colors and yet is backed by the Alps."

"The Alps?"

"Yes, the Alps end in northern Greece. In Greek they are called the Pindos mountains. It's where much of the fighting took place during both World War II and during the Greek civil war. Usually on islands you can't get such altitude as a backdrop. You're right. It is an enchanted place."

The picturesque town ran along the ridge below the fort and down into one of the bays. In that bay were two tiny islands, rocky yet wooded. But it was the bay to the north of town that enticed us. Its foliage was reminiscent of Hawaii and two sparkling streams ran through the beach. When we tried to follow the streams inland, the foliage prevented our passing. There were ferns, broad-leaved tropical plants, many trees, and a crude irrigation ditch along one side served the many plots of vegetables.

We lay on that enchanted beach all afternoon next to a freshwater stream. "We" excluded Bill, who was so deep into *The Source*, in anticipation of his September visit to Israel, that he couldn't tear himself away. Ann took the *Albatros* out and returned with a loving cup of scotch which we sipped (struggling to be fair) while watching a fisherman bring in his catch.

And then the hop-skip-and-jump to dreary-looking Lefkas. "I wonder why Captain Antonio brought us here?" I addressed the world at large, "I was eager to see Cefalonia [famous for all the shipowners it had produced], but Captain Antonio insisted on Lefkas."

"Perhaps something special is going on there, Mom. Look at all the flags." Sure enough, there were brilliant colored flags and banners fluttering everywhere, and many people were dressed in costumes which *definitely* were not Greek. Just then a group of Africans wandered out on the breakwater for a swim. Bill went over to talk with them and found that dreary little Lefkas was the host for two weeks for folk dancers from some twenty-two countries. We never did find out why.

The town had been transformed into festival land. The whole town-square was filled with cane and canvas chairs and jammed with people. During our one evening in Lefkas we watched some spectacular dancing; Italians, Yugoslavs, Dutch, Bulgarians, Liberians, Ugandans, Lefkas had them all. Finally a group of tall handsome Cretans completed the evening's festivities as they performed with superb skill their traditional dances. All this while other groups were practicing their dances inside or in front of various taverns.

Late that night Helen came rushing below, clad in her infinitesimal lace bikini underpants and a large blue blanket. "Mother, it's so late, and when I went up deck to sleep I looked all around and couldn't see anyone, so I dropped the blanket to make my bed. Just as I finished I looked up and saw the owner of the yacht next to us sitting in the pilot's cabin. Now I'm too embarrassed to go to bed."

Reassuring Helen, I laughed, remembering Wendy's concern earlier in the day. She often slept sans clothing as it can be very warm. We all did, with a cotton sheet thrown on top. "It's so embarrassing, Mother, and I don't know what to do when Jorgo is there closing the portholes and if I wake up and if it's been too hot and I've thrown off the sheet — well, it's embarrassing!"

"Don't fret, Wendy. It is the same for all of us. After all, it's Jorgo's job." Wendy thought a moment;

"Boy, he sure has a jazzy job."

"Well, do you think that we can finally go to sleep? Are they all safely bedded down?" Ann teased me all summer about my psychiatric couch, knowing how dubious I felt about that profession. The only saving grace was that I was on the couch! If I ever climbed into my bunk, with its six-inch wooden sides, to read, within minutes one or another son or daughter arrived and pulled up the funny round dressing table stool beside me "to talk."

"Wasn't Wendy wonderful today when we discussed Shakespeare?" Ann pursued the conversation. I giggled.

"It was certainly one of the better exchanges. She really is too much!"

Wendy had been struggling with *Romeo and Juliet* when she turned to Ann (who had been a theater major at college) and asked,

"Why couldn't Shakespeare just say things straight out?"

After much discussion and explanation by Ann, Wendy asked, "Do you think that Shakespeare will still be in style when I get to college?"

Ann clicked off the light. "Tomorrow Olympia. Nite Mimi," and for a while I lay in the dark thinking about being a parent. It certainly was challenging day by day! You never seemed to "have it made." I wondered if in the old days it had been easier with more clearly defined, behavior patterns pretty much accepted and adhered to. The crazy permissiveness since the war — why did it begin? *Someone* had to give a child boundaries. I knew they had to have boundaries in order to feel safe, and in order to have some guidelines to eventually make their *own* boundaries. Why did I "know" that? Was it instinct? It was often hard to say "no" — to one child or another — but if I didn't, who would? Thinking about many of my neighbors in Menlo Park, I considered that they wanted to be liked by their offspring. Maybe if there isn't enough loving in a family, they can't risk not being liked. I wondered. There were certainly a lot of mixed-up kids and I guess that meant mixed-up parents. I sighed, there in the womb of the yacht, and said to myself, "It really is a matter of bringing up mother. Fumbling and stumbling and learning by doing, parents and children really growing up together. Too bad all the experience gained has to go to waste in our culture with its emphasis on each generation starting from scratch. The one thing I know is that I'll never write a book about raising kids."

⚡ 40 ⚡

Winning of The Olympic Games

All day we sailed, fourteen hours on a lake-smooth sea. A perfect day for letter writing, reading, and taking a shower. It had become quite satisfactory — my weekly shower. I would sit on the round stool in the larger of our two baths, and when the hot water was pumped I would furiously lather, wash my hair, shave my legs. "Mother, you never do a good job on your legs," Wendy admonished.

"I know, but I always feel so guilty with Jorgo standing out there pumping all the time. Sorry it distresses you."

"Well, you should have someone else do the backs for you."

The town of Katakalon, on the western coast of the Peloponnesus, is the port for Olympia. We found the telephone office to call Athens about mail. It was an upstairs room, with a floor that sloped at such an angle that a wooden chair by the desk kept sliding quietly downhill. Next we approached a taxi driver to ask about taking us to Olympia the following day. "Yes, I will take you and my friend will take you, too; it will be $30 for each taxi." No way, we told him and bought both drivers an ouzo to soften the rejection.

That night we were served chunks of turnip to eat with our ouzakis. A new wrinkle. But how to get to Olympia? The cafe owner solved the problem by telling us of the train that went every morning *"poli proee"* (very early).

So we relaxed with our drinks and watched a large red fishing boat, floating on the pink sea and docking next to the *Eva*. Soon an elegant yacht pulled in on the other side, flying the Italian flag. Three tall good-looking Italian men ("I put them at young middle-age," Bill spoke *soto voce*) came ashore and with them were three real-life dolls. It was not the first time we had encountered love-boat parties. We had discovered that we were the exception —a family sailing together for months. Mostly we saw two or three couples who had chartered for a couple of weeks, or party boats like the Italian one. The exceptions were Greeks who owned their own yachts and were sailing with friends or family for a weekend or weeks on end.

Our Italians began to bargain with the taxi drivers for *their* trip on the morrow to Olympia. The drivers beamed at the business and we kept absolutely quiet about the train.

At 7:20 a.m. we heard it coming, with a high, shrill whistling. It was "the little engine that could," No. 27504, pulling three passenger cars with their curved wooden-slat seats and two freight cars! The engine uncoupled, rushed to the last freight car and sidetracked it, hurried back, hooked on to the main train, and away we went. Several times, at other villages on our way to Olympia, that process was repeated as a freight car would be subtracted or added. A busy little engine.

It was pleasant, rich-looking countryside, fertile with corn, tomatoes, melons, and many citrus and walnut trees. In the vineyards we saw tiny purple grapes, resting on carefully raked earth, becoming raisins.

As we got off the train in Olympia, we stood and watched a year-old calf being prodded, pulled, and lifted into a freight car. I turned my movie camera on this scene, whereupon the woman who owned the cow ran and got her son, and they—mother, son, and calf—struck a formal pose for the camera. As we walked away they redoubled their lifting and pushing to get the protesting calf into the car.

There were no other people at that enchanted site of the ancient Olympics. It is such a gentle setting, nestled in rounded mountains and with magnificent trees brooding over the mammoth toppled columns from the Temple of Zeus. We wandered at random, walking the perimeter of the hotel where guests and athletes had lived, the street of Treasuries, and on to the ruins from Roman times. When we eventually got to the track, with its marble bleachers, we found the three Italian men and their girls.

Rick walked over to them and said in Italian: "Don't lean out the window." This was his one Italian phrase, learned from signs in the railway cars. Laughter and English followed and all males decided to recreate a track event. After rejecting a race a-la-ancient Greece, without clothing the Italian men and ours did take off their shirts and lined up at the starting line. While the men discussed their race, I made a laurel wreath. "Helen, you crown the winner and Wendy can kiss him."

"I won't kiss him if Robert wins!" Wendy and Robert had fought that morning.

"Okay, Pooh Bear," said Helen, "if Robert wins we'll trade duties."

The race started out in a joking, casual mood, but at the starting signal it became immediately evident that it was "for real." Richard nosed out Italy, got crowned and kissed—to Wendy's great relief.

"Why did I worry about kissing Robert?" Wendy asked. "What if I'd had to kiss one of those strange men!"

After a delicious spaghetti lunch (roast beef, spaghetti, stuffed tomatoes, mousaka, and melon . . .) under a plane tree with serenading cicadas, the busy little black engine pulled us back down to the sea, spraying cinders, running out on a side track for water and coal. I expected to see a train robber on horseback emerge from the woods at any moment. Everyone in the family was quiet, some slept.

Bounding along on my wicker train seat I idly watched the countryside and thought about the day, and Richard winning the race. Olympia is such a focus for Western people, maybe not the place itself, but the idea of Olympia and the games is omnipresent. When Richard was very young, he was very competitive in everything. A friend in California had a children's Easter egg hunt. A gold egg was the prize for the race. Rick lost and was crushed. I remember cuddling him and talking about losing with grace, searching for words and thoughts a five-year old might understand. He learned, indeed, he learned early on. That was good as he also knew when still young that *winning* with grace is just as important, the spirit of Olympics. I looked at my first-born child who sat across from and in front of me on the train, and decided to go and sit across from him. I leaned over and gave him a kiss and hug. "I've been thinking about you."

"Good thoughts?"

"Yes, all good. One of the funniest remembrances was when you returned a golf ball to Bob Hope on the practice green at Pebble Beach. Remember?"

"Oh, yeah, when he said 'Thank you, Tex'?"

"Yes, and you came running over to me and asked how Bob Hope knew you were born in Texas!"

"It must have been the cowboy shirt. Are we going to sail on to Pilos tonight?"

"No, it's too big a sail — seven hours, the Captain estimates. We'll leave early in the morning. Richard," I felt suddenly shy, "I hope these next three years at law school are going to be wonderful ones for you. It will be nice to have you close to home. Just think, you've been away five years, except for summers."

"Don't think *I* won't like it! And I'll have to come home a lot because no one else will know what I'm talking about. What a summer."

✷ 41 ✷

What's A Grownup?

Seven hours on a heaving seas brought us to Pilos. When we arrived a thunder and lightning storm to the west provided a wondrous, if scarey, show. Pilos is located on a large bay, in which lie more than a hundred sunken ships from the Greek War of Independence in 1822, ships of the Russian flag as well as French, English, and Greek, all of whom battled with Turkey. As we sailed along the Peloponnesus that day, the Captain told us sea tales of the different Greek wars, taking out a map to give location and reality to his stories. We didn't even go ashore in Pilos as we were to sail early again, for Mani, the middle peninsula of the Peloponnesus and the only port of Greece never under a foreign power.

Mani is the southermost point of continental Europe. It is a stark, dramatic land of stones with sometimes the surprise of a small white beach. Appropriately, our sea had been as dramatic as the land. Deep swells were topped by smaller waves, the whitecaps like feathers tossed against the angry blue of the sea. The winds, working at cross-purpose, tore the tops off waves and spread mist across the large areas. As we sailed around the point of Mani the Captain yelled, "Sails down, quickly, quickly," and all the men fell to in the fierce and frantic wind.

It all matched, wind, sea, and land. Ann, Richard, Wendy, Robert, and I stayed above, getting soaked, as waves dashed across the deck in haphazard glee. Rick had on his bright blue-and-white striped Greek trousers and was topless. He sat in the middle of the deck, his hair plastered against his forehead, water running down his face and chest and a look of sheer delight in his grin.

A deep bay surrounded by high cliffs and endless ruins was our port, but we couldn't get into the bay against the wind and so kept going north, up the east coast of Mani, where we found a shelter and anchorage in front of a tiny fishing village.

Robert and Jorgo rowed ashore in the twilight. We were out of bread. Our family could have gotten by, but for the crew, no bread was simply unthinkable. Shortly the shoppers returned with an enormous round loaf, four kilos they claimed, of un- leavened bread. It would not cut. No knife could make a dent. The Captain got the ship's saw. Even the saw was no match for this bread. Sadly, Jorgo tossed the loaf into the sea, saying that when we got to his home the next day, we would see "real bread."

As we looked ashore to the village, we could make out several of the stone towers we had read about in Patrick Femur's fas- cinating book on the Mani. Homes as well as towers, they served as a family base in its blood feud, and the height of a family tower also indicated their social status in the community. No one knew the beginning of those blood feuds, but from the ninth century until well into the twentieth, the fueds between families domi- nated the life of Mani. One's worst enemy might live in the tower across the road. A family would spend endless hours plotting the ambush of the oldest enemy male. Seldom did anyone know the origin of the feud — somewhere in the dim past it probably began in a dispute over land. But once a male was killed in a family, the next generation were honor bound to murder his murderer. And so it went, century following century, in that land of savage beauty. When wars came along, the Maniots were the fiercest of fighters. They held out against the Spartans, the Romans, and were never subjugated by the Turks. During World War II even the Germans gave up on the Mani.

As long as there was a ray of light, we stayed on deck, sweatered against the wind, but the black of the cloud-filled night finally drove us to our cozy salon. When we were all in it at the same time, it bulged a bit but was nevertheless very friendly. The older children began a game of hearts. Robert, Ann, and I got talking about age and grownups, and gradually our scintillating discussion drew the whole family in. The discussion began with Robert asking, "Mother, are you middle-aged?"

"Well, yes, I guess I probably am."

"No, you're not," Ann spoke with authority, "or if you are you are young middle age." There ensued a confused and animated conversation with all ages eventually catagorized in young-young age, young age, old-young age (I think this group was in the late thirties), and so on, through young middle age, and so on up to the octogenerians. Robert became bored and interrupted, "Why do only children have fun?"

"I don't think that's true, Robert." I thought a bit. "I think children and people who are really grown up have fun."

"What do you mean that they are really grownup?"

"She means they are mature, don't you, Mother," said Helen.

"Yes, I guess that's what I mean. You see, Robert, lots of people get older but they don't grow up. I mean, well, that they stay dependent on others. They never take responsibility for themselves. You know people like that who, even though they may be thirty or fifty years old, are always blaming someone else for everything that happens to them."

Richard abandoned the card game as he began to tell stories of friends at Princeton who blamed their parents, or grandparents, or some teacher, or a brother for any problem at all. "It's such a bore. They never seem to take their own life in their own hands and get on with it."

"But why if you are older but not grownup, can't you have fun?" Robert persisted with his original thought.

"I suppose you can have some kinds of fun, but if you have to spend most of your time posturing and playing roles, you can't have carefree fun," said Ann.

"What's posturing? Is it the same as Mother always yelling at us to stand up straight?" Robert again.

"Chest up, butt in," Bill laughed remembering my constant harping, "Not exactly the same, Rob, but it is from the same word. Get the dictionary."

So we read all the various definitions under *posture* and Robert was satisfied with "to strike a pose for effect" as being different from "assuming different body positions." The presence of the dictionary led us to spend the rest of the evening playing our favorite game, the "Dictionary Game." Every person is armed with a sheet of paper and a pen. One person has the dictionary and chooses a word which no one knows. Then each person writes a definition, trying to sound more like Webster than Webster. The person who chose the word writes the real definition on his paper and when all other definitions have been given to him, he reads them aloud (trying to keep a straight face) and then each person selects the "real one." The most fun is to have several players select the fake definition *you* have written.

The night concluded with hysterical laughter as Helen, choosing a word none of us had every heard of, read each of our eight definitions. When she read, "Merkin — an artificial pubic hair piece," she was shouted down, "Who wrote that?" "Who ever heard of such a silly thing." But *that* definition was straight out of Webster's! So with an esoteric new word added to our vocabulary, we pulled down the hanging bunks, decushioned the couch and prepared the male dormitory. It was such a handsome room — that salon, dining room, bedroom — with deep brown wooden walls. Although the males had not spent many nights below, they all liked the room. "We take it all for granted, Mother, but it's pretty wild when you think of Menlo Park in contrast to a schooner anchored off the Mani. Someday I'm coming back and follow in Patrick Femour's footsteps."

"Oh, Rick, bring me, too." Said Helen as I shooed the girls up and out down into their nest, kissed sons and retreated with Ann to our cabin. Before I slept I thought again of the wild history of the land which lay a few hundred feet from the rocking *Eva*. Its people had led a harsh life over centuries, but a life of total reality in the fight for food, shelter, and safety. I decided that in the Mani it was likely everyone "grew up."

✢ 42 ✣

The Crew

The crew were in a state! Each man changed clothes at least three times during the short sail from the Mani to the most easterly peninsula of the Peloponnesus and their home village—Pahion. Such excitement, to see family, to show off the *Eva* (the crew loved that graceful yacht as much as we), and to give *us* a sense of *their* life. Before setting off for the main village, some two miles up the mountain, we decided to lay in a bit of food—especially bread!

Next to the bakery was a cavernous wine cellar, its great barrels lined up against the wall. "Come, come in. Come and drink." The middle-aged man had a fine wrinkled face and few teeth. He shepherded us into his fold. As we stood among the vats, our toothless friend kept looking me over head to foot and up again. As he drew us wine, he continually made comments in Greek. Rick spoke softly, "All I can tell, Mother, is that he's talking about you and it seems to be good." Now and then he would pause and kiss my hand before drawing another glass of wine. A dozen villagers gathered and I became increasingly embarrassed; I said in my best Greek, "These are my daughters." He grinned, his gums glistening, and answered slowly, *"E matera einai pio ourea apo ta koritsia"* (the mother is more beautiful than the daughters). As he spoke he bowed to me and pressed ten drachmas into my hand. Totally frustrated, and mystified, I pled with Rick, "Please find out what I'm to do with the ten dracs, and please can't we find some way to leave gracefully?"

Rick finally determined that the ten dracs was to buy "the children of the gorgeous creature" (me!) a treat.

With great relief we bid my admirer farewell—leaving him to his wine drinking, "I think he's well on his way," commented Bill, and when we were out of sight, the children dissolved in laughter over "Mother's suitor."

During the morning, Jorgo secured a cousin's truck to take us up to his house for lunch. It obviously had not started life as a truck, but the cousin had built a boxlike structure and attached it to an ancient vehicle. Inside the box, a bench ran along each windowless wall. The bench was lovingly upholstered in chintz. Along the ceiling looped green plastic tubing. Soon we were grabbing in desperation for the tubing as we careened and bumped up the steep road to Pahion. The vehicle stopped short of the village and Jorgo took us into a field adjoining a church. "These are my trees," he gestured proudly, "and my brother owns the land under them." As we ate the figs, Jorgo explained that land had been divided so many times over the centuries that often one child owned the crop and another the field. We passed an elderly peasant woman right out of a Brueghel painting, in her earth-brown dress, a white kerchief tying her hair back from a warm wrinkled face. She laid down her homemade hoe and picked a dozen figs for us before she came to hug Jorgo.

Next we were led in the church, because Jorgo's father had built and painted the *Iconostasis*. "Mother, come quickly, there is water running out from under the church." Robert had lingered outside and sure enough, a spring gushed forth from one corner of the rock foundation of that simple country church.

We chose to abandon our boxlike taxi and walked to Jorgo's home, where we were immediately drowned in a sea of relatives. "This is the wife of one of Captain Antonio's brothers. The one you met on Ios isn't a Captain."

"This is my father's sister's girl."

Smiling and concentrating wildly on the Greek, saying, "*seega, seega*" (slowly, slowly) over and over, we were finally led from the extended family scene and into the living room of Jorgo's home where we found ourselves with only immediate family members plus one grandmother and a few extra children. Handsome people! Father had, of course, built their home. Mother had woven all the rugs on her loom (it sat in the corner of the living room, a black and white cloth partly finished). Another corner of the room held a silver-colored bed with immaculate white sheets and pillows, all hand-embroidered. The tiny balcony was a riot of flowers planted in cans of every size and what a view! Richard kept repeating his latest word as he stood on the balcony gazing over the sea below, "*Ourea thea, ourea thea*" (beautiful view). It was! with the variegated blues of the sea and the island of Kithera as background.

Jorgo's home, and all the village, was built on a steep slope. Under the house was father's workshop. Helen went down to admire the shutters he was making for a house he was helping to build and she returned with a curly shaving which she carried for hours, "so I can smell it." Up behind the house was a tiny area containing a horse, a donkey, two goats, some scrawny chickens, and a kitten. In the backyard was a brick oven. "Yesterday's bread is drying in the oven [to be eaten hard] as the oven cools down from today's baking. Come back inside. My father has drawn some of our wine for you." Jorgo was proud.

"Did you make the wine with your feet, Jorgo?" Wendy asked.

"No, this wine is from my father's feet."

"Sixty-eight kilos of wine a year," father told us, "just for my family."

"How do you get wine with the golden color?" Rick asked. Indeed the color was like sherry, a clear amber.

"We use all colors and kinds of grapes."

As we sipped our wine, we admired the pictures of the family for several generations—boys in their uniforms (military service is compulsory in Greece), wedding pictures, and always grandmothers and grandfathers. Jorgo's sisters arrived with the meal. Stewed chicken and gravy, and brown wheat bread baked by the father. Robert asked Jorgo, "May I break up my bread and put it in the gravy like you taught me?"

"Yes."

Bowls of melon cut in large chunks arrived on the table along with grapes and figs. Jorgo and his parents and grandmother ate with us. The other children waited until we were finished to have their dinner. They clustered in a corner talking, whispering, listening. After an extended meal, Jorgo's mother gave Wendy and Helen each a rose and the rest of us a piece of lemon geranium. We kissed affectionately (always on both cheeks) and went out with Jorgo to explore the village. Everyone spoke to us. Everyone was related. We walked to the end of the village where the village laundry was located next to the fountain. Eight cement stands with water running through them stood in a row — the world spread out below for the laundresses to admire. "A far cry from a laundromat," I commented. Next to the laundry facilities were four open urinals and next to them a water fountain built into the mountainside. Women and girls, including Jorgo's sisters, were drawing water in amphoralike clay water jugs, "Just like the ones we bought on Aegina," whispered Helen.

The Captain's father joined our walk and led us to his porch, covered by a grape vine in full fruit! He brought us a carafe of *his* wine made with *his* feet. Bravely sipping again, we looked far out to the bay and watched a "Mother" fishing boat lead her children boats in a large circle and set the nets. The blood red sun set behind the Mani, the new moon rose, and the acetylene lamps on the fishing boats were lit, looking like enormous fireflies bobbing above the water. One could understand how the Captain and his six brothers felt a yearning toward the sea.

Woozy from vast quantities of resinated wine, we returned to the *Eva* and ate large bowls of lentil soup. I knew it was a blessed day and that we had been privileged to touch the lives of those men with whom we had spent such important weeks. I smiled in contentment, curled up in my bunk, and floated into oblivion on a sea of soup and wine.

✠ 43 ✠

A Summer Without End

"Let's put a step between the eating part of the main room and the living end."

"Be sure and make the built-in couches deep enough. Remember they have to have pillows at the back."

"What are we going to put on the floors?"

There was a massive joint effort going into the house drawings as we suddenly realized the plans would have to be given to Jorgo Drakos before we left in a few days. The only missing family member was Robert, who was curled up in his boat nest, which he lately stuffed with airform pillows before bedding down. Richard's one year of mechanical drawing in high school was paying off as we struggled to make the house have correct proportions. It is hard to work in meters (all Greek houses are done in meters). In our heads we knew that the length of three feet was just under a meter but it is another thing to constantly do translation, "So the living room will be a foot or so longer than fourteen yards?" I struggled as I divided feet into yards and added a bit for a meter!

"Mother," said Rick, "I think I've got it all worked out to have your tunnel from the front of the house to the courtyard."

Knowing that everyone arriving at the house from the beach would be sand-covered, I'd devised a passageway between the living room and the master bedroom—eventually to be covered with grapevines—so that all of us could enter the courtyard where there would be a faucet to wash feet. I figured it would save endless sweeping. The house was built, like a hacienda, around a courtyard and all the rooms opened onto it. "Let's see, the main room, five bedrooms, one bathroom and one *apothiki* [storeroom] will open out. That's eight doors." And so it went, off and on all day as we sailed from Porto Gerakas up the eastern coast of the Peleponnesus. Jagged mountains were gradually replaced by rounded hills. It was the first week of September. The Captain was taking us to the island, Spetse just off the end of the Bay at Nauphlion. The older children could get a ferry back to Athens every day from that island, whereas if they accompanied us out to Ios they might get caught in the *meltemi* and Ios only had two ferries a week for Pireaus.

Our past two days had been idyllic. It had been dusk when we'd sailed into the famous bay, Porto Gerakas. I got up at sunrise the next day and, sipping my coffee, looked out over the loveliest, but one, of the countless bays of summer. The bay at Porto Gerakas was covered with a low mist and with its dimly seen fishing boats and the stands of *kalami* (bamboo) I felt as though part of a Japanese painting. I could barely make out the three little farmhouses whose windows had glowed with kerosene light the night before. I wished I could have understood more Greek when Captain Antonio was telling the stories of Porto Gerakas as we sailed North the previous day. He'd told us that it was "perhaps the most famous of all bays in Greek history because it was so protected from the open sea." Indeed, we had discovered it was invisible from the open sea as it opened to the south of a smaller bay.

I refilled my coffee cup and sat on the prow dangling my feet. So our summer was inexorably ending. I supposed it would be years before any of us would know the influence on our lives of those three months together. What I *did* know was that it had been three months of total and absolute delight! I ran over the family in my thoughts:

"Robert is no longer a little surburban boy. He's a budding sailor who can tie knots well and peel and slice a potato.

"Wendy has discovered that there is a world, an enticing one, beyond Menlo Park.

"Helen has found that romantic love can end and hurt, but arms of brothers and mothers and sisters can ease the hurt and help, giving strength to love again.

"Bill has read endlessly and wants more knowledge of man — in all times, in all ways.

"Rick has come home. He's been gone for five years. Gradually and surely he's discovered each of us — and we him.

"As for Ann and me, perhaps the most important thing has been time. The first part of the summer we both felt a compulsion at least to plow through all those great books in our portable library. Slowly we discovered the pleasures of just 'being.' And," I thought, "it is undoubtedly the only time in our lives that we'll all share the same experience for such an extended time. What a blessing these three months have been, and in a few days I'll get to be with John in New York. Happy day."

Soon everyone was up, and we swam and explored a cathedral-like cave in our rowboat and swam again, "I feel like soaking up the Aegean," said Ann, "Shall we water ski one last time? It seems almost sacrilegious to destroy the peace of this bay, but that smooth surface is too tempting." And on that last day of water skiing Helen managed to leave the yacht in standing position, do fancy skiing and return to the ship's stairs with her hair dry. She had been trying that feat for weeks. Ann kept getting dunked and *she* returned to the *Eva*, "I'm going to change from a bikini to a one piece" and she did and magically it worked as she blithely sailed off on the skis and even managed some one ski antic.

It was good to have the house plans as focus during those final days on the *Eva*. That job took our minds off of our limited togetherness. Before we knew it, we sailed into the old harbor at Spetse and docked next to a sleek sloop flying the Australian flag. During the next day we became friends with our neighbors. That was good as they took my mind off the imminent departure of the older children. The Australian couple, of Greek heritage, had shipped their sloop from Australia to Greece by ocean liner and they had recently flown over to join her. With them was the president of the "largest rum-making plant in Australia." A close friend, and an amateur cook, he was a great addition to their planned trip. His rum was a great addition to our last night together and we drank, ate, sang, and laughed far into the night. At one point I went above to look ashore at the handsome old stone homes lining the shore of the old port. Plaintive music floated across the harbor; a group arrived back from town in a carriage. The horses had cleats and, together with the sound of the iron carriage wheels on stone roads, the stillness of the night was interrupted by sounds familiar to the centuries. A fishing boat fired up his inboard motor. I wondered if he was rushing the dawn or was it really time for the children's ferry to Athens? What an ungodly hour to depart, 3:00 a.m.!

So they left. Grabbing their bags and the guitar, they linked arms and—heedless of the sleeping world—lustily sang "Mr. Tambourine Man" as they walked away from the *Eva*. My heart thumped with love for them. Before I could burst into tears, I heard a shriek. Helen was running back to the yacht. "Mother, I have no money!"

That good old checklist; passport, tickets, money, and I'd forgotten the latter. "What would I have done for four days in London without a penny?"

Hugging her madly, I answered, "Knowing you, darling, probably the crew of the plane would have taken up a collection."

"Oh, Mother!" and she was off again as I chuckled over a favorite family story of Helen running out of money on a ship from Alexandria to London and *that* crew *had* taken up a collection for her.

Ann, Captain Antonio, and I decided on one more rum and tonic. Wendy and Robert spread their sleeping bags near Jorgo. The waning moon lit the skeleton of caïques a-building in the boat yard on shore. We talked about the nearly one hundred nights of summer we had shared. Captain Antonio said, "My friends warned me that it would be a difficult summer, that a three-month charter is very long, and they thought that an American family would be very demanding." He smiled shyly and getting up, came over to my seat, leaned over to kiss me— once on each cheek. "I love all your family, Mrs. Mimi. It has been a fast three months. You are a Greek family in the way you love each other. I looked, I felt and I saw." Then Robert called from his sleeping bag,

"Mom, I can't sleep. There are big lumps in my bed."

Investigating, we found fifty Greek lemon candies in his pocket, stored up for the journey home.

Epilogue

It is April in New Jersey. The first April of the last decade of this century. I sit at our word-processor looking out over the pond and the ten thousand grapevines in our vineyard just north of Princeton.

It was twenty-four years ago this week that I boarded TWA for the long flight from San Francisco to Athens, then climbed the ferry gangplank for another lengthy journey to Syros, Naxos, Paros and — finally — Ios. Jorgo Drakos was there to meet me at two in the morning and after a few hours' sleep we set out for Milopotas Bay. I don't know who was the more excited, I-the-owner or Jorgo-the-builder. Past the three tiny chapels along the path from the village to Milopotas Bay, gleaming white in their newly refurbished dresses of whitewash, and rounding a corner, Jorgo stopped short. "Spiti sou," he shouted, pointing far up the beach. And indeed, there was my house. Built around a court-yard, it looked like a great big white U in the middle of a field of, yes, beans! "We knew you would want a crop." But on closer inspection I found that between the house and the creek, beans gave way to grapes where Jorgo had planted a small vine-yard. The house looked gorgeous to me, even though it was definitely stark, except for a few bright spots of color — geraniums planted by Irini Drakos. The arched windows copied from the Cretan hotel were graceful, the rooms high-ceilinged and spacious. The livingroom fireplace was artistically off center. Now the job would be to turn a house into a home.

Year by year the plantings have grown until today that island house is surrounded by pines, eucalyptus, olive trees, and one palm. We have a small fruit orchard, including figs. We've masses of flowers and the vineyard gives us enough grapes to stomp a barrel of red wine each fall. The house court-yard has an arbor clear around it and by July it sags under the weight of great bunches of eating grapes.

"Buy land, girl."

Richard lived on Ios for nearly three years recovering from infectious hepatitis. He graduated from Berkeley law school three summers after sailing on the *Eva*. Visiting Bill in West Africa he became critically ill and went to Ios for his long recovery. During those years he constantly improved the house; then, with financial help from three Princeton friends, including Tom Singer now a psychiatrist in San Francisco, he bought the bay just south of Milopotas and built three homes.

A few years later, when Rick was heading Amnesty International in Washington, D.C., President Carter asked him to be the Assistant Secretary of Energy. That he did, receiving the highest civilian award anyone can get for meritorious service — a handsome medal. Later he moved to Princeton as an executive with a company making photovoltaic cells. Now, back in the political world, Richard is Associate Treasurer for the State of New Jersey. Nearly every summer he returns to Ios with his family — to his houses and mine.

Bill graduated from Stanford and, having taught in the Peace Corps in Upper Volta, West Africa, decided his career would be buying and selling African art. One day he arrived on Ios for a holiday with several pieces of art from Ouagadougou. One of those pieces, a wooden snake mask, is still mounted above the fireplace of the Ios house. Twenty-two years later Bill still makes a number of trips each year to West Africa. He has a splendid family and the Wright gallery, both in Soho, New York City. Bill has become one of the experts in America on the art of West Africa.

After her graduation from San Francisco State, Helen lived a whole year at our Aegean home and, since she majored in Latin and Greek, she speaks the most proper demotic Greek, with full-fledged, grammatically correct sentences. Helen met her husband in Greece when she was the teacher and he one of the students on a study program. He is now a professor of classics at Harvard and Helen teaches Latin in a boys' school nearby. Over the years Helen has walked the twelve-mile length of Ios island, has explored Homer's grave, and was there to supervise the workmen when they installed electricity in our house a few years ago. No more kerosene lamps to wash and fill each morning. Sometimes Helen's husband works at The American Academy in Rome, and being that close to Greece, with children in tow they sail off to Ios.

Just lucky, I was, and deeply happy when John and I were married the summer of 1968. He had recently resigned as president of San Francisco State University. Those were hard times for college administrators. Probably Governor Reagan would have fired John, as they did not see eye to eye on anything to do with education, the Vietnam War and the meaning of student demonstrations. John was eager to get on with his career and give up being a policeman. So he resigned with a lot of publicity and chose a job offer half way round the world.

The summer of 1968, after a month on Ios with various children, John and I and Wendy and Robert boarded an Ethiopian Airlines plane bound for Addis Ababa and a new life on an old continent. John and I had spent a few days in Addis that spring when he was being interviewed for the Ford Foundation job as Advisor to the President of Haile Selassie I University. Poor Wendy and Robert were horrified when told they were to accompany us to Africa for a few years. "But why? Why? Why must we leave our friends?"

"John has a job in Ethiopia. We have to go where the job is. And we will be much closer to Greece for holidays."

The next day Robert, a freckled thirteen, came racing into the kitchen. "We don't have to move to Africa. I found John a job at the pizza parlor on El Camino Real. I saw a sign in the window and the man said my father can come in and talk to him right away."

It has been difficult to tell others about our time in that most unique of countries—ancient Abyssinia, now Ethiopia. Protecting their Christianity, those handsome Amhars (all the women seem descended from Nefertiti) lived centuries isolated from the world on their plateau, eight thousand feet high. We all struggled with the language, camped in many parts of the country, and John spent a good deal of time with the Emperor who was deeply interested in his fledgling university. Most of all we learned how little we knew about Africa—how complex and varied that massive continent. We were much closer to Greece and for the next few years we got to Ios at Easter as well as summers. Wendy and Robert thrived at the British School in Addis with children, including Ethiopians, from forty-two countries. But when they finished that fine school, each had to have two more years of high school. My choice was the American School in Lugano, Switzerland. That did it. From those years onward my two youngest children have divided their time between the old world and the new. So far the old world has dominated, but there are signs that, in the end, we will all live in the northeastern part of the United States. What an admission for born and bred westerners!

Wendy took her college degree at the University of Bologna, one of the oldest universities in the western world. By then in love with an Italian lawyer, she spent the next three years doing high-fashion modeling in Italy. Ialian-perfect, she worked a few years in New York in public relations with Italian companies only to move east again, this time to Greece where she has been assistant to the head of the College Year in Athens—a program in which university students of the classics take their junior year abroad. She has managed the house on Ios, by making countless ten-hour ferry trips. But she has also had the joy of several whole summers in that serene stone house—baking bread, working in the vegetable garden and swimming miles each day.

"Now that I am fluent in Greek as well as Italian, I fall in love with a man from Germany! At least he lives in the United States, and he *is* terrific." And he is also one of the finest vinters on the East Coast. Now Wendy is back on this side of the Atlantic planning a wedding.

During Richard's years at Princeton I would visit that unique old New Englandish town when I could. Especially during basketball season as Rick was playing first-string with the championship team led by Bill Bradley. After flying to the East Coast, I would take the train down from New York, get on the little shuttle train known as "the dinky," and disembark mid-campus to walk across the street to the quaint Princeton Inn. "If I ever lived in the east," I would say to Richard, "I would choose Princeton." It was an unlikely possibility.

Yet, unlikely or not, here we are. Well, almost Princeton. Our farm is just seven miles north of the center of the handsome old town with its fine houses and ancient trees. While we lived in Ethiopia John was offered the job of heading all College Board programs at the Educational Testing Service in Princeton. PRINCETON! Incredible.

It took a couple of months to find a home. "We would like to be right in the center of town or out in the country, please," I was firm with the real estate agents. We found a splendid colonial farmhouse on six acres. It had an old swimming pool, a screened porch, acres of grass to mow, and room for all children — if you counted the basement. The day we were closing our 'deal' the agent said, "The thirty acres adjoining your new house have just come up for sale. The price is good and you might want to buy them." The price *was* right — affordable — and we did buy those rolling acres, which included woods along Fox Creek and a metal sheep barn, painted baby blue.

"Buy land, girl."

Children came and went. We had four in college at the same time — John's two daughters and Wendy and Robert. John's small son adored the farm, built a tree house in the woods and every second day asked "when are going to Ios?"

I began a study program for high school students to work and study abroad. I rode my bicycle on back roads to my Princeton office where John would pick up the bike and me and ferry us home at the end of the day. John worked at ETS four years and got rid of the heavy debt the College Board tests had accumulated. Then he took a leave. We spent much of it on Ios, really settling in as we worked the land, fixed up the stone cottage and rebuilt a stone wall. I re-covered cushions, endless cushions when they are done with a Singer sewing machine which has to be turned by hand. "That will be the epitaph on my tombstone," I told John — "Between New Jersey and Greece she covered two hundred pillows."

When John's leave was over, we returned to New Jersey and sold the big white house and built one of logs at the end of a line of ancient wild cherry trees. We built a cottage as well, for returning grown children and their families.

Our farm had horses when we acquired it. When the lease was up for those fattening horses, we bought sixteen Black Angus cows. If you have a farm you must farm. We learned more than we ever wanted to know about beef cattle, delivering calves, making a surrogate-mother cow.

John took on a new job at ETS as head of the international programs. He encouraged the development of innovative programs in adult education and experimented with ideas like an educational passport. We settled in. . . .

Then, flying home for Ios one fall and thirty-thousand feet above the Alps, I was idly reading the latest issue of *Time* magazine. "John, John, why don't we plant grapes on our farm? Look, here is an article about three fairly new vineyards in England. If they can produce wine, why can't we in New Jersey?"

So began the saga of the grape. We now have 10,000 vines and bottle about twenty-five thousand bottles a year in the new red sheep barn-turned-winery. The wine is called "LaFollette." I'm sure my Huguenot ancestors would approve.

During six of those ten years, while the grapes matured, we spent much of the year in Greece. But not on Ios. It was then John became president of Athens College. Those were marvelous years at an exciting school of more than three thousand Greek students. We lived in "the most beautiful house in Athens" in the middle of the wooded campus. John began new educational programs at the college and fought to preserve it from the socialist government headed by alumnus Andreas Papandraeou. John was asked to stay on longer; I loved my job running the college theater, and we were close to Ios. But the grapes beckoned us back to New Jersey—not to mention our children and grandchildren.

While we lived in Athens, children came and went and then one day Robert came to stay. Robert had studied hotel administration, two years in Paris and two in the United States. After working briefly in America, longer in Africa, Robert came to Greece to run a small resort. The owners have the largest cruise line in Greece with a dozen ships and they next asked Robert to become head of quality control for those ships. What a job for a young single man! He flew to Alaska, the Amazon, and over and over to Mediterranean ports as he checked on services. He could only have that job because he spoke fluent Greek (although he still cannot read the alphabet). Greek learned as he spent early summers with Jorgo's son. Two young boys, each on a donkey, struggling endlessly back and forth to the village of Ios as they shopped for the Stellios family taverna.

Robert met his wife, an English girl, in Greece and now they both work in England, Robert as development executive for a large building company involved with restaurants. Robert flew home for harvest last fall where he joined his brothers and sisters and a hundred other volunteers for the three-day pick, big home-cooked lunches, and grape stomping. That's just for fun. Thirty-five tons is a lot of grapes and we thank God for the big mechanical bladder press which we rent for the harvest.

Ann comes visiting sometimes. She graduated from law school in Boston when she was fifty, practiced a few years and now is painting essentially full time. And she is good.

How twenty-five years have raced by! Life is full, indeed, as we work very long days in the vineyard. I am the chief "wine solicitor." A grandmother salesman. John drives tractors, prunes, and tests, and is the chief winemaker. We all bottle, some of us cap and label, and as the grapes ripen, everyone chases birds away from the sweetening fruit. Candide may have found peace in his vineyard, but one thing is certain—he worked hard.

Our vineyard has become a part of the New Jersey "Farm Preservation Program." We have sold our development rights to the State. So the farm will always be here—for grapes or horses or sheep—or family.

GREECE,